URBAN LIFE AND URBAN LANDSCAPE SERIES

the poetics of cities

DESIGNING

NEIGHBORHOODS

THAT WORK

mike greenberg

OHIO STATE UNIVERSITY PRESS

Columbus

A Sandstone Book

Library of Congress Cataloging-in-Publication Data

Greenberg, Mike, 1947–
    The poetics of cities : designing neighborhoods that work / Mike Greenberg.
      p. cm. — (Urban life and urban landscape series)
    Includes bibliographical references.
    ISBN 0–8142–0656–5 (cloth : acid-free paper). —
    ISBN 0–8142–0657–3 (paper : acid-free paper)
    1. City planning—United States. 2. Neighborhood—United States—
Planning. 3. Community development, Urban—United States.
I. Title. II. Series.
HT167.G75 1994
307.3'36216'0973—dc20
                                              94–26658
                                                CIP

Text design by Donna Hartwick.
Type set in Centaur.
Printed by Braun-Brumfield, Ann Arbor, MI.

9 8 7 6 5 4 3 2 1

FOR DUAINE

may all his ballparks be outdoors, with natural turf

contents

a confessional preface
Why I wrote this book

I don't like what has happened to my city. I don't just mean crime and drugs and poverty and decay, but something deeper—the failure of community.

My city is San Antonio. I was born here, in the Nix Hospital, a 1920s Gothic-Deco skyscraper that rises above the River Walk. San Antonio today is a popular tourism and convention site. Most visitors think of San Antonio as a gracious and beautiful city of well-tended historic neighborhoods, walkable and verdant, culturally rich, diverse, community-minded, easygoing, and fond of public celebrations in a multitude of public spaces. That is the part of San Antonio that the tourists see, the part that still works. Some of this part of the city is fakery, made just for the benefit of tourists, but most is genuine—a real city of real neighborhoods where real people really live.

There are other San Antonios that the tourists don't see—inner-city neighborhoods of desperate poverty, illiteracy, and violence; neighborhoods drained of economic activity existing within sight of the convention hotel balconies; once lively middle-class neighborhoods vanishing under parking lots; the vast ring of generic suburbia, fragmented, congested, and ugly, where most San Antonians now live without being, in any real sense, San Antonians.

We have lost track of something. The old San Antonio, the pre-1940 city of about forty square miles, was and is a city of neighborhoods. Some are rich and some are poor; most are middle class; many are a little of each. Although neighborhoods are more or less identifiable by age, architectural style, ethnicity, or economic status, there is no radical break between rich and poor. No walls carve the city into tribal enclaves. Ethnic and economic concentrations exist, but their boundaries are blurred, permeable, changeable, and in large measure irrelevant. Walls of custom and law used to divide ethnic groups, and economic injustice has yet to disappear. But when racial and ethnic discrimination was outlawed in the 1960s, the old San Antonio took to the change with few problems, by the standards of the time. People discovered that they could get along because, in little, seemingly trivial ways, they had already been getting along without realizing or admitting it. The idea that we were all in the same boat was constantly if subtly reinforced by the unifying street grid, the sidewalks, and the neighborhood centers and parks, most serving diverse nearby populations.

Despite its many failings and frustrations, Old San Antonio commands an almost mystical affection and loyalty from its people. San Antonio is not, of course, unique in that respect. Many old American cities, in touch with their traditions and blessed by unique histories or cultural mixes, inspire a similar piety—Chicago, San Francisco, New York, Charleston, Boston, New Orleans, St. Paul, among others. The basis for Old San Antonio's claim on its people's loyalty is hard to explain. Life here has a peculiar fragrance, color, and timbre. Culturally, Old San Antonio was shaped by the clash and blend of Mexican, Indian, Spanish, and German traditions; by its status as a frontier and borderland metropolis; by its poverty; by the sensual and communitarian tendencies of the Catholic Church; by a sense of farce that can arise only from a finely honed sense of tragedy.

Old San Antonio is notoriously a city of parties, fiestas, carnivals, parades, music festivals, ethnic celebrations (Greek, Italian, German), church fairs—the most perfectly named being the Our Lady of Sorrows Fun and Food Fest. Much of the partying occurs outdoors in parks and plazas, along the famous River Walk, on the grounds of the old Spanish missions, in amphitheaters and parking lots, in grand and modest backyards and patios.

Through its ubiquitous and almost ritualistically formalized celebrations, Old San Antonio attaches itself to the senses—the smell of tamales and fajitas, the strings of colored lights, the accordion and bajo sexto of conjunto music, the heavy summer air lightening with the night, the tufts of breeze from the distant Gulf of Mexico. The parties and fiestas, Old San Antonio's most highly developed form of theater, are central to our shared life, our public life in public places.

Old San Antonio's sense of community is inseparable from its physicality. We could not have a shared life and shared memories and shared absurdities without places for sharing to happen. We are implicated in each other's lives, made participants in the whole, by the old city's richly interlinked streets and neighborhoods, by its civic spaces and parks and sidewalks. We have a sense of community because we have the reality of community, a patrimony of places that we hold in common, places that have value to us and that we jointly—in our sometimes conflicting ways—must cherish. Places and memories and memories of places bind us together. We live here as we live in our own skins. We may go elsewhere for a time, but we can never leave our skins.

In the forty years between my early childhood and my middle age, San Antonio's population has doubled to about 1 million within the city limits, and about 1.4 million in the metropolitan area, in early 1994. For as long as I can remember, population growth was regarded as a good thing, something to hope for and celebrate, because more people would mean more opportunity, more variety, greater intellectual and cultural growth, a stronger economy. But in a lot of ways the promise didn't pan out. The poor are still poor and more isolated from economic life than ever before. Many of our old neighborhoods have steadily lost homes, businesses, people, and joy even as the city's gross population has increased. New jobs, new industry, even a new university and a new medical school did not bring to the community at large heightened creative energy or a climate that nurtured innovation. Although the cultural landscape has improved in many ways, thanks largely to heavy public funding, San Antonio still cannot sustain a well-stocked bookstore or CD store, an opera company, or professional theater and dance.

Despite a dramatic rise in the number of noses, it would distort the

truth to say that San Antonio has grown much since I was a child. Growth is
something that organisms do, organically. The ankle bone's connected to the
shin bone, the shin bone's connected to the ham bone, and they all grow and
develop as an integrated ensemble. San Antonio grew until World War II,
and then it stopped. Since the war, and especially since about 1960, San Antonio has grown mainly as a sunken ship grows, by the accretion of bar-
nacles—hundreds of separate subdivisions, each with its protective shell,
having little to do with each other or with the city to which they are attached.

Most San Antonians today live in a wide ring of post-1960 suburban
developments that we Old San Antonians disparagingly call Loopland after
the beltways that girdle the metropolis. In Loopland nothing connects with
anything else. Loopland's commercial corridors are ugly, congested, and
hard to use; its residential enclaves are graceless and cheap—even where they
are exquisitely pricey. There are no civic spaces and few parks. There are no
neighborhoods, only insular subdivisions. Many of the new residential enclaves are surrounded by walls and protected (flimsily) by guards and gates.
Their parks, swimming pools, and streets, and even a large portion of their
taxes, called more politely the dues or assessments of their homeowners' associations, are strictly private, for use by their own residents only. There are
no places in Loopland for the bonds of community to take hold. Loopland
has little in common culturally or economically with Old San Antonio. If
Old San Antonio is a distinctive place, its unique history inscribed on nearly
every city block, Loopland and its way of life could be anywhere. There is no
shared life in Loopland, no historical memory, no soil to sustain roots. It
is a location to be occupied for a while and then abandoned without sentiment, turf to be guarded, not a garden to be husbanded. It's like a parking lot
for lives.

More troubling, Loopland and its people are radically disengaged
from Old San Antonio. Routine movement between the old and new cities is
increasingly difficult, uncommon, and, with the flight of jobs and shopping
to Loopland, unnecessary. Many Looplanders come downtown only when
their visiting relatives must be shown the Alamo and the River Walk. Many
say they fear to come into the city to attend a symphony concert or visit a
museum or eat at a restaurant—a fear based more on myth than reality.

Looplanders are not stakeholders in the Old San Antonio, nor are Old San Antonians stakeholders in Loopland. The two have little to do with each other socially, politically, or economically. We are all impoverished by the division.

The story that I have told you about San Antonio could be repeated, with slight variation, about most American cities and even about the countless small towns sucked dry by the Wal-Mart and the shopping plaza on the expressway. In our rush to build houses and roads and shopping malls and office parks and guardhouses—lots of guardhouses—we neglected the basic principles of sustainability, livability, and economic progress. We built things, but we forgot how to build communities.

We have been brought to this pass partly by the greed, thoughtlessness, and laziness of developers and business leaders, partly by the timidity and cupidity of local politicians, partly by the failures of the civil engineering and planning professions, and partly by the shortsightedness and inattentiveness of ordinary people—myself included—who did not understand the long-term consequences of their actions, or their inaction.

In this book I try to help you understand some of those consequences, and I suggest alternatives that I believe return to basic, proven urban design principles while accommodating the realities of modern life. This is not, however, meant only as an intellectual exercise. It is part of a personal crusade to reclaim my own city. I hope that you will make it part of a personal crusade to reclaim the city that is yours.

I owe a great debt to the *San Antonio Express-News* for having given me a free and secure platform from which to observe urban planning issues since 1979. Some passages in this book have been tried out, in somewhat different form, in my newspaper column. The newspaper's editor-and-publisher emeritus, Charles O. Kilpatrick, deserves particular credit or blame, depending on one's point of view, for having nudged me in the direction of urban criticism. Innumerable readers have shared insights, gripes, and magazine clippings with me. Their lively concern with planning issues has been a great encouragement. It's nice to know that someone is listening.

Many individuals in the fields of planning, architecture, and real estate development have been invaluable as sounding boards, foils, reality checks, inspirations, and idea generators during and before the preparation of this manuscript. Here are a few, some of whom may not have been aware that they were being used: Robert Ashcroft, Rosemary Catacalos, Ed Cross, Larry DeMartino, George Geis, Kate Martin, Michael O'Neal, Patricia Osborne, Andrew Perez, Jeff Pilarski, Boone Powell, the late Cathy Powell, René Ramirez, Genevieve Ray, Roland Rodriguez, Eloy Rosales, Steve Tillotson, and Cy Wagner. My close friend Duaine Jackola, a biophysicist, provided cogent criticism of the manuscript and suggested some productive paths of analysis drawn from biological themes. My editors of the Urban Life and Urban Landscape series, Henry Shapiro and Zane Miller, provided constant encouragement, shameless flattery, and gentle but always useful questions and suggestions. I am especially grateful to Ohio State University Press Managing Editor Ruth Melville and to copyeditor Nancy Woodington for their sensitive reading and insightful editing.

Although I didn't realize it at the time, long observation of my parents' experience as small retailers greatly influenced my understanding of urban design issues and informs many pages of this book.

Because nothing, or at any rate very little, in this book is original with me, the greatest debts are to those critics whom I have been able to admire only from a distance—Lewis Mumford, Jane Jacobs, and Ada Louise Huxtable. Standing on the shoulders of these giants is out of the question, but perhaps I can aspire to cling to their knees.

■ a theory of cities

 Before deciding what to do, it's a good idea to figure out why we want to do it. In Part 1 we consider the city in general terms. What is a city, anyway? What is it good for? What are we trying to get at when we use such phrases as "economic development," "quality of life," and "community" to talk about urban progress or decline? ■

■ the map and the community

 Let's begin with a thought experiment. Our guinea pig will be Chicago, a city whose people have been known to gripe on occasion about narrow streets, inadequate parking, the Cubs, and each other.

Suppose that all the people, businesses, and institutions of Chicago have been relocated to New Chicago, a fully planned utopian city that has been designed to avoid all the errors and inconveniences of Old Chicago. The streets are wide, and the parking lots stretch as far as the eye can see. In place of Old Chicago's gridiron street plan (which made it too easy for people of different economic classes and ethnic groups to annoy each other) stand New Chicago's hundreds of insular residential enclaves. To protect families from the dangers of commercial activity, stores and offices are located far from homes, and there are no sidewalks connecting them. The Cubs play at the convergence of expressways on the edge of town, in the Wrigleydome. In short, New Chicago looks like suburban Anytown, the utopian dream of traffic engineers.

The residents of New Chicago bring with them a rich network of customs, habits, and patterns that had been established over the years in Old Chicago. But in New Chicago some of these cannot be sustained. You can't walk around the corner to the neighborhood bar or bookstore; you have to drive to the nearest mall or entertainment strip. Other patterns can be sustained only with difficulty. Once-strong networks of affinities and friendship, now diffused across a larger geographical area, become thin and brittle. Because every errand, whether for pleasure or necessity, now requires a separate automobile or bus trip, errands of marginal importance drop from the daily routine. Some businesses that thrived in Old Chicago die in New Chicago because they are no longer situated on pathways that connect them effectively to their customers. Other kinds of businesses, more suited to the setting, take their place. People who tended bar in neighborhood taverns or acted in neighborhood theaters find new jobs as cashiers at self-service gas stations and stock clerks at Wal-Mart. Family-owned ethnic restaurants are supplanted by McDonald's and Jack-in-the-Box. Nobody walks anywhere. Motorists in their wheeled cocoons have few opportunities for serendipitous encounters or spur-of-the-moment decisions. Daily life becomes more fully planned, more inward-turning, and more static—more cellular and less social.

What are we to do with all those empty buildings left behind in Old Chicago? Let's repopulate Old Chicago with people, businesses, and institutions chosen by lot from throughout the United States. Nordstrom's occupies the former Marshall Field's stores, Florida State takes over the University of Chicago campus, and the Astros play in Wrigley Field. Much that is distinctive about Chicago is lost—the ethnic neighborhoods and, with them, the concentrated markets, traditions, and information exchanges that make possible large numbers of good ethnic restaurants; the loyalties, shared memories, and stable patterns of behavior that bind individuals into communities; perhaps the special role of the Catholic Church, with its sheltering neighborhood parishes and schools. Because nearly everyone is a stranger to everyone else, this repopulated Chicago starts out with no social or (what amounts to the same thing) economic networks. Everyone is an individual cell.

But if the physical city remains the same, many of the old social patterns will quickly reassert themselves on the new people. A city that is organized in a particular way lends itself to some ways of being used and resists being used in other ways, whether the users are newcomers or long-time residents. Within a few weeks the new residents of Old Chicago, formerly strangers to each other, will be gathering as friends at their neighborhood taverns to grouse about the Astros and the shortage of parking.

This book is an exegesis on a maxim attributed to Winston Churchill: "We shape our cities, and then our cities shape us." If that is true, then we need to take care to shape cities that will shape the us we want to be. But "we" is a presumptuous pronoun, including within its scope many individuals with many points of view about how they wish to live. I'll tell you my point of view, and you can decide if you like my version of "we."

We are diverse, prosperous, and free.

We imagine and make things to enhance one another's well-being. Our urban economy gives small, local, independent entrepreneurs access to concentrated markets and a fair shake in competition with national, mass-market retailers. We share in a lively, creative market for goods, services, and ideas, for the arts and sciences as well as for industry.

We have freedom of access to the whole city on uncongested roads and good mass transit, but we also have freedom of access to and within our own neighborhood centers on sidewalks that work. Our neighborhood's children have safe and easy access to many positive, stimulating experiences outside home and school. Our neighborhood welcomes and meets the needs of many kinds of people—the elderly, the handicapped, single people as well as one-parent and two-parent families, and people with a wide range of incomes.

We live in a neighborhood, in a city of neighborhoods. By "neighborhood" I don't mean just a developer's subdivision or a sector on a street map, but an integrated urban microcosm with ample opportunities for shopping, recreation, culture, and socializing near our homes. We enjoy the intangible pleasures and tangible security of community—an environment in which neighbors are not just people who watch television in living rooms situated on the same street, but who also have a shared life on the neighborhood's sidewalks and in its parks, stores, and restaurants. We are able to invent and express our individual selves, but we are also participants in a community.

That is the "we" I think we would like to be. But neither the individual nor the community has been well served by the patterns of building that have shaped America's expanding cities and suburbs since World War II, and more particularly since about 1960. The litany of complaints is all too familiar: the new way of building honors the automobile over the person, the real estate speculator and developer over the community, concrete and asphalt over trees, plastic fast-food homogeneity over local culture, giantism over the little guy, conformity over individuality, ugliness over beauty.

In many American cities, the public policies that allowed or encouraged the new way of building have been justified in the name of something called economic development, always, for some reason, seen as the polar opposite to something called quality of life. In my city, San Antonio, the polarizing rhetoric attained the absurd during the 1980s. Mainstream politicians and business leaders seriously asserted that, if the city adopted planning policies to promote efficiency, convenience, sustainable growth, environmental responsibility, and beauty, McDonald's and Kmart would abandon the city, jobs would dry up, and all the people would starve. Or words to that effect.

The opposing camps too often talk past each other, staking out positions that do not adequately serve either's purposes. The "economic development" folks advocate policies that they call "pro-growth" and "pro-business" and oppose public planning frameworks that encroach on private prerogatives, but "pro-business" policies have turned out to have antibusiness consequences—growth that exceeds a community's capacity to serve it at a politically acceptable cost, geographic dispersal and dilution of the market (and thus of sales and profits), traffic congestion and its associated costs, and ultimately, in many cities, an antigrowth, antideveloper backlash. On the other side, the "quality of life" folks too often demand, and are satisfied with, such purely aesthetic measures as landscaping standards and sign controls that may prettify the city while leaving it a functional mess; in the name of property values and security this side often demands solutions that cause more problems than they solve.

I don't believe that quality of life must be bought at the cost of less economic development, or vice versa. I believe *economic development* and *quality of life* are two shorthand terms that refer—not exclusively, but in large measure—to the same phenomenon, the propensity of people to create value for other people and to engage in free, peaceful, mutually beneficial, and multifaceted exchange. Some ways of organizing the physical space of a city contribute to that propensity; others inhibit it.

We need to reconsider what *economic development* and *quality of life* mean and to ask how they relate to each other in the concrete and steel and glass and grass and flesh and flux of real cities, real neighborhoods, real people living real lives.

THE GREEKS HAD A WORD FOR IT

This book's title may strike some readers as odd. Poetics? To the Greeks, the term *poetics* was not restricted to what we now call poetry. One modern translator of Aristotle's *Poetics*, Kenneth Telford, suggests that the Greek might better be rendered as "productive science" and understood to cover "any kind of making, including the products of both useful and fine art, but only in respect of their production, not in respect of any external criterion or purpose they might serve. A 'poem' is therefore *anything* made or produced."[1] Homer's *Iliad* was a poem, but so are a bridge, a coffee grinder, an algebraic equation, and my lovely but immobile 1980 Fiat roadster. (Some poems, after all, are made badly.)

And a city, too, is a poem. As Aristotle was concerned with the characteristics of a well-formed play, I am concerned with the characteristics of a well-formed city. Because poetics deals with things that are made by people, the rules of making are not inscribed in natural law but drawn from experience, practical reason, and discussion. The method of poetics is to develop an ethos, based on our experience of the poetic objects and the people who use them, about how things should be crafted to do what they're supposed to do.

To Aristotle, in the *Poetics*, *ethos* meant character, in the sense of personal qualities. To us, *ethos* means custom, or how things are done—the character-in-practice of a social group or nation. I might just as well have used the more familiar *ethics*, although the two English words have slightly different colorations. If *ethos* refers broadly to the standards and assumptions of a given community, *ethics* carries a more personal force, dealing with how you and I ought to treat each other. Poetics has an ethical dimension in that any object made for human use is a surrogate for the maker's conduct toward the user. To make an object well or ill is to treat the user well or ill. To make an object is also to make assumptions about the user and to change the user's life, if only in a small way. Poetics is ethics at one remove. The poetics of cities is also the ethics of cities.

| One concern of this book is to consider how we can treat our neighbors ethically by crafting the physical city in such a way that it can be easily used by all its people—so that not only able-bodied, well-off adults with cars but also children, the elderly, the poor, the blind, the halt, and the lame can have freedom of movement and convenient access to all the good things that cities offer. We can strive for no less if we imagine ourselves to be a just and ethical society. Political and economic freedom in the abstract mean little without practical freedom of movement and action. |

| Good urban design enables people to get around safely, efficiently, and in pleasant surroundings, creating value in a fairly direct and obvious way. But good urban design also creates value indirectly by enabling a city's *people* to create value and make it available to others through free exchange. At one level we're concerned with the city's hardware; at another level we're concerned with the software—with what people *do* in the city. As we shall see, the most important thing that people *do* in cities is exchange things—goods, services, and money, but also ideas, beliefs, knowledge, and love—with other people. |

⊢ Exchange depends upon proximity. And proximity is the business of cities. |

Or at least it used to be. After World War II, and increasingly after 1960, urban form fundamentally changed with the rise of the regional shopping mall, the large discount store, the fast-food franchise, the office park, the interstate highway system, the insular residential subdivision, and the functional segregation brought about by land-use zoning—in sum, suburbanization, American style. Proximity and connectedness—which were a matter of course in the more compact, intimately scaled city of the past—have been replaced by fragmentation and separation, both in the expanding peripheries and, increasingly, in the decaying and urban-renewaled interiors of cities. Exchange of goods, knowledge, and ideas is inhibited.

Television, radio, computer bulletin boards, and other electronic media now provide an artificial proximity, but this is a pale imitation of the real proximity of a glance at the shop window and a visit to the neighbors.

I am not a geographic determinist. An arrangement of urban space that facilitates exchange will not solve all urban ills. Connectedness and proximity are, I believe, necessary conditions for a healthy economy, culture, and community, but they are not the only necessary conditions, and they are certainly not sufficient conditions. Nor do I entertain nostalgic yearnings for the supposed golden age before automobiles, expressways, television, and Wal-Mart. (Well, maybe Wal-Mart.)

I do, however, entertain a reasonable and practical hope that these and other features of contemporary culture can be integrated into a coherent framework that facilitates many kinds of exchange and preserves not just the sense of community but the fact of it. That is the guiding principle behind a poetics of cities.

There is a lot at stake in this project. The intense creativity and democratization that occurred in cities from the Middle Ages through the late industrial period were, I believe, associated with the physicality of those cities—not just with the fact of concentration but with the *how* of it, with certain characteristics of scale and density and the way the parts interrelated. The compact city of the old style is now valued, where it survives, mainly for its "historic charm." But it also was and is a highly efficient technology for fostering innovation, supporting diversity, and extending freedom while at the same time maintaining a stable base of historical consciousness, tradition, and social cohesion. I don't want to dismiss the undeniable difficulties, dangers, and injustices of life in the premodern city, but it seems to me there was something about the way historic cities were assembled that brought people, things, and ideas together in a self-sustaining, continually spiraling cycle of exchanges that created value.

In its essence, the city is a technology and a medium of communication. But in that case, haven't advances in electronic communications made the city obsolete? Isn't the old city of streets and stores and theaters and offices being supplanted by the new city of fiber-optic cable and dispersed work stations?

I do not believe that the communitarian city of personal contact is obsolete, either economically or socially. It used to be predicted that thirty or forty channels of cable television would keep people glued constantly to the TV. But in the decade since cable television came to my city, the use of parks, theaters, and recreation facilities has increased, not decreased, even in inner-city neighborhoods where population has declined. People still want to get out of the house and enjoy community life in the company of their neighbors. It seems that the more options are available electronically, the more we appreciate what electronics can't give us. Corporations whose idea workers can now do their jobs in private offices, connected to their colleagues only by computer networks and telephones, have learned the importance of architectural features that encourage, even require, serendipitous social contact at strategically placed water coolers and lounges, which is where much of the real work gets done.

Well-made cities and city neighborhoods have certain essential capabilities that lie beyond the scope of other communications media. The advertising slogan notwithstanding, a telephone is useless if you want to reach out and touch someone, or some thing. Face-to-face (or face-to-object) contact is qualitatively different—indeed, even quantitatively different, measured in terms of the bits of information exchanged—from any existing or foreseeable form of electronic communication, including virtual reality. And it is face-to-face contact that the city as a communications technology is designed to achieve. Neither a fulfilling personal life nor an advancing economic life can be detached from a healthy community life. There is a value-creating energy in the well-formed city that cannot be duplicated by other technologies, however powerful and brilliant and liberating they may be. The task before us is to regain and revivify cityness so that we may make full use of this creative power.

THE PLAN OF THE BOOK

In chapters 2 and 3 I begin to dig beneath the surface of "development" and "economic development." City leaders err, I believe, in identifying "development" with new construction, irrespective of how the new construction relates to its surroundings, and "economic development" with new jobs and the importation of money, irrespective of their contribution to citizens' well-being. The question to be asked is not How can we create more jobs and construct more buildings in the fourth quarter? or How can we get more corporate headquarters this year? but rather How can we set in motion a self-sustaining spiral of value creation and exchange? We will see the well-formed, economically healthy city and neighborhood as a community in which wealth increases as people create things of value and exchange them with each other. The opportunity to engage in free exchanges of many kinds, with many kinds of people, is the principal advantage that cities have over other patterns of settlement, and the principal reason that cities exist. Exchange, moreover, is essential both to commerce and to much of what we think of as quality of life, and certainly to its cultural components. If a city is organized in a way that encourages exchange, then both commerce and culture (which in its broadest sense includes commerce) will benefit.

In chapters 4–9, I show how physical pathways and connections affect exchange in cities and, more particularly, in neighborhoods, whether in urban or suburban contexts. Chapter 4 introduces the notion of the urban matrix, a framework for collaboration in city-building, and chapters 5–9 consider how an urban matrix designed to foster exchange might be applied both in the large sense—"urban form" in the jargon of planners—and in the small, in the minutiae of sidewalks, parking lots, shop windows, front porches, and their connections with each other. A major objective is to bring the lasting lessons of the traditional city to bear on the planning of new suburban development, in the hope that the values of community, connectivity, and free exchange may eventually supplant the insularity and fragmentation that suburban development practices of the past thirty or forty years have brought about.

While many American cities have made the wrong decisions in recent decades, some models exist (here and abroad) to show that the automobile and modern business realities can be domesticated and made compatible with the city's needs for proximity and connected pathways. With careful planning, it is not necessary to throw out the baby with the bath water.

But meaningful planning is never an abstract enterprise. Planning and urban design policies inescapably reflect the tugs of political interests. Chapter 10 surveys some of the political realities and serves as a reminder that, if you want your city and neighborhood to change, you have to immerse yourself in the political process. In chapter 11 I hope to persuade you that the stakes are worth fighting for.

■ porches, sidewalks, and the gift community

 We will begin by sticking our heads out my front door, because it is at front doors like yours and mine that the geography and economy of a city begin. A blurry transitional zone links the private space of my home with the public space of the city. There are no curtains on the tall arched window that faces the street; anybody can look into my living room, and I can look back. The front door opens to a porch, the size of a small bedroom, shaded by a metal canopy and bordered by a low stucco wall. Sometimes I sit on the wall and watch the passersby on the street and sidewalk.

/ A porch is an odd kind of place—not quite private, even though it is well within the property line, and not quite public, even though it may be open to the elements and vulnerable to strangers. Because it is usually built a foot or two above the street level, a porch shares some of the characteristics of a balcony, but is less off-putting. /

In *The Politics and Poetics of Transgression*, Peter Stallybrass and Allon White wrote:

> The gaze/the touch: desire/contamination. These contradictory concepts underlie the symbolic significance of the *balcony* in nineteenth-century literature and painting. From

the balcony, one could gaze, but not be touched. The gentle-man farmer who presided over a harvest feast would com-monly arrange the table so that he could sit at its head *inside the house*, distributing hospitality through an open window or door. Similarly, the bourgeoisie on their balconies could both participate in the banquet of the streets and yet remain separated.[1]

If this passage gives off a faint odor of antielitist disapproval, I don't share it. To "participate in the banquet of the streets and yet remain sepa-rated" is the signal gift of the city to its inhabitants. The front porch and the balcony were great advances in the technology of the city—while they lasted.

From the very fact that I have a proper front porch you may have guessed that I live in an older neighborhood. The impression is confirmed by the proper sidewalk, separated from the street by a strip of grass, locally called a "parkway," five feet wide. The sidewalk is well used. From my perch on the porch I see young couples pushing baby carriages or walking their dogs, older folks on an evening stroll, the blind man tapping with his cane, families carrying grocery bags from the supermarket around the corner, teen-agers going to visit friends or walking to and from the high school five blocks to the west. The sidewalk, like the porch, is a transitional space in the geography of the city—less public than the roadway, less private than the porch. Legally the sidewalk is public space, lying outside my property line and within the street right-of-way, but I am still responsible for maintaining it and its environs. As pedestrians on the sidewalk pass in front of my prop-erty, they enter my sphere of influence. They enjoy or endure my landscap-ing and the architecture of my house. If I happen to be outside they might catch my gaze, and I theirs. A brief and distant intimacy connects these strangers with me because the public space of the sidewalk brings them, in a socially authorized and (usually) nonthreatening manner, into my world; when I use the sidewalk to pass in front of their houses, the intimacy is recip-rocated. A very different and colder kind of relationship obtains in neigh-borhoods where there are no sidewalks and pedestrians must walk in the street. But we will talk about such things in more detail later. For the moment, let's stroll west toward the high school while I tell you about my neighborhood.

My part of San Antonio was built up from the late 1920s to the 1940s about three miles northwest of downtown. An aerial photograph taken in the early thirties shows neat, nearly treeless blocks stretching for about a mile west and then yielding abruptly to a dairy farm. The new neighborhood attracted the expanding merchant and professional classes. For several decades, until the early sixties, the area was especially popular with Jewish families. Lutheran, Disciples of Christ, Baptist, Methodist, and Presbyterian churches lie within an easy walk of my house. The Conservative synagogue is a little farther west on my street, but the congregation is preparing to move to new quarters several miles to the northwest, in a newer suburban area where the Jewish community is now centered.

The houses in my neighborhood range from modest one-story cottages to imposing Mediterranean-style villas on two levels. As we proceed west along the sidewalk, you can see that the architecture is extravagantly eclectic. From my vaguely Pueblo-style stucco house with its flat roof and historically improbable arched window, we pass the sturdy brick bungalow with its broad, low-pitched roof next door and, across the street, the charming fairy-tale cottage of stucco mixed with brick under a steep pitched roof of red clay tiles. Here we have a very distant echo of Palladio, with an otherwise plain stucco exterior highlighted by a trio of arched windows—two narrow ones flanking a wider one—centered under a moderately pitched roof. Note the rustic house of irregular stone with the half-timbered gables, followed by a pair of white stucco Spanish colonials decorated with painted Mexican tiles. Further on, we meet Norman-French designs with pointed-arch stained-glass windows befitting a church, plain wood-frame cottages and bungalows, Tudor half-timber affairs, echoes of Italianate, and very strange things with delightful facades of brick randomly mixed with rock dug up during construction.

It is important to note that not all parts of my neighborhood are eclectic in the same way. A walk of several blocks will take you into several distinct tonal regions, to borrow a musical term. Some blocks tend to have more rock houses in vaguely English rustic styles, while other nearby blocks tend to have more modest cottages of wood, depending on the developers and architects who happened to work in those sectors of the neighborhood. But the whole area is unified because the same architectural themes that are dominant in some blocks may also appear here and there as highlights on other blocks. In a concentrated area in the northwest part of my neighborhood, for example, there are more than thirty houses and small apartment buildings that were designed by an underappreciated architect-developer of the 1930s and 1940s, Nathan Straus Nayfach, who dreamed of making quality architecture available to the middle class. But isolated examples of his work (which was itself eclectic but identifiable by signature details of craftsmanship in stone or brick) can also be found a few blocks away from that concentration.

Many of the houses, regardless of architectural style, include a feature that is most typical of the bungalow. The front porch, usually eight or ten feet deep and framed by heavy columns or arches, extends across roughly half of the facade from the front door to the driveway and often continues a short distance around the side. This device creates a sheltered path from the car to the front door, theoretically for the convenience of visitors. In practice the residents themselves usually park next to the porch (rather than in the detached garage at the rear) and enter by the front door. Their comings and goings are visible to neighbors, not just as the movements of four-wheeled shuttle craft into and out of garages equipped with remote-controlled doors but as the movements of actual people, with faces. In this way architectural design helps bind a collection of homeowners into a community. People in my neighborhood are made visible to each other in a routine way, brought into the quasi-public space of the front porch, without in any sense submitting to an invasion of privacy. Architectural design is not just a matter of inert aesthetics.

But aesthetics is nothing to be sneezed at. Although many of these were "developer houses," as they would be called today, they benefited from the handiwork of locally important individual artisans. My fireplace, for example, is faced with a Mayan bas-relief design executed in plaster by (I'm told) a man who did much of the interior work in San Antonio's historic Aztec Theater. In other houses, one sees the metalsmith's hand in the distinctive lighting fixtures, the master mason's craft in unusual patterns of brick and stone, the tile worker's art from Mexico. It is a neighborhood with Character.

My part of town is called by several names. Some of the original subdivision names are still seen on modern maps—Woodlawn Terrace, Monticello Park, Furr Addition. But the area is most widely known as the Jefferson neighborhood, for Thomas Jefferson High School, which opened in 1932. We're approaching it now. With its silver domes (originally colorful tile) and rich Spanish baroque detailing, its division into a cluster of variously massed wings and buildings connected by arcades and courtyards, its grand placement on a slight rise amid a broad and gracious lawn, Jefferson is still one of the nation's finest examples of school architecture. It is a national landmark—listed on the National Register of Historic Places—and was used as the location for a 1930s film. It is also, of course, a neighborhood landmark, a focus of neighborhood pride. The place still gives me a thrill every time I pass by, even though I attended its snootier and newer crosstown rival, Alamo Heights.

Beyond the high school is a residential area that was built up mostly in the forties and fifties, although a few houses, including a mini-Alhambra with a Moorish-arched porch, are earlier. A few blocks west of the high school is a neighborhood retail hub that was alive with shops through the 1960s and now has fallen on hard times, although the original hobby shop remains in business. But our concern now is with the older part of the neighborhood, so we'll reverse course and walk back east from the high school. As we walk, I'll tell you more about the neighborhood's history. It's a familiar story, repeated in countless inner city neighborhoods throughout the country.

The same process that brought merchants and professionals to the Jefferson neighborhood in the thirties and forties sent them to still newer subdivisions farther north in the sixties and seventies. They wanted larger and more modern houses on larger lots, they wanted better schools, they wanted semirural serenity, and—let's be blunt—some of them wanted to get away from people of color.

Unlike many older neighborhoods in San Antonio and other cities, however, Jefferson never fell into ruin as a result of suburban flight. The neighborhood just sagged a little, and although patches of blight appeared, they tended to be small and isolated. The flight of wealth wasn't complete: Many of the early residents stayed, especially those whose children had finished high school and who continued to have strong bonds with neighborhood churches and synagogues. Those who departed were generally replaced by middle-class families of various hues. Many were the upwardly mobile sons and daughters of the West Side, the low-income Hispanic neighborhood that begins a couple of miles south of Jefferson; now successful professionals, civil servants, and tradespeople, these individuals are kept close to home by strong family loyalties. Many young families are returnees—people who were raised here, moved to newer areas as adults, and then came back to their old houses when their parents died. There is a fair share of newcomers to the city, people who simply like older neighborhoods and the opportunity to restore or renovate old houses. And many bargain hunters were drawn to Jefferson by the low housing prices relative to comparable houses in the city's pricey historic districts. Today the neighborhood closely reflects the ethnic and economic mix of the city as a whole, but with the economic extremes lopped off. Property values in Jefferson didn't rise as quickly as they did in other parts of town during boom times, but neither did Jefferson see the blight that set in on other inner-city neighborhoods.

Why? In part, I think, because of the architectural character of the neighborhood and its landmarks. People take a little extra care to preserve things that have a little extra value, and many of the houses in the Jefferson area have that extra value—not in terms of sale prices, but in terms of the human care and individual attention put into their architecture. The tile work, the cartouches, the quoins, the eccentric masonry, the improbable little turrets and porte cocheres, all the other improvisatory and non-mass-produced touches are gifts from the hands and imaginations of their makers. In the strict sense this is not true, because the makers were paid for their labors, and their artisanry entered the system of commodity exchange along with the plumbing and electrical systems, the roofs and walls and foundations of basic shelter. Nonetheless, while I intend no disrespect toward the building trades, there is a difference in kind between a plumbing or electrical system based on standard, manufactured components put together according to preordained rules and products of the imagination. The value of imaginative labor is not quantifiable and bears only an arbitrary relationship to the price or wage paid for it. There is usually a surplus of intangible value, not accounted for by price or wage, and that surplus is a gift.

In his wonderful book *The Gift: Imagination and the Erotic Life of Property*,[2] the literary critic Lewis Hyde shows how a gift remains a gift only so long as it remains in circulation, freely passed on to other members of the "gift community." While a gift remains in circulation, its value increases, in the sense that a table service passed down from mother to daughter through the generations has more value than one purchased new at a department store, even if the new one is fancier and more expensive than the old one. If a gift is hoarded by the recipient, its value diminishes, and in some cultures the deadending of a gift may even carry a curse. At a minimum, removing gifts from circulation damages social cohesion and function, just as a blown fuse or a thrown switch will stop the circulation of electrical current and prevent your appliances from operating.

Now I, sitting in my living room, cannot see or enjoy what is distinctive or gift-like on the outside of my house. I can, however, see and enjoy the houses across the street, and the residents of those houses can see and enjoy my house. To the extent that we take care of our houses, preserve for the enjoyment of our neighbors the beauty and distinctiveness that was first given to us by our houses' makers, we participate in a gift community. In this way we continually exchange gifts with each other, are bound to each other, even if we never speak. One leaves a community like this only with reluctance.

If you have a house that includes a goodly measure of gift, you are subtly impelled to take better care of it than you might if the house did not reveal the hand of the maker, did not include a measure of gift. You take better care of the lawn, you keep the stucco patched and the walls neatly painted. And if most of your neighbors take care of their property in this way, they establish a neighborhood ethos, a habit, that tends to rub off on you even if your particular house happens not to be very interesting.

In the vulgar jargon of the real estate business, houses that are made and maintained in this special way have "curb appeal," something that might translate into an extra $5,000 or $10,000 in resale price. But most houses, most of the time, are not up for sale. Most houses, most of the time, are people's homes—links in the chain of a neighborhood, a gift community. It seems reasonable to suppose that, if people are willing to pay a high monetary price for curb appeal when a house is for sale, then curb appeal must correspond to something of nonmonetary but real value when the house *isn't* for sale—when it's just a home rather than a commodity. Call it satisfaction or pride of ownership if you want, but I think that this value must have at least as much to do with giving as with owning. Except perhaps in the ritziest neighborhoods—which often aren't really neighborhoods, anyway—people do not generally buy or build beautiful houses with fine front yards only to hoard them, hide them from the view of their neighbors behind high walls. Nor do most people choose a neighborhood, a house, or a shrub solely on the basis of a calculation of their future resale value. The vitality of the gift community is intrinsically valuable to people while they are living there, not just when they are ready to sell their houses and move on.

The gift community is not just a matter of static aesthetics, however. A healthy gift community is valuable in all sorts of unromantic, hard-nosed ways, providing benefits for security, social order, and economic development. The exchange of gifts—that is, the exchange of the surplus value we create for one another—entails movement of people, goods, and ideas, including ideas about how we should conduct ourselves and relate to one another. Thus pathways and proximity are essential to a gift community. Where the pathway ends, where proximity is denied, the gift community also ends.

WHERE THE GIFT COMMUNITY ENDS

Walking back toward the east, we pass my house again and, at the corner, see immediately that something is wrong. Facing us on the other side of the street are the ramshackle rear ends of commercial buildings, a Dumpster, a used car lot, weeds. The gift community has come to an abrupt stop.

Something used to be wonderfully right about the retail hub that anchored the eastern end of my neighborhood. The retail center was built up in stages during the 1930s and 1940s along Fredericksburg Road, a major artery running northwest from downtown. (As its name implies, Fredericksburg Road was originally the road to Fredericksburg, a picturesque town of German settlers in the Hill Country northwest of San Antonio.) A few of the smaller buildings of the thirties reflect Spanish Colonial or Mission Revival styles vaguely related to that of the high school. The Woodlawn Theater and its attached retail center—with a bowling alley on the second floor—came in the 1940s and were in the Art Moderne style, with deep blue Vitrilite cladding on the outside. The theater was one of the later efforts of architect John Eberson, who designed many of the nation's most flamboyant atmospheric movie palaces of the 1920s, including San Antonio's recently restored Majestic Theater. John Wayne's film *The Alamo* had its world premiere at the Woodlawn. Terrible movie; nice theater. The attached retail building was designed by Nayfach.

In its heyday this neighborhood retail hub, extending for several blocks along Fredericksburg Road, had just about everything you might want. There was a cafeteria, a men's clothing store, a women's shoe store, a hardware store, a grocery store, a bakery, a drugstore, beauty and barber shops, the lumberyard (cunningly disguised behind a retail front) where my father bought sand for my sandbox, a barbecue place, gas stations in Mission Revival and Moderne styles, and the Italian restaurant that introduced pizza to San Antonio in the 1950s.

If you drove into my neighborhood from almost any other part of town, you almost certainly drove through the Woodlawn retailing hub. Because of the pattern of arterial roads, this area serves as the most probable gateway to the Jefferson residential neighborhood—but not, in the early 1990s, the sort of gateway to inspire the current residents with pride or potential new neighbors with confidence.

The retail center saw increasing vacancies as regional shopping malls lured away the customers and the shops. The changing economics of the movie exhibition industry made the big, single-screen theater unprofitable; the Woodlawn was divided into a three-screen complex, struggled for a short time, and then went dark, reopening intermittently and briefly as a live theater and then as an evangelical church. Similar pressures closed the bowling alley, which had only about a dozen lanes. The businesses that remain constitute a mixed bag of neighborhood retailing and light commercial or industrial firms (a small barbecue restaurant, a small manufacturer and retailer of ice cream bars, a billiards supply place, a T-shirt printing shop, an industrial supply company) and commercial schools (a ballet academy and a beauty college, the latter until recently called the University for the Arts and Sciences of Cosmetology).

If you were to add up all the neighborhood-service retailers within a four-block span, you'd find a nice assemblage of useful, even indispensable, shopping. A liquor store, a beauty shop, a waterbed store, an optician, an ice cream parlor, a dry cleaner, two convenience stores, and a health club seem to be holding on, as are the hardware store, barbershop, and meat market dating from the forties. The grocery store, part of a large regional chain, grew up to be a supermarket with a congested parking lot. The Laundromat is doing well. While some storefronts and buildings have been recently vacated, new businesses have come in. A savings-and-loan opened a busy branch in what had been a long-vacant convenience store. A bakery thrift shop opened where a tire store had been.

But simple enumeration of stores and businesses doesn't tell the whole story. Many of the retailers are marginal. Several have opened and closed—one by arson—while I was writing this book. Patches of blight, vacant buildings, and bare parking lots separate the businesses from each other. Few buildings or storefronts are attractive, and most are poorly maintained. While the Woodlawn Theater's handsome marquee remains, the shiny blue Moderne exterior has been replaced by an insensitive drab stucco finish. A forest of utility poles and a web of overhead lines further mar the area's appearance. Parking is awkward, and walking is unpleasant. Weeds poking through broken asphalt constitute virtually the only greenery. The place is a jumble, neither physically nor visually considerate to potential customers.

Because the businesses are dispersed, the clientele of one shop is not encouraged to visit the shop next door—often there *is* no shop next door, or at least not the kind of place that fits into a typical shopping pattern. People do not customarily run down to the corner for a quart of milk and a bucket of industrial fasteners. These conditions tend to depress the customer base and inhibit sales. As a result, existing businesses and property owners have few resources to improve the environment, and potential new businesses are discouraged from moving in.

Because this retail center is the neighborhood's gateway, it exerts subtle long-term forces on the residential streets that radiate from it. One of these forces is psychological. As residents unavoidably, several times a day, drive or walk through the retail center, they are not made to feel good about their neighborhood. Neither are potential new residents; the appearance of the retail hub raises a question about the trajectory of the neighborhood—is it going up or down?—and the wisdom of investing in a house there. A psychological force can also be an economic force.

Another force is an urban variant of the Second Law of Thermodynamics: without constant vigilance and intervention, disorder—of both the material and behavioral kinds—tends to increase. Blight and commercial incursion spread from the disordered area and weaken the residential area surrounding it. I have been concentrating on the Jefferson neighborhood just west of the retail center and Fredericksburg Road, but similar observations could be made about the smaller Keystone neighborhood—more modest but with an extraordinary collection of populist Spanish Colonial houses—east of the Woodlawn retail hub and the working-class Los Angeles Heights neighborhood to the north. Because several arterial roads and bus lines converge within the Woodlawn retailing area from all four cardinal compass points in addition to the southeast and northwest, the retail area (whose old core is the shaded area in figure 2.1) occupies a strategic location for a large swath of the city. A major investment in redevelopment would do more good (or ill) for more people if it were placed here than if it were placed at any other location within a two- or three-mile radius. The same factors that make this location strategic in its positive or negative effects on surrounding

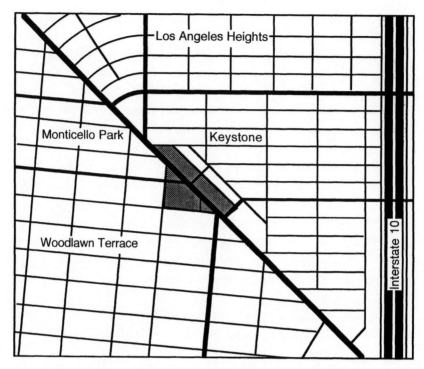

Figure 2.1 My neighborhood and its strategically located retail center.

neighborhoods also give it excellent potential for retail development—if a developer could be found with the vision to recognize that potential and the ability to exploit it in the right way.

A CASE STUDY OF THE DEVELOPMENT PROCESS

A prominent fellow in San Antonio often introduces himself like this: "When my children ask me what I do for a living, I tell them I rob banks and steal from widows and orphans, because I don't want them to know I'm a real estate developer." Real estate developers have become suspect in America, especially after the absurd overbuilding of the 1980s and the inevitable real estate collapse (which contributed to the financial industry collapse) of the early nineties. Real estate developers are not necessarily bad people. The problem is that few of them are actually in the business of *developing* real estate, as opposed to speculating in it. Development in the genuine sense is a complicated and long and often painful process.

I'd like to introduce you to someone I know. His name is George Geis. He's a small-scale developer and contractor in San Antonio. When I moved into my house, just half a block from the old Woodlawn retailing hub, I called George and asked his opinion about what could be done to revive it. To my surprise, he soon began working in earnest on a redevelopment plan. It turned out he had been interested in this neighborhood for several years. The project he has in mind is still far from coming together—it may never happen at all—but the planning process that Geis is following, in concert with neighborhood associations, provides an insight into what the gift community means in terms of the physical space of the city and the social space within which decisions about physical space are made.

Geis did many of the things that any other developer would do. He studied traffic counts and neighborhood demographics; he consulted with neighborhood merchants and with bankers to get their sense of the area's potential; he found out who owned the various parcels of land and how much they wanted for them; he talked with potential anchor tenants to determine their interest and needs—the basic groundwork that any speculative developer would have to do before deciding whether a retail project might be feasible.

The initial auguries were favorable. Traffic counts, expressway access, and crosstown street access were excellent. The bankers said the neighborhood had ample disposable income. An impending reconstruction of Fredericksburg Road might, during the months of construction and inconvenience, help to persuade property owners to sell at reasonable prices. The auguries were not, however, so favorable that Geis could simply take out a big loan, buy some land, bulldoze it, and build a new retail center—if he had been the type to do business that way in the first place.

He decided that, in order for the project to succeed financially, it would have to meet a lengthy and difficult list of criteria:

• **Critical mass.** It would do no good to redevelop one or two blocks to high standards while leaving the surrounding commercial blocks unchanged. A retail project's success depends on the synergistic effects of critical mass. It needs a concentration of a large number of shops of a wide variety in a context that encourages one-stop shopping—parking the car once and walking to several businesses. Geis decided that, in order to accomplish this goal, he would need to redevelop the entire hub, roughly four blocks on both sides of Fredericksburg Road—a very ambitious and costly prospect.

• **The right retail mix.** In order to obtain financing, Geis would have to entice several large chain retailers to make long-term lease commitments to the project. The commitment of these well-known and stable retailers, with built-in customer bases, would also be necessary in order to attract the smaller shops and restaurants that would fill out the project, give it character, and raise its value in the eyes of the surrounding neighborhoods. Geis met with the relevant neighborhood associations to ask what sorts of retailers they needed to have in the area, and what sorts they didn't want; but he also considered his own intuitions and experience about the retail mix needed for a viable neighborhood center.

• **Match the visual context of the neighborhood.** There could be no sharp visual demarcation, no psychological barrier, between the retail center and the surrounding residential neighborhood that would provide the main customer base. The project would have to fit in with the look, scale, and rhythm of the neighborhood in order to help solidify a community relationship between retailers and potential customers. The site plan would have to be a village-like cluster of buildings, with generous landscaping and street trees similar to those commonly seen in the neighborhood. The rhythm of solids and voids, the choice of materials, and the style of detailing on new buildings and restyled older ones would have to be related to those of the neighborhood. The older landmark buildings would have to be retained and integrated into the project. Geis studied the architecture of Jefferson High School and the neighborhood houses. Working with an architect, he began to develop a design vocabulary for his project.

• **Visual focus.** The chaotic appearance and layout of the retailing hub would have to be replaced by coherent order and a clear focus—a "town square" with a landmark visual feature at the center of the development, to give the visitor a sense of arrival at a special place, with the rest of the project radiating from this center in a way that is easily understood but not so symmetrical as to be uninteresting.

• **Sufficient parking.** Both the city code and the requirements of large chain retailers meant that Geis would have to provide more parking spaces than currently exist, and the retailers wanted to have more of those spaces closer to store entrances. The parking demand, however, conflicted with the three criteria listed above—the need for critical mass, the need to fit in with the neighborhood, and the need for a visual focus. Much of the design process was concerned with bringing these conflicting requirements into harmony, carefully dispersing parking spaces to help keep front doors of businesses close together.

• **Remove overhead utilities.** The existing utility poles were unsightly, interfered with pedestrian movement and potential landscaping, created a visual division between the two sides of Fredericksburg Road, and constituted a traffic hazard. Geis and the neighborhood associations worked on persuading the electric utility to remove the overhead lines. (As this book goes into production, early in 1994, the utility lines are being buried and the city is planning landscape and pedestrian improvements to the area, thanks to a grant from the federal Economic Development Administration. The grant application emerged from discussions several years earlier among the neighborhood associations, Geis, and city officials.)

• **Functional linkages.** The project would have to be easily and pleasantly accessible to drivers, pedestrians, and bus riders. Some minor street realignments and very careful placement of parking lot entrances would be required. Sidewalks would have to line up with those of the neighborhood grid and encourage foot traffic throughout the project. The center would have to open up more invitingly to the Keystone neighborhood, to which the original commercial buildings turned their backs. Bus stops might have to be moved, and attractive bus shelters would have to be built: Geis believes, rightly, that a city can be judged in part by the way it treats its bus riders.

• **Mixed use.** Apartments would have to be included in the project to provide a transition between the predominantly single-family residential character of the neighborhood and the retail project. Furthermore, Geis's experience in another project showed him that the presence of apartments enhances security for the shops, and vice versa. Together, these two uses assure continuous mutual surveillance from early in the morning until late at night. Office space would also be included to make use of second-floor space that could not be leased for retail.

In attempting to achieve all these objectives, Geis sought the cooperation and participation of several components of city government (the public works, traffic, and planning departments, the city manager's office, and the City Council representative for the district); the city-owned electric utility and transit authority; the local housing authority and the housing trust (a semi-independent authority that invests in private-sector housing, mainly for low- and moderate-income families); the urban renewal agency; the neighborhood associations; existing landowners (some of whom might have to be brought in as equity partners in the project); potential retailers; the state highway department (because Fredericksburg Road is technically a state highway, maintained with state funds); federal agencies, such as the Economic Development Administration and the Department of Housing and Urban Development, that might provide grants or loans for certain aspects of the project; the financial community; and, not least, the project's potential customers and residents.

In order for the project to be built and to enjoy long-term success, all these diverse and partially conflicting interests would have to be made participants in the redevelopment program. How could all these forces be made allies of the developer? One time-honored way is the use of smoke and mirrors. Lenders and government agencies are remarkably susceptible to bamboozlement. But while this strategy can get projects built, it can't sustain them. Real economic development, over the long haul, requires something more substantive.

Over the course of two years, Geis and his architect laid out three or four radically different site plans and innumerable evolutionary variants in an effort to meet the needs and desires of all the interests whose participation was required for his project to work. At certain points in the site-design process, Geis would utter the magic words "I think, by doing this, we're creating value for them," where "them" referred to whatever interest was served by the particular design detail that Geis and his architect had sketched.

To review:

1. Geis realized that he could not build a successful project wholly on his own. He would have to persuade many different forces, with many different agendas, to make financial or operational commitments to the development process.

2. The way to persuade those diverse forces to participate in the project was to create value for them—that is, to create a diversity of values, each modeled to satisfy the desires of a particular interest.

3. Obviously it is impossible for a real estate development to satisfy all the desires of all the participants that need to be brought into the development process. The developer's unique role is to find the points—or, more realistically, the somewhat fuzzy regions—at which these many diverse agendas intersect. Geis's evolving site plan is, in effect, a map of that complex intersection of agendas, to the extent that they can be seen to intersect within the geographical and functional boundaries of a coherent project.

What Geis is doing is very different from what the usual retail center developer in San Antonio does. George is collaborating, consciously and deliberately, with the past and future builders of that neighborhood. The usual retail center developer just buys a piece of real estate and plops a building on it in the middle of a big parking lot. If he's a very good, very sensitive developer, he might leave a native tree standing and spend a few bucks to make the building pretty. But rarely does a developer think about how his project will work in concert with the larger neighborhood—how people will get to it, how they'll feel about it, how easy it is to see the products the stores are selling, how the stores in one block can share their customers with the stores in the next block. Most developers have no sense of collaboration; they're acting as individual freebooters on insular plots of real estate. That's one reason their projects so often end up vacant and in foreclosure.

The collaborative design process is the thing that creates value in real estate. An underlying theme informs that process—the idea of reciprocity. Although he never stated the matter so explicitly, Geis understood intuitively that the way to create value for all concerned was to lay out his project on a matrix that would encourage mutually advantageous reciprocal relationships, both in the initial development of the project and in its long-term career. The design of the project, therefore, is not just "a map of that complex intersection of agendas" that statically coexist with each other, but also a map of dynamic reciprocities. Both within the project's boundaries and in its address to the surrounding neighborhoods, the project design had to create or re-create the physical matrix of a gift community. It is important to notice, moreover, that the "dynamic reciprocities"—who gives what to whom in return for what—were inscribed in and inseparable from the design process. The urban design process is first of all a matter of negotiation among diverse interests, and only then a matter of translating the results of those negotiations into drawings of the city's physical circuitry. Urban design provides the greatest economic and social satisfactions when the design process is most intensive—that is, when the negotiation process is most inclusive. It is relatively easy to design a retail project to satisfy the wishes of developer, lender, and prime tenant. It is harder to design a project that also satisfies the nearby neighborhood association, the adjoining property owner, the design review commission, and the city bureaucracy, and it is harder still to include the needs of children, the handicapped, the elderly, and the poor. But as the design process includes more kinds of people and interests at the negotiating table, the designed product—the arrangement of streets and sidewalks, landscaping and store windows, parking and bus stops—creates more value by including more people in the gift community.

In practical terms, it is impossible for every project to be preceded by so intensive a process of negotiation and design. It takes a lot of time, for one thing, and time is money. It is, however, both possible and useful for a city to undertake an intensive, highly inclusive negotiation process whose aim is to design a general framework or matrix into which individual projects must fit. With such a matrix as their rule book, multiple developers are obligated to behave as though they were collaborating with each other and seeking intensively to satisfy diverse interests.

Every city has at least a sketchy development matrix consisting of a zoning code,[3] setback standards, major thoroughfare plans, and the safety or technical imperatives of the fire marshal and the traffic and utility engineers. Most often, however, the component regulations or plans evolve independently of each other, each aimed at narrow goals, and do not add up to a coherent or comprehensive framework. Many interests, moreover, do not sit at the table where regulations or plans are negotiated. The planning commission does not, for example, generally include a slot for a fifth-grader, an oversight that may account for the failure of many suburbanized cities to organize neighborhoods in such a way that children have safe, convenient access by foot or bike to schools, recreation, entertainment, and stores.

| One objective of this book is to model an intensive and inclusive negotiating process by trying to consider both the interests that are most often represented at the negotiating table and the interests that are not, and to suggest the outline of a planning framework that might harmonize them. | I hope that people in the business of public policy and planning might find this outline useful as a guide for a city master plan and its implementing ordinances. I would also hope that private-sector developers might find in this book ideas that can be profitably incorporated into their projects, and that ordinary citizens may find increased understanding of how their desires and dissatisfactions fit into the whole so that they may speak more confidently at the policy-making table.

To all, let me say here—and repeat several times over the course of the book—that my diagrams and pronouncements are not to be taken as dogma or as one-size-fits-all templates to be applied to all circumstances, irrespective of climate, terrain, culture, history, or serendipitous opportunities. Outcomes may differ considerably from region to region, from city to city, or from neighborhood to neighborhood. What matters is the process by which urban design decisions are negotiated and implemented. I think it reasonable to suggest that the process should be inclusive and intensive, and it should aim at coherence—a planning framework in which the parts work as an ensemble. | The relevant question to ask is How should the pathways of your community be shaped to optimize exchange where you live? Not all gift communities look the same, although they have many schematic features in common. |

Before examining those features, however, I want to step back a bit and speak in more general terms about economic development, value creation, wealth, and what it means to be a human being.

■ what is the city about?

What is a city?

The poverty of our language is such that the little word *city* must distend itself to cover Paris, France, and Paris, Texas; Tokyo and Phoenix; Detroit and Vancouver; Renaissance Florence and modern Las Vegas. We use the same word to describe places that differ vastly in tone, pace, scale, richness, variety, comfort, economic base, and everyday details of life. Because in ordinary language *city* can mean so many different kinds of places, the word has been drained of meaning. What is left, what is common to all, is hopelessly vague and even more hopelessly bland . . . a city is a somewhat limited geographic area where a lot of people live and work, and "a lot of people" can mean twenty thousand or twenty million. We need to understand *city* in a more nuanced way if we hope to arrive at usable criteria for a well-made city.

It's sometimes useful to dig into the origins of words. The English word *city* comes from the Latin *civitas*, which originally meant citizenship—not just the passive act of inhabiting a town, but the network of rights and duties governing relations among individuals and families within those towns. The Latin *urbs*, from which we get *urban*, denoted a walled city in the bricks-and-mortar sense, but even this word had relational implications—a clearly demarcated relation, first of all, between the protected space within and the vulnerable space beyond the walls; and the laws and customs determining who had the right to come inside and under what conditions. (By analogy, *family room* denotes a physical space, but it also connotes a set of relationships, behavioral expectations, memories, and psychological goods.)

To the Greeks as well, a city was neither a mere collectivity of people nor the passive receptacle that held them, but a network of relationships. The *polis*, or city-state, was a kind of extended family. In the *Politics*, Aristotle described the polis as a form of *koinonia*, a word that can be translated as "community" or "association." The term implied active exchange, not just propinquity.

The same is true today, for us. When we understand *city* in its weak sense as only a large aggregation of people, dwellings, workplaces, and infrastructure, we miss most of what the city, as a form of organization, is about.

Before we can judge whether a poem is well made, we must know what the poem is supposed to be about, what effect it is intended to have on the reader. Before we can judge whether a city is well made, we must know what the city is about, what effect it is intended to have on the people in it. We will be asking what a city as a form of organization enables.

Cities being human creations, it is obvious that human goals are central to the plot of the urban poem. But it is not very helpful just to say that cities exist for the sake of their people. We still must specify what it is about human life that cities are peculiarly equipped to enable. Before we can say what cities are about, we must begin with an understanding of what *people* are about. This is not the place (nor I the thinker) for an extended essay on human subjectivity, but for present purposes I would like to offer four assumptions:

• **Assumption 1.** The boundary of the person is blurry. As a physical object, I may be wrapped up in a neat (well, somewhat rumpled) package, but as a subject—as a person who sees, feels, thinks, believes, imagines—I do not end where my body does. My identity is shaped in part by the things, beings, situations, and ideas that I encounter. Many such encounters leave their marks on me and vanish. But many others remain durably a part of my environment—my family and friends, my house and furniture, the computer on which I am now writing, the social and political structures within which my life is channeled, and so on. All of these durable and nondurable, tangible and intangible goods structure in varying degree the way I see and understand the world. In the absence of such a preexisting context, a person has only a very limited framework on which to weave a unique identity. Life beyond the most elemental animal processes would be impossible.

• **Assumption 2.** The boundary of me as an agent—as a person who does things in the world—extends beyond my body to include the tools with and upon which I work. The carpenter isn't just the body in the overalls, but a vast open-ended system that includes the hammer, the nail, the wood, and the industrial and natural processes that made them. Add to these the carpenter's teacher, the architect, the blueprint, the client—even the banks. One can't be a carpenter (or a composer or an accountant) in any but the most abstract sense unless a substantial part of that support system is in place, and in the right place at the right time. I am not just immersed in my support system; in some measure I am constituted by it. No man is an island.

• **Assumption 3.** People both create and are creatures of their cultures. Much of who I am is not determined by biology but formed by what and how I have learned from other people and their works. Invention (whether of mechanical contraptions, styles of art, or scientific theories) does not spring forth spontaneously from the brains of individual geniuses. Invention happens when certain features of the culture are processed in new ways—often only slightly new ways—by those geniuses. Invention cannot hatch, and once hatched cannot be refined through criticism and trial, in the absence of processes that conserve, recombine, and transmit culture.

Consider, for example, creativity in its seemingly purest, least material form—music. When Beethoven's music first crashed into Europe's salons and concert halls, it was startlingly, shockingly innovative. Yet this singular vision could not have happened if the composer had not been trained in music as a child, had not been immersed in the styles and assumptions of Mozart and Haydn, had not encountered the *Sturm und Drang* literary movement, had not been thrilled and then disgusted by Napoleon's exploits, had not had available to him the technical innovations of the early piano or the evolving symphony orchestra, had not been able to enter a preexisting system of patronage and publishing, had not been familiar with the dance and song forms of folk cultures, had not been able to travel from city to city. All these and other experiences were necessary (though not sufficient) conditions for the phenomenon called Beethoven.

• **Assumption 4.** For most people, life is not perfect all of the time, in every respect. Things could be better, and even when they do get better they have an annoying tendency not to stay that way. This assumption is more complicated than it might seem. To recognize that life is not always as we wish it to be, and to imagine that things could be better in this world (as opposed to an afterlife), is to buy into the idea of progress; and the idea of progress is controversial. New, after all, does not always mean improved—often it doesn't even mean new—and technologies or ideas that seem like advances from one point of view can seem like retreats from another. We can never fully understand ahead of time the long-term consequences of "progress," and thus the term asks to be accepted only provisionally until we have had a chance to see how the story turns out. Indeed, the unintended and unfortunate consequences of auto-centric urban planning—which seemed to many a sign of progress—is one of the main themes of this book. Diseases, too, can be progressive.

Yet in a restricted and weak sense progress is . . . well, progress. Even those who believe that things in general don't get better in some ultimate sense can likely agree that particular things can get better for particular purposes. If the ballpoint pens you have been using leave messy blobs of ink on the paper and your fingers, you are likely to cheer the invention of a pen that has all the good traits of the old one while eliminating the blobs. In that narrow context, it would be irrelevant—though in a larger context it might be trenchant—to lament that people write too many words anyway, and that the ballpoint has led to a tragic decline in penmanship. That the glass is half-empty does not negate the thirst-quenching value of the half that is full.

The point is simply to suggest that most people seek to improve their lives. A lot of what people choose to do is directed—often, to be sure, with poor aim—toward making things better, whatever "better" means to them. For thousands of years, one thing that people have chosen to do to improve their lives has been to congregate in cities.

THE CITY AS GENERATOR OF WEALTH

Cities have grown from several species of embryo—from military camps, religious shrines, manorial households, the crossing points of trade routes. But not all such concentrations developed into enduring and growing cities. Military camps can disappear without a trace when the battle is done, and all over modern Europe the tourist can see the brooding ruins of castles, cities that might have been.

Whatever the reason for the founding of any particular place that eventually became a city, and whatever the circumstances that caused particular cities to disintegrate, the city as a form of organization was a successful evolutionary adaptation, as biologists would say. No law of physics or logic dictated that people and their cultural resources should have coalesced into special kinds of clumps called cities rather than spreading out more or less evenly across the inhabitable landscape. The reason that the human map is lumpy rather than smooth is that the city enabled people to do things that other patterns of settlement did not enable them to do so efficiently.

Gross geographical features have much to do with the success of particular cities—the availability of fresh water and nearby agricultural land, location on trade routes that provide access to wealth from abroad. But a city is not just the passive result of external geographic opportunities and limitations. A city—at least, an economically healthy one—is not like a lake, which *is* the passive result of topography, gravity, and an external water source. A city is not just a location to which external, preexisting wealth gravitates. A city is also a generator of new wealth. A lot of the variation among cities with similar geographic endowments can be traced to variations in the efficiency and repair of their internal wealth-creating apparatus. That apparatus exists in only rudimentary form in settlement patterns that aren't cities. That's why the city has been such a successful evolutionary adapta-

tion. There is something about cities that increases the propensity and capacity of people to create value for each other.

What that something might be is foreshadowed by my four assumptions: Things could be better. If by our actions we have made things better
for ourselves or someone else, then we have, by definition, created value. Our
capacity to create value depends on who we are in the first place. But by assumptions 1–3, who we are is shaped by our support systems, our learning,
and our tools—in sum, our culture. As these grow richer, more extensive,
and more varied, our collective capacity to create value increases. Even our
notion of what "better" might mean becomes more refined and demanding
as our culture expands.

But our culture, or any other, exists only as a statistical fiction. Culture
exists only to the extent that it is transmitted to individuals. To the extent
that every individual's life experience is unique, every individual's culture is
unique. The differences in the ways culture is transmitted to individuals
make people interesting. If *the* culture were transmitted equally to everyone,
there'd be little point in getting to know anyone. If everyone's thoughts were
the same as your thoughts, you might as well just converse with yourself.
More important for our purposes, variation among people is a source
(maybe even *the* source) of value creation. Because people are not culturally
or genetically identical, one person or group may possess a piece of the
puzzle—or an idea for a new puzzle—that another person or group lacks.
Although genetics and the accidents of early neurological development contribute some variation, differences in the transmission of culture are, it seems
to me, vastly more important to value creation, which can also be called cultural evolution.

Transmission of culture occurs only through exchange, by definition.
Thus, if value creation depends on cultural richness and variety, then the
central event in value creation is exchange. And not just exchange measured
statistically, on a macro level, but the microexchanges that transmit culture
differently to every person. The more options we have to custom build our
diet of learning and experience, the more bountiful and accessible our
choices from the world's buffet table, the greater the likelihood that we will
be able to create new value. The city has been a successful adaptation because

(and to the extent that) it was a highly efficient technology for facilitating differential exchange and thus for fostering the creation of value.|

By "exchange," I mean the full range of voluntary interactions, whether of an intellectual or a commercial nature. High-minded readers may be put off by the stress I place on retail trade in later chapters. In part this emphasis is just a matter of convenience: "Stores" and "shops" are shorthand for a more inclusive, if awkward, formula such as "places where goods, services, knowledge, ideas, beliefs, and ethical principles are exchanged." But even re-tail trade itself has a transcendent function beyond crass financial gain. As Aristotle recognized in the *Nichomachean Ethics*, commercial exchange is a key element of *koinonia*—community. After dismissing several alternative views of justice and the state, Aristotle writes:

> But in associations that are based on mutual exchange, the just in this sense constitutes the bond that holds the associa-tion together, that is, reciprocity in terms of proportion and not in terms of exact equality in return. For it is the reciprocal return of what is proportional <to what one has received> that holds the state together. People seek either to requite evil for evil—for otherwise their relation is regarded as that of slaves—or good with good, for otherwise there is no mutual contribution. And it is by their mutual contribution that men are held together.[1]

A few lines later, Aristotle relates the abstract notion of proportional reciprocity to the more concrete case of money and trade:

> For a community is not formed by two physicians, but by a physician and a farmer, and, in general, by people who are different and unequal. But they must be equalized [if their services are to be exchanged proportionally]; and hence ev-erything that enters into exchange must somehow be compa-rable.
>
> It is for this purpose that money has been introduced: it becomes, as it were, a middle term. For it measures all things,

<not only their equality but> also the amount by which they exceed or fall short <of one another>. Thus it tells us how many shoes are equal to a house or to a given quantity of food. The relation between builder and shoemaker must, therefore, correspond to the relation between a given amount of shoes and a house or a quantity of food. For if it does not, *there will be no exchange and no community. . . .*

. . . Therefore, the price of all goods should be fixed, for in that way there will always be exchange, and *if there is exchange there is a community.* Thus money acts like a measure: it makes goods commensurable and equalizes them. For just as *there is no community without exchange,* there is no exchange without equality and no equality without commensurability.[2]

In contrast—and erroneously, I believe—Lewis Hyde excluded commercial exchange from his recipe for the glue of community. Writing of the complex interfamily marriage gifts on a Polynesian island, Hyde notes, "After a marriage like this everyone is connected to everyone else in one way or another. Imagine what it must be like after half a dozen marriages and as many initiation ceremonies and funerals (whose exchanges are even more complicated than those of marriage). There will be an ongoing and generalized indebtedness, gratitude, expectation, memory, sentiment—in short, lively social feeling." But suppose all gifts were to be converted to "cash purchase," so that exchange occurs only as arms-length commercial transactions. In that case, Hyde writes, "if every exchange were to separate or free the participants from one another there would also be no community."[3]

Hyde contrasts, for example, the member of the "scientific community," who contributes ideas freely to the community through scientific journals and discussions, with the commercial scientist who is "paid a cash reward that compensated him for his time while simultaneously alienating him from his contribution. A researcher paid by the hour is a technician, a servant, not a member of the scientific community. Similarly, an academic scientist who ventures outside of the community to consult for industry expects to be paid a fee. If the recipients of his ideas are not going to treat them as gifts, he will not give them as gifts."[4]

But even academic scientists of the purest sort do their work for a fee, called more politely a grant, stipend, or chair, and it is customary for scientists to direct their research into paths where the money is. Even poets would like to be paid for their work. Conversely, it is hard to imagine how a scientist (or artist or laborer) could so compartmentalize his personality as to withhold the gifts of imagination from any project that engages his interest just because he or his employer expects financial gain. It would be mean-spirited to lament that Mozart got a little money for *Don Giovanni*, or to suggest that it might have been a better opera if he had not been paid for it.

But whether the product in question is an opera or a kitchen gadget advertised on late-night TV, anything that is made must first be imagined and designed. There is something inescapably gift-like in the process of imagining and designing, unmeasurable mental activities that cannot, in principle, bear a linear relationship to payment received. Every commercial product carries with it, as a gift, the imagination, curiosity, passion, wit, tastes, and knowledge of its creators. I grant that there are qualitative differences in the gifts that are applied to and transmitted by various products, and I do not intend to equate a great painting or scientific theory with a box of laundry detergent. I admit that many products reflect a niggling or thoughtless creative process. I will also concede that some products reflect a generous portion of their creators' gifts and may yet have destructive consequences. All of this is true whether the product is a commodity in commercial exchange, an artwork or scientific advance in the not-for-profit market place of universities and cultural organizations, or an outright gift that circulates through the community.

The point is this. The gift community exists to the extent that people recombine what their culture has differentially transmitted to them, create new value from those recombinations, and make that new value available to each other through exchange—irrespective of the money that might or might not also change hands in the process, and even if the new value is only seen in a shop window and not purchased and possessed. Even crass, for-profit commodity exchange has a role to play in solidifying a gift community. Conversely, commodity exchange cannot be sustained for long in the absence of a healthy gift community. If there is no exchange to establish mutual bonds of relatedness and interdependence, there is no community; but if there is no community to transmit culture richly and differentially to individuals, there is no new value to exchange. |

ETHICS, VIOLENCE, AND THE CITY

The centrality of exchange in the urban project asserts itself in ethics as much as in art and industry. Aristotle claimed that the intellectual and moral virtues are formed by, and could not exist in the absence of, participation in the life of the (just) *polis*. It is only through the practical experience and habits of behavior, which (justly organized) urban life affords, that mature ethical and intellectual judgment can develop. Ethics cannot be sustained outside of an ethical community—an actual, not an abstract, community in which individuals learn ethical discernment and practical wisdom by direct example, practice, conversation, and interaction.

As it relates to ethics, the community is a generative, creative force. The give-and-take of community life continually produces more refined ethical distinctions, new ways of applying general principles, sometimes even new general principles. As a result of the evolving conversation, what was once acceptable may become unacceptable (slavery), what was once mandatory may become voluntary (Jewish dietary laws), what was once prohibited absolutely may become permitted in certain circumstances but not in others (for Christians, lending money at interest). Community, particularly the city, is the engine of change in ethics. At this moment in history the general trend of ethical changes over the course of the past several thousand years seems to be in the direction of greater justice and freedom.

Yet one must acknowledge that the "engine of change in ethics" can sometimes operate in reverse. An urban geography that facilitates peaceful exchange can also facilitate violent exchange. One way to understand this ambivalence might be through the work of the literary critic and biblical anthropologist René Girard.

Girard has argued that desire is mimetic; that is, we desire something because we see somebody else desiring it. Children tend to imitate the behavior of their parents and peers and role models—that is, the activities that their parents, peers, and role models find desirable. Adults imitate the hairstyles of the stars and the attire of successful businesspeople, aspire to join the best clubs, own the most prestigious cars, and live in the right neighborhoods—that is the clubs, cars, and neighborhoods desired by other people. Fads and trends in clothing styles, architecture, music, television programs, cuisine, and political leanings are not the result of mass coincidences of wholly independent choices. Our decisions for ourselves are shaped in part by what we see others doing. Sometimes mimetic desire is manipulated by advertising, as when we see an apparently successful, happy, attractive couple driving a particular make of car or using a particular brand of soap. But beyond the realm of explicit propaganda, imitation of desire is driven by all manner of formal and informal, routine and unusual social interactions. In the street, the school, the office, the club (or gang), the restaurant, the living room, the park, the store, we see what others have and how they behave. That is, we see the things and attitudes that others value or desire. If we want to be more like Tommy and less like Jimmy because we have noticed that Tommy is popular (or rich, or smart, or spiritual, or whatever attribute seems most important to us) and Jimmy isn't, we are likely at least to consider copying some of Tommy's behavior. If it works for him, it might work for us. Thus we may adopt the head cheerleader's hairstyle, or we may pursue scholarly studies like those of an admired professor.

While mimetic desire can be silly or destructive, it is also, I believe, essential to the process of invention. Without desire, there is little motivation to create something to fulfill that desire. Advances in technique are at heart Promethean attempts to give to the many the goods or abilities that previously had been reserved for a few. The wealthy could enjoy a cocktail while their servants washed the clothes or the dishes; with the invention and manufacture of electrically operated appliances, the middle class could enjoy a cocktail while Westinghouse or General Electric did the chores. Innovation begins with a statement of the form, Gee, I wish I could do what X can do. The innovator may be in large measure simply trying to satisfy his or her own desires, but if the product (or idea or belief or discovery) is to reach a public, the innovator's desire must coincide with, or imitate, the desires of potential buyers.

In either case—the marketing of existing products or the invention of new ones—desire depends on proximity. To desire an improvement in your own condition, however you define "improvement," requires first an awareness of the possibilities for improvement, an awareness of the things that can be done or had beyond your own current abilities. By "things that can be done or had," I do not mean only the products and services that are available in commercial trade, but also ideas, knowledge, beliefs, ideologies, habits of thought and behavior, ethical standards—whatever falls under the wide heading of transmission of culture.

That's all well and good, but then we run into the dark side of Girard's hypothesis, the converse of Hyde's. Girard analyzed myth, ritual, and tragedy to show how imitation of desire sets off a reciprocal cycle of violence:

> Two desires converging on the same object are bound to clash. Thus, mimesis coupled with desire leads automatically to conflict. . . . By a strange but explicable consequence of their relationship, neither the model nor the disciple is disposed to acknowledge the inevitable rivalry. The model, even when he has openly encouraged imitation, is surprised to find himself in competition. He concludes that the disciple has betrayed his confidence by following in his footsteps. As for the disciple, he feels both rejected and humiliated, judged unworthy by his model of participating in the superior existence his model himself enjoys.[5]

This relationship sets off a reciprocal cycle of violence:

> If desire is allowed to follow its own bent, its mimetic nature will almost always lead it into a double bind. The unchanneled mimetic impulse hurls itself blindly against the obstacle of a conflicting desire. It invites its own rebuffs, and these rebuffs will in turn strengthen the mimetic inclination. We have, then, a self-perpetuating process, constantly increasing in simplicity and fervor. Whenever the disciple borrows from his model what he believes to be the "true" object, he tries to possess that truth by desiring precisely what this

model desires. Whenever he sees himself closest to the supreme goal, he comes into violent conflict with a rival. By a
mental shortcut that is both eminently logical and self-de-
feating, he convinces himself that the violence itself is the
most distinctive attribute of this supreme goal! Ever after-
ward, violence and desire will be linked in his mind, and the
presence of violence will invariably awaken desire.[6]

Girard derived this analysis from the great tragic figures of myth and
literature, but it applies with astonishing precision to modern urban gang
violence. Like peaceful and constructive exchange, the reciprocal cycle of desire and violence is a form of exchange for which proximity and connectedness are necessary conditions. Many of the features characteristic of suburbia
are explicitly meant to inhibit violent exchange and bad influences—that is,
imitation of the wrong desires—on the young. The strict segregation of residential areas by economic class and housing type, limited access to residential subdivisions, and the absence of efficient links between residential and
retail districts are all calculated to restrict freedom of movement and lower
the temperature of exchange. Many parents who buy suburban houses do
not want their children to have contact with apartment dwellers (who are all
drug dealers and rapists), or ride their bikes to a neighborhood retailing hub
(where they will be corrupted by pornography and commercial entice-
ments), or shoot baskets at a nearby public park (where kids from a less af-
fluent subdivision will steal their sneakers and virginity).

The fear, if often disproportionate to the real threat, is not wholly irra-
tional. No reasonably free environment can be risk-free. But the usual suburban strategy of inhibiting most forms of exchange strikes me as counterproductive. In the first place, it doesn't work. Nobody can escape or hide for
very long from violence, whose practitioners are determined and mobile.
Even guarded and walled enclaves are not secure. The isolation that is intended to protect young people may itself breed violence, drug abuse, or
other socialization and developmental difficulties. Furthermore, when we
seek to avoid violence by inhibiting *peaceful* exchange, we lose more than we
gain. When we eliminate opportunities for beneficial exchange, we also re-

move the most effective preventives or deterrents to destructive exchange, especially by the young. Young people need models of ethical behavior, productive work, peaceful interaction. While the immediate family (if the child is fortunate) may provide the best models, the opportunity to routinely observe and interact with other adult models, in a variety of public settings outside but not far from the home, can help to bond the child to the community. By having a rich variety of places to go and things to do and people to see outside the home, the child comes to see herself as having a role to play in the community, and she begins to learn how to play it.

If the urban community is an engine of change and growth in ideas, ethics, and knowledge, it is also an anchor of stability. Growth comes from differences in the transmission of culture; stability comes from the cultural transmission that occurs in common. Both depend on the exchanges that proximity and connectedness facilitate.

ECONOMICS VERSUS THE ECONOMY

Let's take a fresh and cheerfully untutored look at what "the economy" is.

We moderns divide our lives and the world around us into boxes. It begins at least as early as grade school, where we are taught separate "subjects." As we advance through high school and college and career, the walls grow higher and more numerous, dividing the world into more and smaller boxes.

One of those boxes is labeled "the economy." People called "economists" pack into that box all sorts of numbers that have something to do with money and jobs—construction spending, the purchasing managers' index, the consumer price index, the savings rate, the Dow Jones Industrial Average, the unemployment rate, the prime rate, factory orders, housing starts, the trade deficit, the price of pig snouts for March delivery, and so on. Dozens of "economic" indicators are watched obsessively by the people who watch such things.

But what is really interesting about the box labeled "the economy" is what *doesn't* go into it—namely, most of the things that make up the economy (without quotation marks) in the real world. The real world isn't divided into boxes, and when we imagine it that way we overlook a lot of what we want to know. "The economy" is a simplified mathematical abstraction of a complex reality that includes social, political, aesthetic, cultural, customary, and geographic dimensions. The economy isn't fully described by measuring how much money changes hands. We must also consider how, where, and why it changes hands, or not. More important still, we must consider what money is exchanged *for*. The economy isn't just money, but also the things we buy—even the economists will agree to that much—and the motives, emotions, desires, imaginations, capacities, and limitations of the people who make and buy those things.

Economic development is a term that has also suffered from tunnel vision. As it is most commonly used by policy makers, "economic development" is synonymous with "economic growth." That is, policy makers assume that if "the economy" grows, as measured by jobs, construction, population, and income, then the economy (without quotation marks) has developed.

What's wrong with this picture? Lots. First, if "the economy" grows, but the population grows faster, the result is a net decline in per capita income—hardly a favorable result, but still "economic development." Second, if "the economy" grows, but a larger share of it is concentrated in fewer hands, the result doesn't look much like economic development to the people on the short end of the growth. Third, if "the economy" of a city grows dramatically enough to attract new workers from outside—for an overheated construction industry, for example—and then just as dramatically stops growing, the result is often not economic development but economic catastrophe for the workers (and investors) who were left in the lurch. Fourth, if "the economy" of a city grows in an outward-spreading ring, leaving behind desolated neighborhoods, empty workplaces, and crumbling schools in the center, the people living in those neighborhoods must expend substantial new resources to maintain a decent standard of living; the benefits of "economic development" can be fully consumed, and then some, by the costs of sending one's children to a private school, driving greater distances to work and shopping, or trading one's inner-city house in a buyer's market for a suburban house in a seller's market. "Economic growth," measured statistically across an entire city, doesn't necessarily mean economic development for you and me.

Whatever economic development means, it is supposed to be something good. When we speak of economic development, we mean something more than mere maintenance of the status quo, something more than just getting by. We expect to be better off as a result of economic development. (I'm assuming that we don't get to be better off just by borrowing or stealing; in the United States, this proviso had some bearing on the "economic development" of the 1980s.)

"Better off" has both quantitative and qualitative dimensions. It could mean that we have more money to spend—but only if we also have more good things to spend it on. In general, "better off" means a quantitatively larger number of options (more cable TV channels, for example) *and* qualitatively more agreeable options (TV programs that you actually want to watch).

But being better off does not just mean being able to buy more or better material goods. It might also mean shorter or more pleasant commutes to work or shopping; cleaner, safer, more beautiful, and more diverting parks; better schools and more fully stocked libraries; more enjoyable music on the radio and more interesting exhibits at the museum; more opportunities to make new friends and keep old ones. Even in the mundane world of commodity exchange, "better off" entails more than purely quantitative improvements. It can involve intangible emotional, sensual, and intellectual rewards—the unexpected pleasure of the Indian restaurant that didn't exist last year, or the new computer software that allows me to be more creative in my music hobby, or the new chair design that's more comfortable and looks better than anything you'd seen before.

Many of the good things that fall under your or my definition of "better off" are things that can be acquired with more money. If "better off" means a $20,000 car in your garage and a $50,000 playground at the neighborhood park, compared to your present $10,000 car and the park's unembellished grass and trees, then obviously it takes more money for you and your local parks department to acquire them. But for most people some aspects of "better off" are not directly or exclusively related to money—and I'm not referring only to those best things in life that, as the song has it, are free. Many of the things we do and the products and services we buy offer greater or lesser psychological rewards depending on the skill, knowledge, experience, or wisdom of the people who provide them. And while people with greater skill, knowledge, experience, or wisdom may command a higher price for their services, the acquisition of these qualities does not necessarily hinge on the expenditure of more money. Maybe the dance company in your town gives better performances this year—not because it has hired better dancers from New York, but because the same dancers who were with the company last year have been working together longer, have honed their skills and developed their muscles, have learned and assimilated more techniques; the dance company now offers you more value than it did last year. Maybe your doctor, having recently seen a patient with the same symptoms as yours, is now better able to diagnose and treat your illness than she would have been a year ago; that doctor now offers you more value. Maybe the cook at your favorite restaurant happened to dine one day at another place where he got an idea for a refinement to one of his own dishes; that cook now offers you more value.

Often, the increase in value has consequences for "the economy," in the conventional sense. If the sharpened skill of the cook at your favorite restaurant induces you to eat there three times a month instead of twice a month, and maybe to bring some friends along, then the cook's new skills have been responsible for increasing the rate at which money circulates in the community. If five or six other restaurants have increased their volume in the same manner, one of their suppliers might have to hire an additional worker, who in turn may spend money in ways that directly or indirectly benefit you. Maybe she buys clothes from the department store where you work, helping to sustain your job, or maybe she helps to support your favorite bookstore, which without her purchases of science fiction novels might not be able to offer the Kant and Camus titles that you want. Eventually, other things being equal, some of the additional money you spend at the improved restaurant comes back to you, either in the form of money or as other satisfactions.

But increase in value also has more fundamental economic implications. A product or service conveys more than satisfaction or utility to the purchaser, more than circulation of money to the economy. Whether explicitly or implicitly, every product and service is a vehicle of information, and to increase the value of these products and services is to increase, or change the qualities of, the information they convey. If I produce and sell to you a washing machine, you also obtain—for free, as it were—the information that such a thing as a washing machine is possible and that the unit I make has such-and-such characteristics of water usage, noise, and safety for your clothes. You obtain some information about the unit even if you examine it in the store but don't buy it. You obtain far more information when you put the unit into daily use in your home. You learn how durable and reliable it is, you learn how appropriate its settings are, you learn that it does some things well and other things not so well.

Such information may seem trivial, but it isn't. If a product doesn't perform to your complete satisfaction in every respect—that is, if things could be better—your likely impulse will be to desire an improved version of it. If a product is exemplary, your likely impulse will be to wish every other product were made so well. In either case, the information you gain from the products and services, things and occurrences around you sets up a tension, a dissonance, between ideal and real, and that tension propels the creation of value. To make something—whether a new symphony or an improved washing machine or a new law—is implicitly to analyze and criticize what has gone before. But you can't criticize what you don't know about.

Knowledge drives desire, which drives the creation of value, which also creates new knowledge. This sequence must continue as a progressively spiraling cycle for real economic development to occur. Economic development occurs when value is created in a self-sustaining, accelerating reaction, so that value begets more value. We want assurance that we will be better off tomorrow, and still better off the day after tomorrow. Economic development is not a static condition, but a dynamic process.

VALUE, WEALTH, AND ECONOMIC DEVELOPMENT

Being better off means being able to enjoy the fruits of value that we or others have created—which means that value has to be created in the first place and then distributed to people. But *value* is a difficult term to grasp.

Because there is no direct or necessary connection between monetary price and intrinsic value, intrinsic value has come to be understood as a sort of metaphysical fiction having no place in the study of economics. The value of a product (or labor, for that matter) is defined as the amount of money it sells for on the open and free market. As a corollary, *wealth* has come to be understood, especially in America, in strictly monetary terms (even though Adam Smith, whom Americans honor more in name than in reading, shot that horse in 1776). As a second corollary, *productivity* is generally understood quantitatively as the number of widgets that a worker produces (*output*) per hour in relation to a specified *input* such as raw materials or energy or wages, but without concern for the intrinsic qualities of those widgets. Again, price is understood to be at the heart of the matter. A worker who produces more widgets brings in more dollars just by virtue of producing more widgets— not by producing better widgets. This notion of productivity is almost plausible when the widgets are refrigerators or tons of steel, but it becomes problematic when the widget is a Supreme Court opinion, a music video, a computer program, a package design, or a satisfied tourist. How does one measure the productivity of a teacher, a physicist, an artist, a philosopher, an architect, a counselor, a state legislator, an industrial designer?

Before even a mundane kind of widget has a price attached to it, it is first of all a thing. It has its own qualities, which are more or less attractive to me as a potential user. If I am considering a purchase I might ask, in a linguistic shorthand, whether the qualities offered by that product are worth the price asked for it, but that does not imply an equivalence between price and product. You can eat a dollar's worth of bread, but you can't eat a dollar. Price and intrinsic value are two different things, but both are part of the economy. Some notion of intrinsic value is inescapable if our goal is to achieve a condition in which people are continually better off—if our goal is economic development.

Intrinsic value—I'll just call it "value"—is hard to define because, unlike money, it is not a uniform substance. Value is whatever has the potential to improve somebody's life. But the creation of value does not, in itself, improve people's lots. People are better off only to the extent that more value is made available for their use through the social act of sharing or exchanging. Wealth is value that has been made available to people in this way.

Economists define *wealth* as goods and resources having economic value, which would be fine if economists understood "economic value" more broadly than they do. Wealth includes far more than money and the things that people buy for their private use. In the context of cities, it also includes such public facilities as libraries, parks, and sidewalks, and such intangibles as convenience, pleasure, security, and knowledge. Money and priced goods do not encompass all the wealth available to an individual; for an economy, the sum of the monetary prices of goods and other resources does not encompass all of the wealth that exists. In particular, money and priced goods do not encompass all of the kinds of wealth that engender wealth—those intangible and not-for-sale goods that contribute qualitatively but nonmeasurably to the creation of value.

Endeavors that seem to have little or no direct commercial value often propel the creation of commercial value by creating new needs and desires. If one's goal is economic development, it is prudent in the long run to have an economic development policy or theory that does not discriminate between increments of value that have direct commercial consequences and those that do not.

In *Cities and the Wealth of Nations*, Jane Jacobs has a cogent treatment of this theme: "'Industrial strategies' to meet 'targets'... express a military kind of thinking. Behind that thinking lies a conscious or unconscious assumption that economic life can be conquered, mobilized, bullied, as indeed it can be when it is directed toward warfare, but not when it directs itself to development and expansion." Jacobs continues:

> An emeritus professor of the Massachusetts Institute of Technology, Cyril Stanley Smith, points out that historically, necessity has not been the mother of invention; rather, neces-

sity opportunistically picks up invention and improvises improvements on it and new uses for it, but the roots of invention are to be found elsewhere, in motives like curiosity and especially, Smith noted, "esthetic curiosity." Metallurgy itself, he reminds us, began with hammering copper into necklace beads and other ornaments "long before 'useful' knives and weapons" were made of copper or bronze. Alloying and heat treatment of metals started in jewelry making and sculpture, as did casting in complicated molds. Pigments (which, incidentally, were the first known uses of iron ore), porcelain and many other ceramics, glass and the practice of welding all started with luxury or decorative goods. Possibly even wheels were at first frivolities; the most ancient known to us are parts of toys. . . .

"All big things grow from little things," Smith comments, with this cautionary addition, "but new little things are destroyed by their environments unless they are cherished for reasons more like esthetic appreciation than practical utility."[7]

Smith's observations about the ancient past remain applicable today. The desires of composers and performers for new sounds led to a lucrative industry in synthesizers and digital samplers. Much that is distinctive about the Macintosh computer responds to the desires of graphic designers, animators, artists, and composers for increasingly flexible means to realize their aesthetic visions. The advanced mathematics and physics that led to computers, nuclear power, and a host of other engineering achievements grew out of interests that were "more like esthetic appreciation than practical utility."

More generally, once subsistence has been assured, or even before, people yearn for art, entertainment, fashion, pleasure travel, luxuries, a richer palette of knowledge and ideas. These yearnings are not generated by economic rationalism or practical needs. But these impractical, uneconomic yearnings have practical, economic effects—directly, by fostering industries to satisfy these desires; and indirectly, by expanding the pool of knowledge, metaphors, interests, and lines of thinking that may lead to other, unanticipated industries.

Industries don't produce anything; people do. Whatever is made, is made by people who are immersed in networks of information, ideas, knowledge, skills, experiences, myths, expectations, desires. All these intangibles, and their lively exchange, are essential features of the economy. The richer the networks and the deeper the immersion, the greater is the likelihood that new value will be produced. The field in which this network operates is not an abstraction but a real place, a physical place of social and cultural exchange—the market place. The dictionary shows *marketplace* as one word, but I break it apart as a reminder that we are talking about a physical, not a metaphorical, place. And because noneconomic exchange is as important to the creation of value as economic exchange is, such noneconomic places as parks and sidewalks are as essential to the market place as shops and offices and factories.

While "the economy" of the economists inhabits an abstract number-space, the economy of the real world happens in physical space, in the places where you and I and our neighbors interact. Increasingly, we meet on the telephone or the fax machine, in movies and on television or over computer networks. But historically, and indispensably, we have met in cities.

Imagine a highly detailed map of your city. This map shows not only the streets and major landmarks, but all the sidewalks and plazas, the front doors and windows, the shops and office buildings that make up your physical city. This map is also the map of the channels along which people carry their ideas, beliefs, knowledge, biases, desires, and money. But people do not hoard these things. As they move about the city, they interact in manifold ways with other people, institutions, and things. Ideas, beliefs, knowledge, biases, desires, and money are exchanged, shared, made available to others. Thus the map of a city is also a map of the possibilities for (and impediments to) exchange that the city affords. As we have seen, exchange is the central event in both the creation of value, because value creation depends on the differential transmission of culture, and in the expansion of wealth, because the value that you create becomes wealth only through the social act of exchanging or sharing.

Now look through the other end of the telescope. Suppose you were to set out to create a type of human settlement that optimally fostered and encouraged those social acts of exchanging and sharing. You would invent a place where many people live and work in close proximity and routinely interact with one another; where many kinds of activity are linked together; where physical, legal, and social impediments to free exchange are minimal; where there is ample diversity of thought and custom; and where that diversity is not kept isolated and inert but encouraged to recombine in unexpected ways. You would, in short, invent something like the traditional city, with its neighborhoods and neighborhood centers, its compactness and integration of functions, its diversity and serendipity. The city was a successful adaptation because the pace and ease and breadth of exchange were optimized by the proximity, diversity, and connectedness of city life.

But proximity, diversity, and connectedness are the very qualities that modern planning policies and real estate development practices increasingly, fanatically, sought to eliminate from American cities in the decades after World War II. Urban and suburban areas that grew up after the war don't behave like cities, don't look like cities, don't work like cities—*aren't* cities. The name is the same, but the phenomenon is different.

■ a practice of cities

In the six chapters of Part II, we examine the built environment of cities—their streets and sidewalks, neighborhoods and shopping areas, parking lots and architecture—to show how the way we build cities affects the way we live in them. Do various features of the built environment promote or inhibit the circulation of people and their money, goods, ideas, and beliefs? Does a particular arrangement of pathways advance or retard the transmission of culture, the creation of value, and the bonding of individuals into a community? What strategies can we find to accommodate the car and large, mass-market businesses while at the same time making the city more congenial to pedestrians, children, small business, and neighborhood life? ■

■ the urban matrix

 A city is a palimpsest, a document with many layers of accretion and imperfect erasure, many glosses and commentaries and marginal notes. No city was summoned into being in an instant, by the will of a single creator. Any city reveals the traces of its development over time and space.

If a city is a collaborative artwork, as it has been called, it is a very strange kind of collaboration, a partnership between people who may never know each other, who may live centuries apart, who may practice different architectural styles and building technologies, who may begin with very different assumptions about how people go about their daily tasks, who may act on behalf of widely varying kinds of public and private institutions. Yet despite the diversity of its creators, in certain places the built environment looks and behaves like a unified ensemble, a collaboration.

Even if it's hard to define, most of us can recognize a successful collaboration when we see it. In our travels, particularly in Europe and in older cities of this country, we often find ourselves in a neighborhood that is comfortable but not dull, unified but not uniform, varied but not fragmented, focused but not rigid, stable but not ossified, lively but not congested, intimate but not claustrophobic. Most of us have probably seen neighborhoods where buildings from three or more centuries stood cheek by jowl, or where a modernist apartment tower rose thirty stories above the tops of nine-teenth-century brownstones. We have walked joyful and entranced down streets whose buildings differed widely in style, age, scale, and use, perhaps without a single building of architectural distinction, and found that these streets nonetheless formed coherent unities.

But our concern is not solely with aesthetics. A successful urban col-laboration is a gift community, a place where individual goals and aspira-tions are expressed within a unifying public framework designed to promote exchange.

Too often, especially in the automobile suburbs and even in many cen-tral cities of the United States, we see something altogether different. Even with the same traffic counts, the same demographics, the same mix of uses and architectural periods, the same density of population and businesses, the same amount of parking, a square mile of one place may be dispiriting, insu-lar, congested, inefficient, ugly, and sociopathic; while a square mile in an-other place may delight the eye and the foot, bring people together, and stimulate commerce and art. The difference is not so much what we do but how and where we do it. Successful collaboration happens when the builders of every generation share an urban ethos, a sense of the city as a special kind of settlement, distinct from the village or the suburban gulag and not reduc-ible to the sum of individual habitations or profit centers.

Despite history's changes in transportation, communication, trade, the family, governance, and social relations—in many of the principal activities that happen in cities—some things have remained constant. The human body retains roughly the same gait, the same ability to hear, the same range of vision, the same tempo of conversation, the same social interdependence with other providers of goods and services, the same need for sleep and food and exercise. We are not like Superman. We cannot see through solid walls or leap expressways in a single bound. While the pace of technological, so-cial, and intellectual change has accelerated, the rate of neuronal processing in our brains has remained more or less constant. We may have instant access by telephone to a billion people, but we still learn to trust or fear them, love or leave them, one at a time, at a tempo based on the deliberate speed of hu-man speech rather than on the race of electrons through wire or photons through fiber-optic strands. We may drive past a sign or a storefront or a potential mate at fifty-five miles an hour, but it still takes as long as it always did to comprehend the sign's message or assimilate the store's display or discern the potential mate's charms. Indeed, these things probably require more time now, given the expansion of verbal and visual language, the acceleration of technology and product development, and the increased diversity of erotic standards.

If human bodies haven't changed all that much over the centuries, it follows that certain physical features of urban settlement must also remain constant if we hope to preserve the function of the city as a market place, a place where people and ideas and goods peaceably meet, test, amplify, and influence each other, a place where the human lot can be improved. If many of the activities of cities have changed, the framework in which those activities occur must still be molded in large measure by the constants of the human body if we want human bodies to engage in exchange.

Much of value can be learned from looking at well-preserved streetscapes and neighborhoods from the past. I am not concerned here with the more commonly recognized values of the historic preservation movement, although these values are worth reiterating. First, the high level of craftsmanship, the hand of the creator evident in buildings from certain historic periods, stands as a challenge or a reproach to modern builders. Second, the maintenance of old buildings as part of a vital present helps to preserve the continuity of a city as a distinctive place worthy of the care of its citizens; a city that remakes itself entirely with each generation is rootless. Third, it is wasteful and faintly immoral to destroy sturdy, beautiful old buildings long before their usable life has passed, only to replace them with chintzy, cheesy ones. Fourth—and I mention this with a sigh—historic sites and structures are good for the tourist trade.

But it is a different aspect of historic preservation that I want to stress in the context of urban design. Intact, well-maintained historic neighborhoods and streets demonstrate what I call the *urban matrix*, a conceptual framework or imaginary grid that governs the location and design of a city's pathways. A well-formed urban matrix, expressed in a city's streets, sidewalks, and neighborhood structure, connects the individual pieces of a city to one another and binds them into a whole in which person-to-person exchange can occur with optimum efficiency.

An analogy might help to explain what I mean by the urban matrix. Consider the model train set. When you go to the hobby shop, you can buy lengths of track in a variety of shapes and specialized functions—straight, curving to the left, curving to the right, switches and so on. You can also buy bridges, signal lights, and whole Alpine villages. And of course you can buy the railroad cars and locomotives that will run on the tracks—coal cars, cattle cars, box cars, hopper cars, even car cars. With all these options at your disposal, you can create a setup that's quite elaborate and different from anyone else's. The thing that makes possible so much freedom and variety is modularity. You might have a hundred pieces of rolling stock, each one unique, but you can still line them up as a train because at each end of every car there is a coupler that matches the couplers on every other car. Similarly, the lengths of track are designed to plug into each other at their ends, whether the pieces you are connecting are curved or straight. The pieces of an electric train set can differ vastly from each other, but the train will still go if all the individual pieces have a strategic uniformity—if they are designed to plug into each other at their ends. Without that strategic uniformity, the train set may have some aesthetic virtues, but it won't work.

If you ignore all the differences between the pieces of a train set and focus instead on the strategic uniformities—imagine a row of naked couplers chugging down the tracks—you will visualize the *matrix of connectivity* for the train set. Lincoln Logs, Tinker Toys, and Erector sets are among the other toy kits that are based on a matrix of connectivity. If you prefer adult toys, the integrated office system is yet another example.

Note that the matrix of connectivity, both as an abstract idea and as a physical expression of that idea, must be determined at the beginning of the design process. Only after the matrix has been designed does it make sense to design and build the specific pieces that plug into it—to design the railroad cars that will fill the spaces between their front and rear couplers. The matrix of connectivity is the pattern or principle according to which individual pieces aggregate into a coherent, functional whole. The matrix is also the principle by which a system expands, or replicates itself.

The matrix of connectivity is a liberating discipline. The individual objects in the train set do not have to be all alike—indeed, no two need be the same, even in a set of a billion pieces—so long as they connect properly at their ends. And the matrix is a framework for collaboration. The individual objects can be designed and built by many different people, at different times, to serve different ends and satisfy different tastes, and still these objects can form a functional train set.

A similar framework of collaboration is needed in cities if their many individual parts are to hang together as a coherent whole, for the mutual benefit of all. In a city, "hanging together" is a matter not of static adjacency but of the movement of people through time and space—a matter of pathways. While the internal details of property development are the prerogative and responsibility of the individual property owners (whether they are private developers or public entities), the pathways that connect one front door to the next—like the coupling system of the electric train—are the responsibility of the public. The location, condition, and usefulness of the pathways are matters of public concern, because if the pathways don't work, if the pieces of a city are not adequately connected to each other, exchange is inhibited. Laying out the system of pathways is one of the most important and pervasive ways by which city governments create (or fail to create) value for citizens.

In typical modern suburbia, the system of pathways is poorly developed and often discontinuous. Moreover, the pathways of the public realm are most often uncoupled from those in the individual private realms: the public sidewalk in commercial areas, for example, usually goes from parking lot to parking lot, not from door to door. The pathways do not have a clear structure or sense of direction; they don't have a rhythm that propels people along them. Finally, the diverse activities or land uses of suburbia are often not organized, in relation to each other, in such a way that pathways can connect them efficiently. If pathways are too long and roundabout, resistance to exchange is high.

We are now ready to say what the urban matrix is:

• First, a grid indicating the pathways for all the means by which people move about a city and engage in exchange with others—by car or truck, by mass transit, by bicycle, and, most important because it is most fundamental to exchange, by foot or wheelchair;

• Second, the rhythmic structure that urges people along those pathways;

• Third, the rules by which individual places (homes, stores, offices, libraries, whatever) align with the pathways of the public realm; and

• Fourth, an organizing principle by which places of exchange activity coalesce into nodes—an urban form that allows places of exchange to be efficiently and richly linked with each other and with people's homes.

A well-designed urban matrix is like a jazz chart, a framework for improvisation as well as collaboration. No two performances of "April in Paris" will (or should) be alike. Soloists elaborate the tune and explore its harmonic terrain in unique ways, and musicians respond to each other differently in every performance, yet the underlying melodic and chordal structure of the song is still (usually) audible. The chart is not a means for strict regimentation. It enables the musicians to be individual, together.

Conceptually and schematically—we are not yet ready to pour concrete—the urban matrix looks something like Piet Mondrian's late painting *Broadway Boogie-Woogie* (reproduced on the cover to this book). Mondrian is best known for his starkly simple geometrical abstractions—pure rectangles of primary colors in a grid of straight (usually black) lines on a white background. But in his own way Mondrian was really and always a representational artist—he was showing us the world around him. The focal plane, however, shifted as he reached toward his mature style. In his early years he sought to represent the surface appearance of things, with their particular, accidental shapes in the three-dimensional, touchable here and now. But soon he began looking past the particular to the universal—the underlying structure of the object that, before, he had seen as surface color and shape.

Broadway Boogie-Woogie, which dates from 1942–43, came near the end of Mondrian's lifetime of thinking about and representing the underlying structure of things. The painting could be seen as an abstraction or distillation of Manhattan. The rectilinear character of the composition suggests Manhattan's street grid, but Mondrian does not represent the map in a literal, reductivist way. Rather, he portrays the map as a rhythm of intense and muted activities. Significantly, the pathways in Mondrian's painting are not just uniform black lines, as in most of his middle-period paintings. The pathways are shown as red, blue, and yellow pulses—short and tightly spaced to suggest a frenetic pace on the north-south avenues, longer and less varied in color to suggest a more serene pace on the east-west streets. The pulses are not uniform in length or in color sequence—not a constant disco beat, but a flexible, organic rhythm that has everywhere a sense of direction or tendency. Mondrian's brilliantly accurate insight, expressed in both the title and the design of this painting, is that the pathways of a city are not just static ribbons of concrete, but also (and in their essence) movement and rhythm—not a rut, but a groove, in the jazz sense.

The urban matrix looks a little like Mondrian's painting in being a complex plaid of pathways—streets and roads, sidewalks, transit routes, bike paths—that are continuous, that penetrate deep into the fabric of neighborhoods, that come together in nodes or concentrations at strategic places, and that are rhythmic. This plaid of pathways is the public realm.

But the public realm does not exist for its own sake alone. The pathways are meaningful only to the extent that they clearly, efficiently, and usefully connect places where people do things with each other for their mutual benefit. For want of a better term, we'll call those places, collectively, the private realm, even though some of the places are publicly owned—schools and libraries, for example. The boundary between public and private realms—the vertical plane where they meet and provide access in either direction—is a critical part of the urban matrix because pathways are defined by their boundaries. The many places of the private realm need to stand in an intimate boundary relationship with the pathways of the public realm if the pathways are to work.

In Mondrian's painting, a discreet silence is observed regarding what happens in the blank spaces between the pathways of the city. It's a free country, after all, and people are entitled to do whatever they wish in their private realms. But the boundaries of the individual private realms impinge on and define the public realm. The rhythmic pulses of color that form

Mondrian's matrix are not, we can assume, painted on the pavement. They represent the public face of the private realms, the alignment of private spaces with the public matrix.

I don't suggest that Manhattan's extremely intimate relationship between private and public should be normative for every neighborhood or every city—only that an urban matrix should define pathways sufficiently to allow them to do what they're supposed to do. That degree of definition is achievable in low-density suburbs as well as in high-density downtowns, in new neighborhoods or old ones.

In the built city, the urban matrix may be seen in three aspects, or three levels of analysis. First is the physical and visual matrix of connectivity expressed by the width of streets, the sizes of blocks, the scale and setback of buildings, the rhythm of columns and windows along a building line, the rhythm of solids and voids, the continuity of sidewalks, the relationships between sidewalks and front doors—all those repetitive features that solidify connections from door to door and from block to block. These and other physical features hang together as a nested ensemble in traditional cities, but they form a different kind of ensemble, akin to chaos, in typical post-World War II suburbia.

The second aspect of the urban matrix is expressed by a functional mix that, in old town centers, puts housing, shopping, culture, recreation, and schools within an easy and pleasant walk from each other rather than, as is the usual practice today, radically separating the activities of city life.

Superimposed on the functional matrix is the social matrix: if diverse activities are connected in traditional neighborhoods, then, unavoidably, diverse kinds of people are also brought together in these neighborhoods.

CIVIL SPACE

But America's urban dwellers are ambivalent about diversity. There are two radically different tones of voice in which to say: "You don't know who you might meet in the street." We like diversity, but not too much, not uncontrolled, and not too close to home. Fear of diversity—racial, economic, generational—contributed to the evolution of the segmented, insular, suburban style of land development of recent decades. The cure may have been worse than the disease. Suburban parking lots are among the most dangerous places to be if you're concerned about being assaulted or killed by a stranger. Even the residents of ritzy walled-and-guarded subdivisions are discovering that the security they pay so dearly for is largely a chimera: seclusion allows resident teenagers to burglarize their neighbors' houses and deal drugs with impunity.

Let us acknowledge that the world is a risky place and accept that there are no guarantees of safe passage anywhere—nowhere, at least, that is free enough to be worth traveling to. But an important characteristic of a well-formed urban matrix is that it tends to normalize diversity and make it benign by bending it into coherent channels. I say "tends to" because no system of urban design can cure all social ills. People do bad things to other people for lots of reasons, and better streets and sidewalks won't fix them.

A well-formed urban matrix can, however, help to define what I call "civil space." The conventional distinctions between private space and public space, or enclosed space and open space, or solids and voids, overlook the active, formative role played by shared space as a shaper of civil society. Civil society is a game whose rules must be learned and followed if the game is to proceed peaceably. It is a game that requires a game board or playing field. A baseball field or Monopoly board is neither an undifferentiated space nor a random assortment of real estate, but is ordered to promote the progress of the game according to its rules. Civil space is that portion of the common realm that, by virtue of its intimate relatedness with homes, stores, and other places of exchange, promotes the game of civil society. Civil space is that portion of the public realm where the rules of civil society apply. It is a space where I observe others and am observed, where people share fairly narrow channels and must, for convenience, develop conventions for sharing that space. It is the space where, coming into close proximity to the many offerings and activities of civilization, I learn about them and how to behave in relation to them. It is the space I own in common with my neighbors ("own" not in the real estate sense but in the sense of benefiting from and feeling responsibility for), as opposed to the space that is nothing more than a void between destinations.

The particular circumstance that suggested the concept of civil space to me was a series of violent incidents, including a fatal shooting of an elderly woman who was caught in a gang cross fire, at a park-and-ride bus stop on the property of a suburban San Antonio shopping mall. The transit stop was at the fringe of the mall's parking lot, near an expressway access road, and bore no close relationship with any place of business or other activity. There wasn't even a pedestrian way from the transit stop to the mall entrance. This space served passably as a game board for the game of parking, but certainly not for civil society. It was the perfect example of a void in the fabric of the city, and it is not to be wondered at that un-nice people would do un-nice things there. (The bus facility has since been evicted from the mall property.)

The ways in which people choose to organize their space reflects their ideals and aspirations about how they and others are expected to behave in that space, whether the space in question is the interior of a private home or the public space between private places. The space that is thus designed subtly or unsubtly enforces those ideals and aspirations on its users.

It is well known that blank walls attract graffiti, while walls that reveal the hand of civilization tend to remain clean. Even in gang-ridden ghettoes, a large mural or architecturally interesting wall may remain untouched by graffiti for many years, while nearby blank walls are smothered in spray paint. Buildings that are occupied and well maintained are much less likely to be vandalized than buildings that are vacant and decaying. The preference of graffiti artists for blank walls, and vandals for vacant buildings, is partly a matter of practicality. If you want to write something, it makes sense to use a clean sheet of paper. But a deeper reality is embedded in that practical one. If a piece of paper is already written on, it implies an invitation to read it and to respond in ways that are appropriate to the text. Especially if it is not just a quick, careless scribble, but a neatly printed or written page, the document expresses an orderliness—and, underlying that, a human intentionality—

that asks to be respected. Writing on a blank page is not an act of disorder, although it may be done in an undisciplined or hateful or destructive or inept way, but an attempt to create order where none existed. Similarly, the blank spaces of a city, whether in the vertical dimension as blank walls or in the horizontal dimension as asphalt wildernesses, are awkward silences in the conversation of civil society—gaps that are subject to being filled, possibly in disturbing ways, by people who may otherwise have been excluded from the conversation.

By virtue of its organization, including the relationships of buildings to each other and to the common pathways, civil space subtly models socially responsible behavior for all who use it. Civil space keeps the conversation going and makes it inclusive. It allows diverse behaviors, cultures, opinions, classes, and tastes to coexist as distinct utterances in the same conversation.

Civil space, however, has been all but squeezed out of suburban-style site planning. Suburban space is both overdetermined and underdetermined—overdetermined in the sense that insular and functionally segregated land uses linked only by roads, without redundant pathways, allow a city to be used in only narrowly determinate ways, by automobile; underdetermined in the sense that suburban form, with its vast parking lots flowing around freestanding, randomly located buildings, is not coherently organized to give the pedestrian a sequential, ordered, and intimate contact with a wide variety of urban experience, and thus does not afford opportunities to develop habits of accommodation and appropriate response to a variety of experiences. Glimpses of business signs and attention to traffic apart, the space between freestanding suburban destinations is an experiential, cultural, and social void. You drive to one parking lot, and then you drive to another parking lot, and then you drive to a third parking lot. In the spaces between parking lots, you are protected from the influence of civil society by the cocoon of the automobile; in the space between your parked car and the front door of the place you are going to, the only thing you are likely to learn about civil society is the etiquette of the parking lot—information that is not inconsequential, but far from comprehensive.

The well-formed urban matrix is not solely a matter of functional and physical connectivity but also—and fundamentally—an attempt to reclaim from the manifold voids of modern site planning a connected and effective civil space. The well-formed urban matrix *defines* civil space.

THE CONCEPTUAL CITY

If we hope to achieve optimum economic vitality and social and functional integration in the built city, we have to begin with a conceptual city—a complex grid showing how the individual pieces of a city will connect with each other. The grid needs to penetrate far deeper into the fabric of a city than the grid of major thoroughfares—which is about all that public planning policy considers important these days. In order for the pieces of a city to aggregate into a unity, they have to be connected at the microscopic level, for the pedestrian as well as for the driver. The fundamental unit of measurement for the urban matrix is the human body.

Until the beginning of this century—and really until after World War II and the nearly universal spread of the automobile and good roads—builders had no option but to accept the matrix established by the human body. That matrix was the basis of collaboration in city-making.

When most people moved by foot most of the time, all the necessities and many of the pleasures of life had to be found within a compact, walkable span. In the days before electric refrigerators and freezers, one had to purchase meat, produce, breads, and ice on a daily basis, meaning that shops offering these items had to be found close to home. Such shops were most often small, because the accessible neighborhood market was usually not big enough to support large stores, and the technical systems and public infrastructure that are necessary for large stores hadn't been developed yet.

Nineteenth-century construction techniques favored a close spacing of columns, and on facades the prevailing European architectural styles expressed the structural technology—not in the linear, repetitive way of corporate modernism, but in the rhetorical, richly orchestrated manner of the symphony. There was a close but flexible relationship between the rhythm of walking and the rhythm of architectural articulations along the sidewalk.

As in the music of the period, the structure of facades was elaborated according to the principles of variation and development. The pedestrian was drawn along the street from bay to bay, from storefront to storefront, and from block to block, as the listener to a symphony is propelled from phrase to phrase, from episode to episode, from movement to movement.

Before television and cheap color printing, the shop window was the most efficient way for most retailers to entice customers with items whose value depended at least in part on visual appeal—shoes, clothes, furniture, wallpaper, rugs, flowers, even automobiles and foods. Thus it made economic sense to have shop windows, and the buildings in which they were located, coincide with the property line and the public sidewalk. Moreover, for various historical and practical reasons, city blocks were small, on the order of 300 to 600 feet on a side. Space was at a premium in small blocks, so commercial buildings tended to fill the available space. Small blocks also yielded multiple pathways to destinations a few blocks away from the home; because people might take different routes at different times, a larger swath of the neighborhood and its diversity of experience could be routinely encountered and assimilated than if only a single route were available, as in modern suburban-style planning.

Because many or most errands were accomplished on foot, sidewalks were essential. It was particularly important that sidewalks connect homes with neighborhood shopping and with transit routes, so there was no gap in the sidewalk system between residential and commercial streets.

Before air-conditioning, large shaded porches were important living areas in houses, and many of the fashionable architectural styles called for a porch on the front of a house. The porch, with its transparency to the sidewalk, acted like the shop window in mediating between private and public realms and bringing them into intimate relationship, while at the same time reinforcing the privacy of the sanctum behind the front door.

If you ignore the architectural styles and accidental particulars of a historic neighborhood and abstract from it the general form of its pathways, couplings, and rhythms, you end up with a drawing that looks a little like *Broadway Boogie-Woogie.* Conversely, you can begin by drawing a matrix of the general form of pathways, couplings, and rhythms—a matrix of connectivity—and then design or let others design the particular and peculiar pieces that will fit into the matrix and express it in physical terms.

When you set out to design a matrix of connectivity, you begin with a vision of how you want the finished, physical product to function, who will be using it, and what the technical limitations and opportunities might be. The matrix of connectivity for a train set will not be like that for an office system. The matrix one might design today for a suburban neighborhood will not be like the matrix for an inner-city neighborhood of the 1920s, and the matrix for a high-density northeastern city would not be like the one for a low-density Sun Belt city. The presence or absence of rail transit, large universities, or other special conditions, including topography, need to be considered.

Even within a single city, it would be imprudent to aim for a single matrix that doesn't allow for a diversity of neighborhood types. City governments do harm by imposing a one-size-fits-all regimen of design standards for an entire municipality, irrespective of when or where the parts were built. Everywhere, it is useful to have a publicly defined matrix that fosters connectivity, but the same matrix will not be suitable for all historical and geographic circumstances. It is not my purpose to prescribe *the* matrix, or a menu of matrices, for planners to apply, in the manner of a pattern book, to their own cities. Rather, I hope to guide planners, developers, public officials, and ordinary citizens to an understanding of the questions they need to ask as they work together to devise matrices that meet local needs, desires, and conditions. I hope to show how the small details and large patterns of a city affect how people live their daily lives and how they interact with each other in the economic, social, and cultural realms. People in a city need to ask themselves and each other what it is they hope to achieve, how they want to live, what they want their city to enable them to do. Then they need to ask how the patterns on which they will build their city and the pathways that connect one to another can be designed to serve those goals in the context of a particular set of historical, geographic, and economic circumstances.

My appreciation for a variety of means for connectedness should not be taken as an endorsement of chaos. Wherever, however, and whenever people live, the general outlines of the human body and the laws of physics are the same. These constants impose natural limits on the dimensional and topological features of an urban matrix if the pathways are to do their job. The constants guide us to what is essential in a neighborhood as opposed to those features that are accidental.

There are many legitimate criteria against which to evaluate a city's built environment. Is it beautiful? Does water drain off safely after a heavy rain? Is there enough good housing in every price range and in every part of town? Is the air clean? Are historic buildings preserved? Do the sewers run downhill? These and other questions are worth asking. But policies that address such criteria as these in isolation, as ends in themselves, risk stumbling over each other. Good cities are not just the sum of good sewers and drains, housing and beauty. A city's mission is exchange, and that mission ought to be the foundation for a city's master plan and the context for narrower policy decisions. The most useful criterion for measuring a city's quality of life and economy is this: Does the layout of the city, as a whole and in its details, facilitate the manifold processes of exchange?

However obvious this objective may seem, it has been widely disregarded in American cities in the decades since World War II:

• Seeking to keep cars and trucks moving quickly, the traffic engineers widened streets, obliterated sidewalks, multiplied expressways, and synchronized traffic lights. That would all be very nice if the city were about ceaseless vehicular movement. But the traffic engineers' vision provides only very limited opportunities for exchange, and *that* is what the city is about.

• Virtually every type of building program—private and public, residential, commercial, and institutional—has been conceptualized as a congeries of independent cells. The large discount store stands alone on its vast (and usually treeless) parking lot. The strip retail "center"—which is almost never central to anything except a parking lot—scorns pedestrian connections, and often even auto connections, with the adjacent strip center on its left, the adjacent office building on its right, and the residential neighborhood behind it. Commercial buildings are set back at widely varying distances from the street and are usually separated from it by a parking lot, so that pedestrian pathways are poorly defined—if they exist at all. The residential subdivision is an isolation chamber attached to the rest of the city only by a narrow umbilicus leading to a busy road. In San Antonio, a large apartment complex was built directly across the road from the city's biggest civilian employer; the door-to-door distance is perhaps seventy-five yards, yet the only safe or practical way to commute between the two is by car. We build this, and we build that, and we build the other thing, but we don't bind the things we build into a mutually supportive, interdependent neighborhood.

• Urban aestheticians agitate for historic preservation, parks, public art, and ordinances controlling billboards and sign clutter, but they too often neglect to demand a context in which these goods make social and economic sense. We often end up with parks that are in the wrong place, underused, and dangerous; or (usually bad) sculptures that are plopped down in locations that nobody else wants; or sign-control proposals that draw resentment and often insurmountable opposition from business people because, given the typical approach to site planning and road design, the large sign is the only way for a business to make its presence known.

In sum, post–World War II suburbia is ugly and congested, diffuse and confusing, wasteful of land, energy, and time, economically and socially dysfunctional. People moved to the suburbs in hope of finding Arcadian peace and bucolic splendor only to be followed by all the noise, congestion, asphalt, and squalor they thought they had escaped. They are understandably resentful that the promise of suburbia wasn't realized.

But suburbia will continue inevitably to destroy itself by its own success in the absence of a framework for collaboration in city building. Because an urban matrix is a framework for collaboration among many individual property owners in both public and private sectors, it follows that the design and supervision of the urban matrix must be public functions. However good my intentions for the property that I develop, I can't control the way you develop your adjoining property. I cannot require you to build sidewalks or streets that connect with mine, for example. You and I may agree to develop our separate properties to connect as an integrated unit, but it is unlikely that a dozen or a hundred separate property owners can be drawn voluntarily into the same agreement. Furthermore, the public infrastructure itself affects the matrix of connectivity. No individual property owner can dictate the design and placement of crosswalks and traffic signals, or the location and site planning for such public facilities as libraries, fire stations, and parks. If it is to be effective, an urban matrix has to be written into the regulations and policies, including the master plan, of a jurisdiction with authority over zoning and development standards.

The regulations need not be very burdensome or costly. A well-formed urban matrix redirects regulations that are already in place in most cities and may make some design standards less onerous than they are now. The problem with the regulatory regime in most suburbanized cities is not just that it doesn't do enough, but that it does the wrong things. Too many of the rules keep things apart—setback and open-space requirements, on-site parking standards, function-segregated zoning, huge right-of-way requirements for major roads, and landscaping standards that may increase the raw area between buildings without necessarily organizing the space in a more usable way. We need to reexamine the rules to see how they can be rewritten to tie the pieces of a city together rather than pull them apart.

■ sidewalks and the dance of the street

In Charles Chaplin's *Modern Times*, the Little Tramp and the Gamin (Paulette Goddard) escape from the police, run along a street and stop to rest on the parkway in a modest neighborhood. Lounging on the grass, they watch a man in a suit and a woman in an apron enact the tender morning ritual of parting at their front door. When the kisses are done, the husband leaves for work on the sidewalk behind our heroes. The Little Tramp tells the Gamin how nice it would be if they, too, could live in a house like that one. We see a fantasy of their connubial breakfast: a cow stops outside the kitchen door to dispense a pitcher of milk. A policeman interrupts their reverie. Standing behind them on the sidewalk, he orders them to move on. They rise, brush themselves off, and walk away—not on the sidewalk but, as they had come, in the street.

At one level, *Modern Times* is about the destruction of individual worth by the cogs of the industrial machine. More deeply, however, it is about the failure of community, a division between the powerful and the weak, the owners and the workers, Us and Them. The Little Tramp asserts the values of community, mutual responsibility, and individual dignity against an increasingly privatized, insular, and dehumanizing social and economic order. With the simple insight of a great artist, Chaplin exposes the core of his theme in a tiny detail. While the working husband in the suit uses the sidewalk, our heroes—separated from the community by circumstances beyond their control—must walk in the street. They are transformed, metaphorically, into objects with the same status as other machines—cars, trucks, buses.

Sidewalks are the capillaries of community, even the embodiment of community. They connect homes with other homes, offices, stores, and schools. They are democratic pathways, usable by people who do not or cannot drive and—if properly designed—even by the blind, the halt, and the lame. Sidewalks are public pathways, open and free, in the ideal, to persons of every class, belief, age, and interest.

In San Antonio, where my newspaper column often deals with sidewalks, some people regard me as being more than slightly dotty on the subject. Sidewalks, it is said, just aren't that important.

I cheerfully plead guilty to being a sidewalk fanatic, but I hope to persuade you that sidewalks are worth being fanatical about. I believe that the design of the network of public pedestrian paths is degree zero of urban planning. A well-formed pathway system alone cannot guarantee a healthy urban organism, any more than a well-formed vascular or nervous system can guarantee a healthy human body. But if you were to design a living organism, the fine structure of the network that delivers nutrients or information to the functional organs is a limiting condition on what your final design will be able to do. In a city the fine structure of the pathways is a limiting condition for the viability of the more glamorous structures in which vital urban processes—commerce, learning, knowledge generation, the construction of patterns of mutual responsibility—take place.

In too many American cities, especially in suburbanized areas but also in decaying inner cities, planners have paid obsessive attention to the veins and arteries while allowing the capillaries to atrophy. The needs of auto traffic have become the preeminent organizing theme of city planning, but the planners have forgotten that people still have to get out of their cars and go *into* some place in order to do most of the things that people live in cities to do. Pedestrian movement has become the unwanted, neglected, and abused stepchild of the urban enterprise, to the detriment of the city's life processes.

Even the more enlightened transportation planners subsume sidewalks under the category "pedestrian amenities," although, curiously enough, roadways are not called "motorist amenities."

Conventional wisdom has it that sidewalks are no longer essential in most places because hardly anybody walks any more. But people do walk. Look closely at the sides of any busy street that doesn't have sidewalks. You will probably see deep footpaths worn into the grass. Look out your front window. You will see your neighbors walking for fun or fitness or a visit to a friend's house or the ice cream parlor. Look at any bus stop. You will see people walking to and from it. In the supermarket, people do not drive their cars through the door, down the canned vegetables aisle, and past the checkout stand. They walk. Even in that ultimate symbol of suburbia, the shopping mall, people walk great distances. Cars and buses may carry people to the *vicinity* of where they want to be, but in the end most of the exchanges that constitute the life of a city occur on foot. Drive-through car washes, banks, and restaurants are virtually the only exceptions, with the demise of drive-in movies and the failure of drive-in funeral parlors to catch on.

Ultimately, the act of exchange depends on an encounter between a flesh-and-blood human being and some feature of his or her world. Electronic communications and mail-order shopping have not greatly reduced the field of action in which physical proximity is necessary for exchange. You still cannot try on a suit, test the ripeness of a cantaloupe, or make love electronically. Electronic media have given us immense options for learning and entertainment in solitude, but these cannot reproduce the sharedness of the theater, the concert, or the lecture hall, where many strangers participate together in a transformative experience and in that way strengthen the bonds of community. The library and the bookstore, the park, the doctor's waiting room, the shops and restaurants and bank lobbies where people act out their lives in the company of others, all these are places where community building happens in ways that cannot be duplicated by electronics. Physical places matter, and that is why the pathways that connect those places also matter.

Human physical attributes impose natural limits on the ability of the human being to participate in exchange. In addition, some psychological and cultural attributes may be so nearly universal, at least within a particular region or culture, as to constitute additional natural limits—how we perceive time, distance, security, and comfort, for example. Because these attributes are nearly universal, the limits they impose on participation in exchange are also nearly universal—that is, applicable in every part of town for equivalent land uses, but most particularly for those in the consumer sector of the economy: retailing, cultural and recreation facilities, residential neighborhoods, and many kinds of offices.

If our objective is to facilitate exchange, what do human anatomy and psychology imply for the dimensions, surface characteristics, and continuity of sidewalks; or for their location in relation to roadways, on the one hand, and the places where people want to go, on the other?

For the answers, we need only look at the sidewalks in older residential and commercial districts—those built between, say, 1880 and 1940—and understand why they were laid out as they were. The sidewalk was not an afterthought, as it usually is today, nor was it just a ribbon of concrete indifferent to its surroundings. Rather, the sidewalk was part of a coordinated ensemble, a technology that responded effectively to specific problems and opportunities of urban life.

In my neighborhood and others nearby, developed from the 1920s to the 1940s, residential sidewalks were generally about four feet wide (the minimum width that allows two adults to walk abreast) and set back twelve to fifteen feet from the curb. In some older neighborhoods, the sidewalk was closer to the line of houses or apartment buildings than to the street. In some cities, though only rarely in San Antonio, the parkway often included a uniform line of "street trees" planted by the developer. In dense urban neighborhoods such as those in New York and Chicago, the sidewalk might be adjacent to the street but quite wide, twelve to twenty feet, and still punctuated by trees along the curb. In either case, the tree line divided the wide space between building lines into three relatively intimate linear zones—the street corridor itself, which over time would be overarched by a nearly continuous tree canopy, and two flanking ensembles of front yards and sidewalks.

Thus placed on the house side of the tree line and at some distance from the street, the sidewalk afforded the pedestrian protection from the danger and anxiety of vehicular traffic. Even standing rainwater splashed by passing cars would probably not reach the pedestrian path. Furthermore, the parkway established the sidewalk as a transitional zone, both a linear public pathway and a lateral interface between the public and private realms. Placed next to the curb or on the street side of the tree line, the sidewalk's lateral relationships with houses would have been weakened.

The parkway serves many useful functions. It's a convenient place to locate utility poles, mailboxes, traffic and street signs, bus benches, and other public objects without blocking the pedestrian path or impinging on the more private space on the residential side of the sidewalk. In some grander subdivisions, the parkway accommodated stone gateways, decorative fountains, or special plantings, amenities that helped to distinguish one neighborhood from another.

The parkway even affects the sidewalk surface itself. A setback of at least eight feet is generally required to put the sidewalk beyond the slope of a driveway, even on fairly level terrain. A parkway twelve to fifteen feet wide makes a level sidewalk possible in most cases. Placed next to the curb, the sidewalk's level surface is interrupted at every driveway by slopes that, as one elderly and disabled lady put it, "might as well be Mount Everest to me."

One interesting if not especially scientific observation: On several San Antonio streets that don't have sidewalks, I've measured the distance between the curb and the furrow worn into the grass (or weeds or mud) by pedestrians. Where the terrain is relatively flat and unimpeded, the footpath typically lies about six feet from the curb—a distance that approximates average adult height. As a rule adults do not walk immediately next to the curb unless they are forced to. Similarly, on downtown sidewalks I have observed that people do not generally walk within arm's length of building walls and shop windows, but five or six feet away. Given a choice, people tend to choose a comfortable distance from the boundaries of the space they occupy. By happy circumstance, the twelve- to fifteen-foot parkway that was typical of early twentieth-century residential streets yielded a pedestrian-to-boundary distance on the order of five or six feet when the parkway was planted with a row of street trees. The arrangement all but required people to walk where they were most comfortable anyway. The unsurprising result? People felt comfortable walking on the traditional residential sidewalk, and they still do.

In traditional urban neighborhoods, sidewalks formed a continuous and largely unvaried grid. There were gaps at street crossings, of course, but the sidewalk on one side almost always lined up with the one on the other side, and this arrangement continued without interruption from blocks of detached single-family houses through blocks of two- and three-story apartment buildings to neighborhood retail and commercial centers, schools, and parks. Thus it was easy and convenient for my grandmother, back in the early fifties, to wheel her shopping cart from her frame house on Cincinnati Avenue to the grocery store (now deceased) on Fredericksburg Road, two blocks away.

But the benefits of sidewalk continuity extended beyond ease of pedestrian movement. The sidewalk grid was also a subtle psychological linkage. As long as the sidewalk didn't end and didn't appreciably change in dimensions or relationship to the street and buildings, a residential block and a commercial block a dozen streets apart could still hang together, perceptually and functionally, as parts of one coherent unit, the same neighborhood, even if the architecture of the buildings varied considerably in scale, materials, and style.

In all these ways, the traditional sidewalk grid encouraged people to walk to neighborhood retail centers, parks, schools, libraries. Walking was easy, convenient, comfortable, pleasant, and healthy, helping to keep the heart fit and the body trim. In the days when people commonly sat on their front porches, the sidewalk in close proximity to the house served a social function as well. The pedestrian could wave to his neighbors, exchange news and gossip, and keep up with who was moving in or out of the neighborhood. People spend less time on their front porches than they used to, even in neighborhoods that have them, but people still work in their yards, and it was in that circumstance that I met several of my neighbors for the first time as they or I strolled on the sidewalk for business or pleasure. In this way, sidewalks help knit individuals into communities, a process that is inhibited when people travel in air conditioned automobiles with their tinted windows rolled up.

The traditional arrangement of sidewalks came under pressure from many quarters in the decades after World War II, and especially after about 1960. That pressure continues to the present.

• On commercial roads and some busy residential streets, the pavement was widened to accommodate more and faster vehicular traffic. When streets were widened, the parkway was typically narrowed to a scant four or five feet, or even eliminated. One astonishing result of street widenings in San Antonio was that utility poles and other obstructions ended up dead in the middle of sidewalks. (In 1993, thanks to external pressure and internal enlightenment, the city-owned electric utility adopted a new policy against obstructing sidewalks.)

• Local codes governing sidewalks changed over time. Some cities and, especially, incorporated suburbs had no sidewalk requirement at all, at least for a time. The absence of a sidewalk might even be fashionable, underscoring the country-manor aspirations of suburbia, setting it visually apart from the city and subtly discouraging intrusion by pedestrian pedestrians. For those cities that did have a sidewalk requirement, the standards for width and placement in relation to the street might change over the years. Even where the sidewalk grid existed, it lost its block-to-block continuity. In many locations in San Antonio, the sidewalk changes size and position or comes and goes from lot to lot.

• In the hopscotch growth of post-1960 suburbia, each residential subdivision was typically built as a separate entity, at first an island of houses surrounded by farms or undeveloped land. When the blank places in the map were eventually filled out, either by other residential subdivisions or by commercial areas, the sidewalks (if any) did not usually cross from one subdivision to the next, or continue from a residential subdivision to the retail project a block away. Increasingly, developers built walls around their subdivisions, making the main road's sidewalk (if any) more a rebuff than an invitation.

• On suburban commercial roads, the only continuous, publicly mandated sidewalk usually abutted the street, while the front doors of businesses were separated from that sidewalk by parking lots. Thus disengaged from the places people might want to go, the sidewalk lost much of its psychological and functional meaning as linkage. Because the sidewalk didn't actually connect things, there was no point in bothering about continuity across property lines. Moreover, the sidewalk often blended into driveways and parking lots, so while the sidewalk might exist in principle, it did not exist in the real world of human feet and eyes. The public sidewalk became irrelevant, contributing little or nothing to the objective of human interchange. In the old city, by contrast, places of exchange formed a more or less unbroken line; the building line and the boundary of the public pathway were one and the same, for the most part.

CRITERIA FOR GOOD SIDEWALKS

In practice, the sidewalk in older neighborhoods is part of a comprehensive, integrated system. The usefulness of a sidewalk does not depend solely on its own width, flatness, and good repair, but also on its relationships to its surroundings—to the buildings it connects and to the other objects with which it must share the public right-of-way.

By asking what makes the sidewalk an effective, efficient pathway in older neighborhoods, we can derive six criteria for good sidewalks anywhere, whether in dense urban neighborhoods or in suburbs. Some, perhaps all, of the criteria can be met in different ways in different locales. But the end is the same everywhere—to encourage peaceful, voluntary exchange.

1. **Continuous.** The sidewalk should allow continuous, uninterrupted pedestrian movement from every place to every other place—from your front door to the front door of the neighborhood bank and hardware store and branch library. Where the sidewalk stops, the community stops.

2. **Well Defined.** The sidewalk does not blend into a smear of parking lots and driveways but is a clearly defined and bounded pathway, unam-

biguously a pedestrian zone. The need for definition applies to crosswalks as well. Especially in high-traffic areas, clearly marked crosswalks remind drivers that they must share the road with pedestrians.

— 3. **Organized to be unobstructed.** The public space has to accommodate many kinds of objects other than the pedestrian path. The space has to be wide enough and organized in such a way that there is a logical place to put bus benches, light poles, mailboxes, newspaper racks, and other amenities. This rational zoning of the public right-of-way requires planning and cooperation among several public and private entities—the utility company, responsible for street lights and power-line poles; the transit company, responsible for bus benches and shelters; the public works department or private developer that builds sidewalks; the city traffic department, which places traffic signals and stop signs; the postal service, which decides where to put mail drops and regulates the location of residential mailboxes.

— 4. **Safe from vehicular encroachment.** The pedestrian should not feel threatened by passing vehicular traffic, either physically or psychologically. The pedestrian path should be buffered from the street by distance, landscaping, or parked cars—the greater the amount or speed of traffic, the greater the buffer needed. In heavy-traffic areas, clearly defined crosswalks (preferably in a paving style distinct from the traffic surface) and landscaped safety islands are especially important to reinforce visually, for pedestrians and drivers, the sacredness of the pedestrian pathway.

— 5. **Rhythmic.** Depending on the rhythms of architectural features or landscaping along the sidewalk, the same physical distance may seem short or long, and the same physical pace may seem fast or slow. A rhythmically active pathway can encourage walking; a pathway without rhythm can inhibit movement. We need to see pathways not just as static corridors but as dynamic, rhythmically propulsive conveyor belts. We look at rhythm in some detail below.

— 6. **Giving efficient access to places.** The sidewalk should provide direct, efficient connections between the front doors of places where people want to go. This seems like an obvious criterion for sidewalks, but it is almost universally disregarded in modern suburbia, where sidewalks rarely connect anything other than parking lots. Thus, while my general strategy is to avoid proposing radical changes in planning standards, one such radical change is unavoidable. Instead of a *minimum-setback* requirement for commercial property, cities should establish a *build-to line*, a standard setback that allows for slight variation, and should require that the public sidewalk be coupled to that line. In dense urban neighborhoods the build-to line might be most appropriate close to the street, in the public right-of-way; in suburban areas the build-to line might be set farther back from the street, within private property, to accommodate more landscaping or parking. Wherever the build-to line is placed, the continuous, publicly mandated sidewalk should be attached to it.

In figure 5.1, Washington Avenue represents the typical pattern of compact urban development. The sidewalks (the heavy black lines) abut the curb, and the buildings (in gray) and their front doors (the arrows) abut the sidewalk. No problem with connectivity there. Adams Road and Jefferson Boulevard represent lower-density suburban development, where buildings are set back from the street behind parking lots or landscaping. In typical practice, the public sidewalk in such settings remains attached to the street and thus disengaged from the places it's supposed to connect. There is a strong argument to be made against placing a parking lot—as opposed to a single line of on-street parking—between the street and the storefronts in the first place, but if that's where the parking lot *must* go, the diagrams propose a compromise: the planning authority establishes a consistent but slightly flexible build-to line and requires developers to put the sidewalk there rather than at the curb, even if "there" is outside the public right-of-way, on private property.

Such encroachments on private property are not unprecedented. Developers may now be required to provide fire lanes on their property, for example. Moreover, this arrangement allows a developer to avoid spending money on a sidewalk that does no one any good, while the required sidewalk becomes the one that the developer probably would have chosen to build anyway, along the building front.

The crosswalk should, of course, continue the sidewalk line as closely

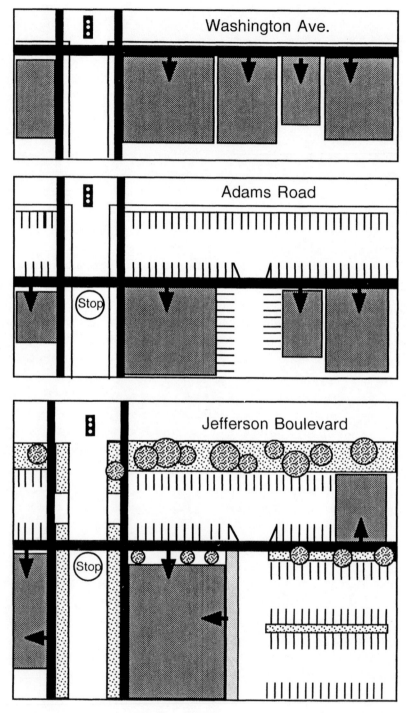

Figure 5.1 In commercial areas, the public sidewalk should always be attached to a build-to line.

as possible. To satisfy traffic engineers and traffic laws, the relocated cross-walk would have to be equipped with its own stop sign, in addition to the sign or signal light at the intersection, or with a sign advising motorists, "Stop here on red."

THE PATHWAY AND ITS BOUNDARIES

The design of the buildings that border a sidewalk have an influence over its usefulness. Again, traditional building practices indicate that the older architects and builders knew what they were doing.

In nineteenth- and early twentieth-century commercial buildings, doorways were typically set back several feet behind the building line, creating a little outdoor foyer. This setback served two important functions. First, a door opening outward—as fire codes now require—does not hit an unsuspecting passerby; the setback frees the pedestrian path from this danger. Second, the entry setback allows for small shop windows that face pedestrians—potential customers—as they walk along the sidewalk.

Windows parallel to the sidewalk are fine for the deliberate shopper, but the casual pedestrian is generally looking forward, not to the side. Windows that parallel the sidewalk thus are limited in their opportunity to entice. The entry setback with display windows—even quite small ones—rectifies that problem. They alert the casual pedestrian that something of interest can be found at this shop. If a little interest is piqued by the one or two items shown in the entryway window, the pedestrian may slow down enough to consider the more numerous items in the main windows paralleling the sidewalk. Some older shops reversed the ratio of large and small windows: A small retailer with narrow street frontage could set the doorway back deep behind the building facade, perhaps twelve or sixteen feet, and put long display windows on either side of this exterior corridor. In this way, a small retailer could get his message across to the passing customer as easily as a large retailer. In the forties and fifties, downtown retailers tried to distinguish their storefronts with oddly shaped display alcoves. San Antonio's then-premiere fashion retailer, Frost Bros. (of blessed memory), had a whole courtyard of display windows in an alcove set back from the sidewalk, and the perfume of the day would waft through this semi-enclosed space, pulling pedestrians' noses to the front door. Such alcoves and passageways, transitional public-private areas analogous to the residential porch, did more than expand display areas. They also added to the mystery and sensual pleasure of the stroll.

But these alcoves and setbacks are old-fashioned now. They're incompatible with the smooth, extruded lines of modernist architecture, they diminish valuable interior selling space, and they are too easily converted to ad hoc pissoirs and sleeping quarters. So a lot of the alcoves went away. Downtown is a less interesting place as a result.

The older architects and builders did not have reflective and dark-tinted plate glass available to them, but it seems unlikely they would have been dim-witted enough to use such glass on street-level storefronts. Granted, these materials can reduce air-conditioning costs—sometimes to zero: there's no point in cooling a vacant store, and vacant is what stores become when they don't have customers. Some years ago, a store selling maps, luggage, and travel accessories opened in the ground floor of a new office building in downtown San Antonio. Stunningly designed in a postmodern deco style by a topflight interior designer, Judith Urrutia, the store earned notice from the national design press and won several awards. Everyone who went inside oohed and ahhed and felt like spending money. But hardly anyone did go inside because casual pedestrians—potential customers—couldn't see in through the office building's dark tinted windows. The store didn't last long.

The older builders had other means to defend storefronts against the sun—awnings and arcades. These low-tech devices blocked the sun's rays more effectively than tinting could, so clear glass didn't pose an energy problem. Awnings and arcades reduced overhead glare, at least in some circumstances, making the window displays yet more visible. And, of course, pedestrians were sheltered from rain and the noonday sun.

RHYTHM

If the function of the sidewalk is to facilitate exchange, then the sidewalk is successful in proportion to the number of points of exchange that are located along it and within easy walking distance of a pedestrian's point of origin. But "easy walking distance" is a flexible concept. As a rule of thumb, a quarter-mile is thought to be the maximum comfortable distance for an errand, but this distance can easily be doubled or even quadrupled. People willingly walk long distances, without realizing how far they've gone, if they're having a good time. Two trips of identical distance may be perceived very differently, one trip seeming long, the other short, depending on the visual surroundings.

Just around the corner from my house is a barbecue restaurant where I sometimes go to carry home a sandwich. The walk takes hardly any time at all—a few minutes each way. My house is the sixth from the corner, or about three hundred feet. From my corner to the restaurant on the next corner is another three hundred feet or so. The total is a little over a tenth of a mile—practically nothing. Seen another way, however, the distance is the equivalent of two football fields. A tenth of a mile past my neighbors' houses is nothing; two whole football fields is a schlepp.

Why is that? Because a football field is boring, a broad and uniform sea of grass punctuated by a uniform grid of white lines and bounded by uniform ranks of bleachers. On my street, by contrast, the distance is broken up, modulated, by a complex layering of rhythms.

If you think of each house as a measure of music, the house's columns, windows, porches, and gables define the measure's strong and weak beats, accents and syncopations, staccato and legato attacks—the phrasing of the street. The phrasing of each house on my block differs from that of the others, as does the instrumentation, the palette of colors and materials. The basic metrical unit doesn't vary from house to house—the lots are all about fifty-five feet wide, and all the houses have roughly the same scale and setback—but there is some flexibility of weight or importance or contour because of the differing roof lines and variations in the assertiveness of the facades. Some grab the attention; others, more modest in form and materials, recede into the background.

A football field is a schlepp because it is an unrhythmic space. The same physical distance on my street is a short stroll because my street has rhythm, and rhythm makes time pass quickly.

An inescapable feature of older European and American streets is their rhythmic character. Even in unprepossessing buildings such as warehouses, factories, and modest row houses, grand or plain-spoken articulations of the facade measure the human gait—not in the rigid sing-song of doggerel but in the supple, organic rhetoric of poetry. Or music.

Architecture, Goethe said, is frozen music. The image is altogether beautiful but only half accurate. Architecture is a kind of music, but is it really frozen? We do not ordinarily conceive of buildings as objects in motion. But only in two-dimensional drawings or still photographs is a building frozen in one eternal pose. A real building is in a state of flux as the people who see and use it are themselves in motion. As one walks along the street, buildings advance and recede, blanch and blush, spin on their toes and play hide-and-seek, reveal their seductive ankles or their proud heads. Even if the viewers are momentarily still, they encounter a building from different angles, see subtly or greatly differing patterns of light and shadow and reflections, stand in more or less intimate relationship with the front door or the loading dock.

If architecture is poetry or music, the city is a dance. You are the dancer, and the buildings are the music—indeed, not just the buildings, but also the trees and street lights and fire hydrants and all the other pretending-to-be-stationary objects along your path.

Architects and architecture critics often talk about rhythm in buildings, and musicians and music critics often talk about architectural structure in the performance of a sonata or jazz solo. The parallels between musical and architectural rhythm are usually taken only as metaphor. I would like to make a stronger claim. Rhythm in music is not just a convenient metaphor of rhythm in buildings and groups of buildings and other objects in the streetscape. It is a precise analogy, and one that holds lessons for the design of cities.

As we move about a city, whether afoot or in a vehicle, we experience the city in time. A sidewalk and its environs are not just spatial features; they are temporal features as well. The linear distance from your office to the public library or the florist's is not traversed instantaneously. The trip, like that from the beginning to the end of a musical composition, takes a number of minutes, which may vary depending on the tempo of your walk. The objects you pass along the way are also temporal features; each occupies the field of vision or the attention for a number of seconds before you reach the next significant object. Music, too, unfolds as a sequence of temporal events.

Now, suppose I were to invite you to attend the eagerly awaited world premiere of my tone poem, *Ennui*. This work consists of a single chord sustained by the strings, loudly, for seventeen minutes and twelve seconds. I will cheerfully admit that *Ennui* is boring. Why? Because it consists of only two events, the beginning and the (excruciatingly distant) end. *Ennui* is a long blank wall.

Matters would not improve much if I were to add a trombone playing identical short blasts at one-second intervals throughout the length of the composition. The music would have a beat, which it didn't have before, and this beat would mark the passage of time as the ticking of a clock does, but few people find the ticking of a clock a fascinating diversion for more than a few seconds. Because all the events are the same, none stands out as an *event*. Adding a steady beat, furthermore, may just make bad worse. If the undifferentiated drone of *Ennui* was a long blank wall, *Ennui 2* is a water torture.

Real music has several layers of differentiation of time. In the *Ennui 2* example, one might give an extra stress to the even-numbered pulses, creating a backbeat. The result, if you add a simple melody and a three-chord progression—changing harmony being another way to differentiate time— is the sort of music that has a good beat and is easy to dance to. Add yet higher levels of groupings and you have yet more complex music. You got rhythm.

The function, or one of the functions, of rhythm is to propel the music forward, to sustain the long arch of a musical structure, and to sustain the listener's desire to follow that arch to the end. Rhythm is not the same as the beat or meter, which marks individual units of time without giving a composition a unique and meaningful shape or sense of direction.

In *The Rhythmic Structure of Music*, Grosvenor Cooper and Leonard B. Meyer explain:

Most of the music with which we shall be concerned is architectonic in its organization. That is, just as letters are combined into words, words into sentences, sentences into paragraphs and so on, so in music individual tones become grouped into motives, motives into phrases, phrases into periods, etc. . . .

As a piece of music unfolds, its rhythmic structure is perceived not as a series of discrete independent units strung together in a mechanical, additive way like beads, but as an organic process in which smaller rhythmic motives, while possessing a shape and structure of their own, also function as integral parts of a larger rhythmic organization.

Grouping on all architectonic levels is a product of similarity and difference, proximity and separation of the sounds perceived by the senses and organized by the mind. If tones are in no way differentiated from one another—whether in pitch, range, instrumentation and timbre, duration, intensity, texture or dynamics—then there can be no rhythm or grouping. For the mind will have no basis for perceiving one tone as accented and others as unaccented. There will be uniform pulses, nothing more, unless of course the grouping is completely subjective. On the other hand, if the successive stimuli are so different from one another or so separate in time or pitch that the mind cannot relate them to one another, there will be no impression of rhythm. The stimuli will then be perceived as separate, isolated tones.[1]

Rhythm, in all its many levels of depth, is essential if a listener is to follow the music through to the end, willingly and with enjoyment and even edification. For the identical reasons, rhythm is an essential feature of the streetscape if people are willingly, joyfully, and attentively to voyage on the sidewalk. The path cannot be a blank space between here and there; it must be punctuated and enlivened by a rhythm of physical events. It follows that the architecture and landscaping along the sidewalk deeply influence the circulation of people—along with their ideas and money.

Cooper and Meyer's two extremes—too little and too much differentiation—have exact analogies in the long blank wall or large parking lot, on the one hand, and in the fragmentation and diffusion of suburban commercial corridors, on the other.

But "too much" and "too little" are relative terms. If the "Minute Waltz" were played so slowly as to take twelve hours, retaining all the relative durational values of the original, the groupings would still be there, in an objective sense, but they would be imperceptible to normal people, those not blessed with attention spans so vast as to make them susceptible to panic at the infinitesimal advance of a glacier. If the same music were compressed into five seconds, the relative durations would again be imperceptible. If groupings are to be perceived, they must fall within a durational range that meshes with the attention span, including, most importantly, the way we perceive the present. We do not perceive the present as an instantaneous point in time but as a more or less extended vicinity of that point—usually, in music, on the order of a handful of seconds. A skilled composer may extend the frame of the present considerably, but the result is usually an increase in emotional tension. If that entire span passes without encountering an event, or if all the events of a piece of music are compressed into a single present, then the listener does not perceive the development of an idea over time. The typical range of perception of the present is a design constraint on the composition of music.

The same psychological mechanism, in tandem with certain physiological realities, is a design constraint on the composition of the streetscape. As we walk, our perception of the present moment is conditioned by our field of vision and the tempo and length of our gaits. One can't quantify how physiology conditions our perception of the present. As Cooper and Meyer say, "Rhythmic grouping is a mental fact, not a physical one." The general principle is that the present—however defined—must contain a sufficient number of ordered events to establish consciousness of rhythm, and that rhythm must propel the listener/walker to the next (and overlapping) present.

How do you apply that general principle? Some flexible, approximate, and undogmatic rules of thumb, based on observation and a bit of intuition, can be suggested. If the stride, roughly twenty-five to thirty inches for most adults, is the basic pulse of the pedestrian's encounter with the city—the beat of the music of the street—then it seems reasonable to propose that the next level of grouping might comprise events that occur at some small multiple of strides, two or three, or at most four. Music provides a precedent and justification for these numbers. Popular dance forms—consider the waltz, the fox-trot, the samba—rarely contain groups of more than four beats, even if one or more of those beats might be subdivided into several quick, short steps, as in the cha-cha. Even non-dance music (in the Western tradition) is most often divided into measures of two, three, or four beats; when the time signature indicates six, nine, or twelve beats, the measure is usually conducted or performed as though the number of principal divisions were two, three, or four. Why? I don't know, but it seems to work.

So our first level of grouping gives us an architectonic event every six to ten feet or so. But as in good music, so in a good streetscape there are more levels of groupings. Two similar consecutive events at Level 2 might be grouped as a pair at Level 3, and two or three consecutive pairs at Level 3 might be grouped as a pair or triplet at Level 4.

In music, these groupings often exhibit a dynamic near symmetry. Figure 5.2 is a graphic interpretation of the first thirty-six measures (roughly thirty seconds) of the less famous second movement (Allegretto) from Beethoven's "Moonlight Sonata." Each vertical line in the bottom row represents one measure, but because the tempo is quick you may think of each vertical line as a single stride. The little gables, arches, and flat roofs in the second row represent the motifs and phrases of the melody. The first motif consists of four notes represented by the first rising roofline, because the last note gives the motif a generally rising contour. This motif is immediately followed by one that is very much like it, but with different harmony and articulation and ending on a lower note, giving this motif a falling contour. This not quite symmetrical pair constitutes the first phrase, the first complete gable in our diagram. Then that whole phrase is repeated but transposed upward; that's the second, slightly higher gable in our diagram. The two gables together are grouped as a period, represented by the horizontal bar. At measure 9, the first eight-measure period repeats again, but in a dif-

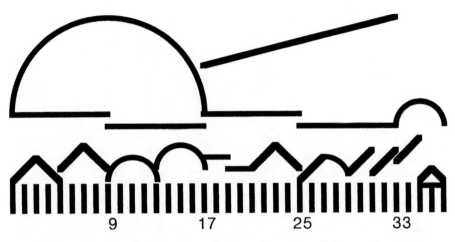

Figure 5.2 Hierarchical rhythmic organization of a portion of the second movement (Allegretto) from Beethoven's "Moonlight Sonata."

ferent rhythm and with counterpoint in the left hand. Because the two periods are much alike in melodic and harmonic content and rhythmic structure, I have tied them together, architectonically, with a big dome.

The second period, starting at measure 17, is less symmetrical than the first. The ingredients that were introduced in the first period are recombined in odd ways in the sequel; the phrase at measure 25, for example, starts like a gable and ends like an arch. Moreover, after the sixteen-measure first period we expect a sixteen-measure second one, but that expectation is violated by two extra measures that increase the tension, leading to a witty payoff. After a short pause, the music drops nearly two octaves and resolves itself in the tonic chord of D flat—the little two-measure folly at the end.

A friend who attended the University of Notre Dame tells me that the dean of architecture at that school would sometimes sit at a piano and "play" photographs of the campus buildings as though they were musical scores. That makes perfect sense, because the hierarchical groupings we hear in music can be seen in certain kinds of streetscapes.

The warehouse district of Louisville, Kentucky, offers a fine example of classical rhythmic structure (figure 5.3). Visible in the photograph are

Figure 5.3　Classical rhythmic structure in the Louisville warehouse district.

three levels of rhythmic grouping at the first floor: the regular or symmetrical spacing of identical columns within each facade; the specialization of bays, seen for example in the symmetrical tripartite division of the first building into two window bays with planter boxes flanking a central entry bay, or the two narrow bays flanking two wider bays in the second building; and the whole facade taken as a unit in relation to its neighbors. The entire line of facades on one side of the street in this block is a higher-order grouping, not visible in the photograph. The warehouse district as a whole might be regarded as one "movement" within the larger—and not altogether successful—symphony of downtown Louisville.

The object of the game is to encourage linear pedestrian movement along the sidewalk and lateral pedestrian movement into the places where exchange actually occurs. What features of the streetscape serve those functions?

First, there is a consistency of texture that establishes the entire block as a single space, as opposed to a collection of separate and unrelated spaces. All the buildings are close to the same height and width, date from the same period, and form an unbroken line along the sidewalk.

Second, within this consistent milieu no two facades are quite alike. One has fluted round columns with Corinthian capitals, the next has square columns and segmental arches. One is divided into three bays, the next into four. One has planter boxes in front, the next doesn't. One is Greek Revival, the next is Italianate. Every fifteen or twenty steps brings a slight change of scene, a slightly different tempo (because of variations in column spacing), and a reason both to continue walking and to notice what's in the windows.

But there is a stasis in the too polite, too orderly rhythms of this Louisville streetscape, which has been prettified by the historic preservation movement. A more exuberant and unruly Romanticism may be seen in the main street of Jefferson, Wisconsin, a small town midway between Milwaukee and Madison (figure 5.4). This collection of facades, seen in a 1975 photograph, is in a sense chaotic, containing a wide variety of architectural styles, some variety of vertical scale, and a lively jumble of signs and awnings. But still the horizontal scale is consistent from building to building, establishing an approximately uniform period length, and the periods are subdivided by a

Figure 5.4　Romantic asymmetry in Jefferson, Wisconsin.

hierarchy of architectural elements grouped according to a dynamic near symmetry, just as in the groupings in Beethoven's sonata. It is important that in some of the facades the symmetry is not perfect—not static. The second building from the left, for example, is divided into two equal bays, but the left-hand bay has a projecting window on the second floor, while the window on the right-hand bay is flush with the facade. The two windows are ornamented differently, too. In music, such asymmetries within a basically symmetrical framework can create a momentary pause in the flow of the music, a moment of repose or of special importance; or they can serve as little thrusts to propel the music forward. Sometimes the same asymmetry can do both, as the fourth step (a turn) in a tango at once interrupts the motion of the first three strides and launches the couple into the next sequence. On the streetscape, asymmetries within a generally symmetrical framework have the same effects on the music of the stroll.

Rhythm is not the exclusive province of older architectural styles.

There is nothing remotely historicist about Fumihiko Maki's Spiral Building in Tokyo, for example (figure 5.5). Though it is clad in commonplace modern curtain-wall elements, the compositionally balanced asymmetry of their arrangement, both horizontally and vertically, energizes the whole block. A more conservative approach can be seen in a Denver office building by Kohn Pedersen Fox (figure 5.6). Here the complex, hierarchical symmetry of financial-district classicism is evoked in a modern idiom. In either case, the architecture establishes a rhythm—not a drone or a metronomic beat—of visual events whose spacing, scale, and variety help to urge the pedestrian along in her dance.

In figure 5.7 we can compare two side-by-side Manhattan buildings of the same scale but of greatly different vintages and rhythms. The older one, on the left, establishes an active, jazzy rhythm in both horizontal and vertical dimensions because of the white arches and sills of the windows that are punched into the red brick facade and because of the complexity of the vertical elements in that facade. The modern building on the right is almost a drone, its horizontal bands of windows punctuated only by thin, widely spaced black panels that express the structural columns behind them; the spandrels are uninterrupted bands of brick in a plain running bond. My eye is drawn to the building on the left, while the one on the right recedes into the background. I feel more stimulated when I look at the building on the left, as though my perceptual pulse rate were elevated. The newer building induces—to be kind—a more serene response.

I don't want to suggest that one is right and the other necessarily wrong. In a real city built by many different kinds of real people over a span of many years, the dance of the street is not all of uniform tempo or emotional affect. A "movement" (to speak of a neighborhood or part of a neighborhood in musical terms) in generally moderate tempo may be punctuated by episodes of calm or frenzy, solemnity or farce. That's one of the things that make cities interesting. But note, in figure 5.7, how the row of street trees softens the differences between the two buildings and binds them into a unity. The similarly scaled (but not identical) storefronts, with their window displays, also help to establish a continuous baseline (bass line) linking two very different fragments of architectural melody.

Figure 5.5 Horizontal and vertical rhythm swirl through Fumihiko Maki's Spiral Building in Tokyo.

Figure 5.6 Financial-district classicism reinterpreted in a modern idiom in a Denver office building by Kohn Pedersen Fox.

Figure 5.7 In Manhattan, jazzy rhythm and dull drone are unified by a line of street trees.

Variations in depth etched yet deeper by shadows in the bright sun are particularly important rhythmic devices. A pair of restored commercial buildings, the Stevens and Staacke buildings, built in San Antonio in the early 1890s, lavishly illustrates the point (figure 5.8). Note the wide range of depth variations: low-relief ornamental friezes, rusticated limestone columns and arches, the pregnant protuberances of bow windows and central balcony on the Romanesque Revival Stevens Building, designed by Gordon & Laub; on the Renaissance Revival Staacke Brothers Building, designed by the great James Riely Gordon, the more demure withdrawal of the third-story curving windows and balcony behind the main mass of the facade, the shadows cast by the shallow balcony overhang, and the stone arches. Because of these shadows, the buildings change aspect constantly under the coursing sun, and their complex three-dimensional rhythmic structure means that they do not reveal all of their secrets all at once to the pedestrian approaching from either side. In these ways, the experience of the street is enlivened and structured in time, particularly if these two facades are but two episodes in a longer drama—as they were before the fine Richardsonian bank building next to the Staacke was demolished for a parking lot.

In much of modern architecture, the complexity of spatial and temporal structure was lost and the experience of the sidewalk impoverished. The postmodern architects sought, halfheartedly, to regain complexity, but even some of them forgot that the complexity that really matters occurs on the first two or three floors, the scale routinely compassed by the pedestrian's eye. Interesting skyline forms bloomed during the eighties, as in the twenties, but the postmodernists often turned a cold shoulder to pedestrians.

Columns and piers, doorways, niches, window mullions, planters, even signs or window mannequins or trees, are rhythmic devices that can contribute to the richness, complexity, and propulsiveness of the music of the street, urging the pedestrian along in the dance.

Rhythmic complexity has a converse worth examining. One passage in Shostakovich's Leningrad Symphony conveys the ruthless, inflexible march of the Nazi brutes (and maybe the Stalinist brutes, too). The effect is as striking in the printed score as it is in the concert hall—even, I imagine, for someone who does not read music. The eye is met by an enormous monolithic

Figure 5.8 Light and shadow accent complex rhythms in San Antonio's Stevens and Staacke buildings.

array of identically articulated and spaced quarter notes. There is no rhythm here, only the deathly, horrific beat of marching jackboots. The music is stripped of the asymmetries and peculiarities that make rhythmic hierarchy possible. Sanitized of difference and humanity, it reveals only a cold and mechanical forced unity. It is the sound and the picture of totalitarianism. It has a certain momentary grandeur associated with raw power, but you wouldn't want to live there. Totalitarianism is like that: it may appeal briefly to the sense of awe and mystery, but before long you realize that if the secret police don't kill you the boredom will.

There is an exact analogy between that page of Shostakovich and the unrelenting, pseudoclassical colonnades of Albert Speer's architecture for the Third Reich, some of it based closely on Hitler's own sketches. Although the ideology and sources may differ, the effects are remarkably similar in much of corporate modernist architecture, especially in buildings from the 1960s and 1970s—the business community's stone-faced and purse-lipped reaction to the social, artistic, and intellectual ferment that reigned on college campuses and in the ghettos. I do not mean to indict all of modernism, some of whose masters have created urban buildings as rich and humane as the best of any period. But too many lesser architects squandered that legacy on buildings that, in their pursuit of formal purity or cheapness, addressed the sidewalk with lockstep marches of columns and dull drones of glass curtain walls, a beat without rhythm. In the infamous reflective glass boxes of the seventies and early eighties, even the beat was muted in favor of a smooth mirror that, in the ideal, would disappear, melding into the sky or borrowing the clothes of its neighbors. In corporate Dallas, more than in Gertrude Stein's Oakland, there was no there there.

Much has been said elsewhere in criticism of corporate modernism, and some of the complaints are overstated. Even corporate modernism has given us some buildings of surpassing lyricism and richness—Gordon Bunshaft's Inland Steel Building in Chicago, for example. But in avoiding asymmetries and complex rhythmic articulation at eye level, the lesser practitioners of corporate modernism stripped the pathways of their horizontal rhythmic impulse. The fashion for "extruded" forms, in which the facade of the first floor was identical with that of the third or the fortieth, eliminated hierarchical organization in the vertical dimension as well, so that a building's facade might have nothing (or very little) to signify the perceptual ceiling of a human-scaled public living room. This puritanical rationalism had a corollary: abstract purity of form should not be sullied by the odor of commerce.

Often the blank walls at street level were explicit expressions of fear. Urban uprisings had rolled across the country during the 1960s and reached their apogee in the calamitous summer of 1967, with riots in Detroit, Newark, Cleveland, and other cities. But even after the fear of Molotov cocktails had faded, distrust of the streets and their benign disorder continued to be reflected in an aesthetic regime that submerged diversity in rigidly and simply ordered forms. The style (though rarely the detailed substance) of Ludwig Mies van der Rohe was deputized to enforce aesthetic martial law. Business signs must be small, "tasteful," and, in the ideal, invisible. Doorways must be flush with the facade and undetectable, like the mad scientist's bookcase that hides a passage to his laboratory. If the philistine developer insisted on having retail space on the ground floor, the businesses should not be obvious; windows (if any) should be tinted to obscure the interior, and there must be no differentiation of bays to reflect the diversity of activity within. Municipal setback standards, which often pushed tall buildings back from the street behind wide, bare "plazas," reinforced the notion of the architect's building as a sanctum, aloof from the world.

If pathways suffer from mute oversimplicity, they also suffer from the opposite—the anarchic cacophony of contemporary site planning along suburban roads and even in old neighborhoods where the original rhythmic structure has been eroded by parking lots or cheap new buildings. Rhythmic complexity is not at all like anarchy. Complexity entails richness of elaboration and violations of expectation within a generally regular framework; anarchy is the absence of a regular framework. A composer establishes expectations of form, key, melodic contour, and rhythm so that violations of those expectations can carry meaning. Similarly, if every visual event on the streetscape is sui generis, detached from structured relationship with its neighbors, the passerby loses the sense of processional, directional movement, the sidewalk and street lose their character as pathways, and the places along the street lose their information content in a welter of noise.

In architecture as in music, rhythm structures the experience of time— and, in architecture, space as well. The manner in which time and space are structured along a city's pathways materially affects the function of those pathways—the tendency of people to use them and the manner in which pedestrians relate to the places the pathways connect. A lively, active rhythmic structure, containing surprises within a generally predictable framework, sustains the stroll and encourages a lively, active engagement of the pedestrian with the places along the way. When rhythmic complexity is replaced by anarchy or sterility, engagement is weakened, and resistance to walking increases.

The sidewalk cannot be conceived in isolation, in narrowly utilitarian terms of width, texture, terrain, and continuity. The ribbon of concrete is only one element of the pedestrian pathway system, ineffectual unless it is part of a comprehensively organized and integrated public corridor. The sidewalk's relationships with streets, driveways, crosswalks, and amenities or potential obstructions are essential features of the pathway's design. So is the pathway's boundary—the proximity of the sidewalk to front doors and shop windows, the rhythmic articulation and visual permeability of building facades, the distribution and aesthetic qualities of solids (walls) and voids (parking lots, plazas, or landscaped areas).

You carry with you the nutrients that are required to sustain the value-creating life processes of a city—your heart and hands, mind and money. The ability of those nutrients to pervade the urban body is limited by the detailed design of the pathways and the manner in which they engage places of exchange. The pathways do not exist for their own sake, but to nourish the organs and systems of a city.

■ the neighborhood
People like us

 In a magazine article about the invasion of his Montgomery County, Maryland, community by a dealer in pornography, David Finkel wrote this moving but disturbing passage about the meaning of neighborhood:

> It is not big, broad, elegant Potomac, this neighborhood, but neither is it the type of antiseptic tract that sprouts up so often these days behind long walls and gatehouses. Rather, it's an old neighborhood of old houses, a reminder of how so many early suburbs began. Out of the city stretched a road. Eventually, it became an artery, with smaller roads veering off into the woods. Houses went up among trees, and when people moved in, they often expected to stay forever. Now, even though we don't stay forever, the neighborhood is no less important in our lives. It is a buffer, a refuge, a place to exhale, drop our guard, feel at ease. Out in the world there is chaos. Within our neighborhood, whose boundaries are defined, whose residents we assume are like us, we have a sense of control.[1]

Finkel beautifully expresses the value of the neighborhood as an extension of the home and its refuge, but the passage is disturbing in its

Us-versus-Them imagery. The neighborhood, in this passage, is not just a refuge; it is also a fortress. In a recent book Robert B. Reich says essentially the same thing as Finkel, but in distinctly unromantic, unflattering terms:

> In real life, most Americans no longer live in traditional communities. The majority live in suburban subdivisions bordered by highways and punctuated by shopping malls, or in tony condominiums and residential communities, or in ramshackle apartment buildings and housing projects. Most commute to work and socialize on some basis other than geographic proximity to where they sleep. And most pick up and move every five years or so to a different neighborhood.
>
> There is only one thing Americans increasingly have in common with their neighbors, and this commonality lies at the heart of the new American "community." It is their income levels. You can bet without much risk that you earn about as much as the folks down the street. Your educational backgrounds are similar, you pay roughly the same amount in taxes, and you indulge the same consumer impulses. The best definition of "community" is now the zip code used by direct-mail marketers to target likely customers. . . . It is known, for example, that the residents of Chelsea, Massachusetts, read the *National Enquirer*, watch Roller Derby, use curling irons and hair lotions, and eat white bread and snack cakes. Belmont's inhabitants play racquetball and golf, use electric toothbrushes, depilatories, and personal computers, and eat white bread and oat bran muffins. Incomes, and the tastes that go with them, increasingly define the new American community.[2]

Well, at least Chelsea and Belmont agree on the merits of white bread. And Reich and Finkel agree on the phenomenon of economic and cultural segregation. Reich decries it as a sign of the failure of community in the large; Finkel romanticizes it as a precondition for the comfortableness of community in the small. However the phenomenon is interpreted, it is a useful starting point for thinking about neighborhoods: our neighborhood is a place for People Like Us.

Economic and cultural segregation are not, as Reich suggests, new phenomena. Immigrant groups have always tended to concentrate into geographically distinct communities—Little Italy, Chinatown, Irish Flats—which for the most part were economically homogeneous (that is, poor, because the people were new arrivals) and, by definition, culturally homogeneous. The Chinese railroad laborers who settled near the Southern Pacific yards northeast of downtown San Antonio were a far cry—economically, culturally, and geographically—from the German and English merchants, bankers, and industrialists who built the fashionable King William district south of downtown, a few miles and a world away.

But there was something integrated about this segregation. A given neighborhood might have a wide range of housing stock; even on the vaunted King William Street, lavish mansions shared the same blocks with modest cottages. One neighborhood shaded into another (apart from certain major barriers such as the railroad yards) on a unifying street grid, which implied social and geographic mobility. Because even the major through streets were narrow and slow-moving, by modern standards, they did not inhibit the formation of walkable neighborhood retail centers. Thus the through streets passed *through* identifiable neighborhoods rather than *between* them.

Modern practice is entirely different, in part because many people fear even the most minimal kinds of economic or functional integration. One example: The city of San Antonio used to require street connections between adjacent residential subdivisions. The first developer to build a housing tract in a new part of the city had to design his internal street system in such a way that it could connect at one or two places with future adjacent subdivisions. The requirement fell into disuse, however, because when the time came to complete a linkage the residents of the subdivision with the more expensive houses would object to being connected—physically or socially—to a subdivision with less expensive houses. Heaven forbid that a child living in a $100,000 house should be contaminated by contact with a child living in a $90,000 house. *They* weren't people like *us*.

It goes almost without saying that functional segregation, too, has become standard practice. While commercial uses gravitated to major thoroughfares and strategic intersections even before the advent of zoning, businesses also would be scattered on the mostly residential blocks between major thoroughfares. Zoning codes, however, typically call for strict separation between residential and commercial districts, and even between areas of single-family houses and duplexes or apartments. Developer practice goes beyond the mere clustering effect of zoning. Street layouts and sidewalk systems (or their absence) may be designed to discourage or prevent movement between dissimilar land uses. Heaven forbid that fourteen-year-old Daryl should be able to bike safely to the neighborhood sporting goods store or bookseller.

Because residential subdivisions under modern zoning practices do not generally include retail, commercial, or institutional uses, nearly all of the places a resident might wish to go fall outside the subdivision boundaries. The commercial corridors and shopping malls of modern suburbia are not part of anyone's subdivision, but occupy a no-man's-land in the spaces between subdivisions. In a technical sense, there is nothing new in this differential deployment of urban space. My house, for example, was built in the late twenties as part of a developer's subdivision, one of many distinct subdivisions that were built at about the same time flanking a once-rural highway (Fredericksburg Road) that became a commercial strip. But the residential subdivisions were built on a common, generally rectilinear street grid, so that one subdivision flowed imperceptibly into another; and residential streets crossed the commercial road at close intervals. A part of my neighborhood is shown in figure 6.1. I have no idea whether my house was built as part of the Monticello Park subdivision or the Woodlawn Terrace subdivision; the two blur into each other without obvious borders.

The shaded area in figure 6.1 is the old retail center, and the circle indicates the perceptual center of the market place, as it existed into the early sixties. Within the circle were the Woodlawn Theater's tall neon sign and marquee, now dark but formerly a strong, landmark presence that gave the neighborhood center a distinct identity and focus. The straight heavy lines are major thoroughfares, albeit only two or four lanes wide. A few duplexes

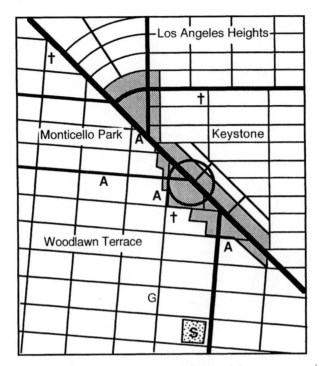

Figure 6.1 In the traditional neighborhood, homes, apartments, businesses, churches, and schools were all interconnected by multiple pathways into a continuous fabric.

and apartment buildings are scattered among mostly single-family houses on the residential blocks and along the diagonal road.

Figure 6.2, which covers the same amount of land as figure 6.1, shows two suburban residential subdivisions of medium-priced single-family houses dating from the late 1970s, each subdivision connected by a single umbilicus to the formerly rural road, now a busy four-lane (plus turning lanes) thoroughfare; a sixty-eight-year-old woman was recently struck by a car and killed as she tried to walk across the road during the morning rush hour. The shaded area represents developed commercial property, not including two large nurseries.

Note that, in figure 6.1, the retail center, three churches, an elementary

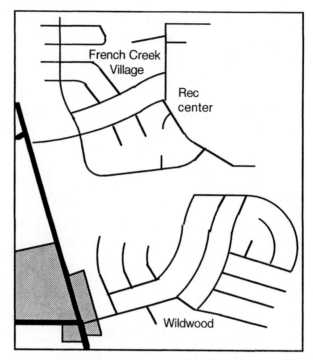

Figure 6.2   In the new suburbia, residential subdivisions are islands unto themselves, and pathways between land uses are minimized.

school and, just off the map a few blocks to the south, a large park and lake are all easily accessible, by multiple low-traffic residential streets, to the entire area. A tiny family-owned grocery and meat market, built before the advent of zoning, is surrounded by single-family houses and serves as an informal community center.

In figure 6.2, by contrast, all activity sites other than the French Creek Village recreation center are accessible only by way of the main road. There are, of course, no retail stores within either subdivision. A large park, mostly undeveloped except for several Little League fields, forms the northern boundary of French Creek Village. A park road is continuous with one of the residential streets, but a gate across the road allows passage for emergencies only; pedestrians can cross into the park by limboing under the gate, but cars have to go to the main road. The adjacent subdivision to the south is accessible only by the main road. Short-distance trips, which would have used local circulator streets in the old city, add to congestion on the main road, which is wide and busy enough to be an effective barrier between the residential subdivisions and the commercial property on the other side. No sane parent would allow a child to ride a bicycle along or across this road.

What is not evident from the diagram is that the commercial area, comprising several stand-alone retailers and a large retail strip, doesn't hang together as a walkable or coherent unity. There are no sidewalks along the main road. Although the northern half of the intersection at the lower left of the map is thoughtfully equipped with a striped crosswalk, a button-operated pedestrian crossing signal, and even gentle handicapped-accessible curb ramps on a concrete traffic separator, both ends of the crosswalk lead the pedestrian immediately into drainage ditches. In this context there is no possibility of a unifying, magnetic neighborhood center. The urban fabric is ripped, the gift community comes to an end, at the boundary of each subdivision.

Because people are accustomed to equating their subdivision with their neighborhood, nonresidential (or even apartment) uses are perceived as falling in the cracks between neighborhoods. Only rarely, when many subdivision-based homeowner associations band together to fight a commonly perceived threat (usually from a commercial or low-income apartment project in their vicinity), does a more comprehensive view of the neighborhood emerge and expose an underlying tension between the narrow concept of neighborhood-as-subdivision—an artifact of the accidents of land development—and the larger intuitive concept of what a neighborhood really is or ought to be. The neighborhood has become not a place among other places in the continuous fabric of the city, but a place apart from other places—and not a place so much as a syndrome, a social pathology based on ever narrower definitions of People Like Us and ever wider definitions of Them.

THE KID-ON-A-BIKE TEST

Let's take a different slice through the concept of neighborhood, one based not on proximity or economic segregation, but on function and community. It's time for a pop quiz. You are going to figure out whether your neighborhood is a neighborhood. You will need a street map of your city, some colored pencils, and a fourteen-year-old kid with a bicycle. If that last item doesn't fall conveniently to hand, pretend you're the fourteen year old.

The test is simple, but it requires some thought and intimate awareness of your environment. Suppose your fourteen year old sets off from home on a bicycle. On the street map, mark with a heavy green line all those streets within a mile of your home that your child could bike continuously and in reasonable safety from heavy traffic. Now mark with a red X all those places your child might want to visit—the homes of school friends, a barbershop, a branch library, a swimming pool or park, an ice cream parlor, an inexpensive restaurant, a CD or video store, a grocery, a sporting goods store, a dentist, an after-school job, and so on.

If a lot of the places you've marked lie on the network of green lines—if your child can safely and conveniently travel to many social, cultural, recreational, shopping, and general maintenance destinations without depending on you to drive—you live in a neighborhood. If not, you don't.

We often think of "neighborhood" in straightforward geographic terms—our vicinity, our neck of the woods, or, more narrowly, our subdivision. But static geography doesn't get at the meaning of "neighborhood" in its deep sense. There is a reason newspaper ads for residential subdivisions almost never call subdivisions *subdivisions*. They are called *neighborhoods* or *communities*. That's because people don't want to live in subdivisions; they want to live in neighborhoods or communities.

These terms imply more than mere propinquity. They connote something warm and fuzzy, a sense of belonging, friendship, mutual trust and caring—neighborliness. More broadly, they imply a dynamic set of social, economic, and cultural relationships among (good or bad, human or institutional) neighbors. A neighborhood is not just a collection of insular cells sharing only geographic nearness. A neighborhood hangs together in some active sense. *Community* conveys an even stronger sense of hanging to-gether—an active *coming together* (not just a passive being together) for com-mon purpose and mutual benefit. This is Aristotle's *koinonia*, a term that Christians use to mean communion.

People do not come together in the abstract. They come together in specific, physical places. Moreover, they do not come together just for the sake of being in the same space. They come together to do things coopera-tively that they can't do by themselves. (Even people watching requires a co-operative, if usually unaware, object.) That is, they come together in particular places for the purpose of exchange, whether it takes the form of buying and selling, teaching and learning, or billing and cooing. By facilitat-ing these kinds of coming together, a neighborhood makes good things hap-pen in the economic, social, and cultural realms. But because people start off in their own dispersed, individual places, they have to get to the spaces where they come together. So a neighborhood or community has three essential el-ements—the dispersed homes where people start off, the places where they come together for the purpose of exchange, and the routes between their homes and the places where they come together.

The kid-on-a-bike test requires that all three elements be woven into a compact, convenient, and coherent whole that is accessible to all. An adult-in-a-car test, which is the one that has governed much urban planning for the past few decades, can be passed with much more widely dispersed sites of ex-change, in environments that are hostile or dangerous to people who aren't driving, and not really safe or pleasant for people who *are* driving. Most kids and many adults do not drive cars, but that doesn't make them any less hu-man in their needs and desires for companionship, activity, and experience outside the home. A good place for raising kids is not a subdivision where the only convenient diversions are drugs, sex, and rock 'n' roll—although, sadly, that's the kind of place many parents look for without realizing it.

The kid-on-a-bike test has implications for urban design—street lay-out, scale, neighborhood structure, and so on. Rather than starting with gen-eralities, however, let's first take a look at a place that passes the kid-on-a-bike test, or at least did when I lived there in the 1970s. The neigh-borhood I have in mind is a near-downtown area of Evanston, immediately north of Chicago along Lake Michigan. Although Illinois winters were not my idea of a good time, this part of Evanston sticks in my mind as a good neighborhood.

To help you understand what made Evanston a good neighborhood, I have to tell you a little about my life there, not because my biography is particularly interesting, but because neighborhoods are about how people live in them. When I moved to Evanston as a graduate student at Northwestern University, I rented a basement room at sixty dollars a month from a family that lived about six blocks from the campus, a similar distance from the downtown main street, three blocks from the park and beach fronting Lake Michigan, and three blocks from the Dempster Street el station. My landlords, Jim and Margo Ladwig, lived in a nineteenth-century two-story frame house, rather plainer than the other houses on their upper-middle-class block. The Ladwigs were in their thirties, and they had three young children. He was building a successful graphic design business; she ran the household, was a splendid cook, and dabbled in artistic business ventures of her own. Nice people.

I kept my room at the Ladwigs' when I started working in low-wage jobs in Chicago's Loop and into the first months of my first real job, as an editorial assistant at *Chicago* magazine. At that point I could (just barely) afford a real apartment, with a legal kitchen (as opposed to my illegal hot plate) and a private bathroom. A big step—but still within the same neighborhood, just eight short blocks west of the Ladwigs'. A few years later, when the Ladwigs' income grew and their children needed more space, they moved into a larger house a few blocks west of my apartment—again, still within the same neighborhood.

To belabor the obvious, this neighborhood of Evanston at that time accommodated people of widely different incomes and family situations. Minimum-wage ribbon clerks and budding journalists lived cheek by jowl with the Mercedes-Benz crowd. Young families and elderly people shared the neighborhood. Expensive single-family houses and inexpensive apartments shared the same blocks. As their incomes grew, people did not necessarily aspire to move up to a richer neighborhood. The neighborhood they started in was just fine. Thus the neighborhood was both stable, because people wanted to, and could, stay there through several stages of their lives; and dynamic, because the people who stayed underwent changes in income, tastes, needs, and family situation.

The neighborhood's desirability stemmed in part from geographic advantages—its location on rail transit lines to downtown Chicago, its closeness to Chicago in comparison with wealthier suburbs farther north, its proximity to Lake Michigan and Northwestern University. But a key element in Evanston's livability was its integration of suburban residential scale with denser urban scale and lively neighborhood retailing.

I had lived in Evanston nearly four years before I bought a car. But a car wasn't necessary—which was a good thing, because the car I ended up with was a Fiat. At the corner two blocks from my apartment there was a cluster of small commercial buildings, of a certain age, containing a ma-and-pa grocery, a dry cleaner, the contemporary furniture store where I bought my first lamps and chairs, even the electronics store where I bought a small color television set so I could watch the Watergate hearings. The el station was a couple of blocks farther east, and beyond that another neighborhood retail hub that offered two hardware stores, a rock record store, a place that sold curtains and rugs, an ice cream parlor, a supermarket, the Whole Earth Store, and even a chess club, all of which—especially the chess club—were part of my routine. Downtown Evanston was also within walking distance, and there I shopped at Laury's for records, Kroch's and Brentano's for books, Audio Consultants for stereo gear, and the Evanston National Bank for money. I bought my first fine art print and was introduced to the charming work of Hundertwasser at Galerie Gunnell. I worked out, after a fashion, in the Evanston YMCA, which was on the edge of downtown a few blocks from my apartment, and on nice Saturdays I'd stroll or bike down to the lakefront.

All this was immediately, conveniently, and pleasurably (except in winter) accessible by foot in a neighborhood that was predominantly single-family residential in scale and verdantly suburban. Even after I bought my car, I would often walk downtown or to the chess club or the grocery store because walking was easier than driving for such short distances (my Fiat often didn't move unless a tow truck was pulling it), and a pleasant experience: Evanston had proper sidewalks, after all.

But there's more to convenience than convenience. Recall Aristotle's strict equation of exchange with the bonds of community. If there is exchange, he wrote, there is a community; and there is no community without exchange. It was the convenience with which mundane exchanges could take place in my part of Evanston that transformed a vicinity (to use the most neutral term of geographic propinquity) into a community. Because so many kinds of exchange could and did take place near people's homes, in the territory they saw every day and which was continuous with their domestic precincts, bonds of neighborhood solidarity, loyalty, and ownership—the relationship that is implied by the phrase "my neighborhood"—were continually reinforced. Every time I bought groceries at the corner store or dropped my clothes off at the corner dry cleaner, I was helping to sustain not just the economic lives of those businesses' owners, and not just my own material well-being, but the very bonds that tied me, those businesses, and our neighbors into a community.

I should stress that I mean "community" in its strong sense, connoting emotional and ethical bonds, not just loose ties of material connection and convenience. I am not the only person who shops at the corner grocery or the stereo dealer or the hardware store or the record shop. When I go to these places, I see other people shopping there as well, people whom I recognize from the street I live on, or from the park or the library, or from previous shopping trips. People who shop at the same stores as we do, stores that are a part of the neighborhood we own, are people like us. They are not mere abstractions or alien creatures whom we may imagine to have horns on their heads. Because they are people like us, we are disposed to include them with us in our ethical community. They are people we can get along with—indeed, must get along with—if only to the degree of standing next to each other in the checkout line. We are less disposed to include in our ethical community those who are distant and invisible.

Not all of Evanston, a city of more than seventy-five thousand people, worked as well as my near-downtown neighborhood. Some sectors were mostly poor, mostly black, and mostly neglected by government and industry. Evanston Township High School experienced some racial tension. Yet racial and economic diversity—not a lot, but not a negligible amount, either—were accommodated peaceably within my Evanston neighborhood during my time there. The presence of such diversity does not, contrary to widespread fear, doom a neighborhood to decline—so long as the neighborhood is designed to foster the manifold little social and economic exchanges that assimilate diversity into a harmonious whole.

THE LOCAL GLOBAL VILLAGE

Now it is true that in our day, rather more than in Aristotle's, exchange is little limited by geographic separation. Modern communications, transportation, and business networks create and constantly reinforce bonds that connect your home to every part of your city, your state, your region, your nation, and every continent. The global market place, as it is commonly called, unavoidably and inevitably has created a global community—or global village, to recall a once-fashionable term—of a sort. The vast geographic extent of trade has brought with it many undeniably good things, not the least of which has been a welcome flowering of understanding and appreciation of diverse cultures. Exchange brings down walls of distrust and fear between cultures and fosters a healthy, creative syncretism and worldwide bonds of mutual responsibility. We discover that people half a world away are People Like Us—some of them, a little. Moreover, when both material and intellectual goods from virtually everywhere are readily available to us, we have freedom to comparison shop, to choose our cultural raiment and attitudes; we are no longer locked into the narrow berth of our birth. That's all to the good. But . . .

While the global village is a useful concept, it's an awfully big place, a different animal entirely from the ordinary kind of village where most people live most of their daily lives. We are all citizens of the world in the sense that we can serve our friends Mexican beer in Czech glasses with French cheese arrayed on Finnish dishes while listening to American jazz on a Japanese sound system. But we are not situated in the whole world in the sense that we can just dash off to Indonesia every time we need coffee. For the most part, the world has to come to us, where we *are* situated, in cities.

But even that is not quite enough. The world has to come to our neighborhoods.

It is sometimes asserted that the automobile, the road, and the express-way in effect expand the boundaries of one's neighborhood to include the whole city, or a much larger part of it than we customarily think of as a neighborhood. That is, the car has greatly expanded our range of routine movement, which now includes shopping malls, "power" retailers, theaters, colleges, parks, and restaurants five or ten miles distant from our homes. In itself, this expansion of our range of movement (for those of us with auto-mobiles) is hardly a bad thing. It's nice to be able to save money on purchases by driving to a big discount retailer. But it's also nice to be able to save time by walking around the corner to a neighborhood store if you just need a few items, and sometimes it's useful to have the personal attention and knowl-edgeable service that discount retailers can't offer. The trouble with the car-and-road system is not that it makes possible a wider range of move-ment, but that it gives so great a competitive advantage to big, high-volume, road-oriented businesses that the smaller, neighborhood-oriented places can't survive.

A while ago I needed to buy some cardboard mailers for computer dis-kettes. In all of downtown San Antonio, with its many thousands of office workers, I could find but one tiny office-supply store, not much bigger than a walk-in closet, with a shockingly limited stock. The diskette mailers, a fairly common need these days, were not to be found. I had to drive to a power retailer seven miles away on San Antonio's Loop 410 beltway. Such power retailers, with their deep discounts, are welcome additions to a city; they help a lot of people keep their heads above water. But this progress comes with a price, the loss of convenience and of neighborhood fabric. When the power retailer drives the ordinary office-supply store out of busi-ness, the result is a vacant storefront. The people who once worked at that now closed store no longer can support other nearby stores and restaurants, which also become threatened.

The automobile's wide range of movement has a second potential advantage in that it can help bring diverse people in contact with each other. It is fairly easy, in a city such as San Antonio, to have dinner at a little Mexican restaurant in the predominantly Latino West Side, go to a play at the Carver Community Cultural Center on the predominantly African-American East Side, stop for dessert and drinks at an upscale bistro on the mostly Anglo North Side, and then return home to my neighborhood on the near northwest side of the city. Such crosstown exchange—to the limited extent that it happens in fact rather than just in theory—can, under the right circumstances, help to tie diverse parts of a city into a mutually related whole. That's a good thing socially and politically. If I occasionally leave my neighborhood and enter yours, where I am affected, if only temporarily, by the conditions that affect you, I am more likely to support public expenditures for streets and drainage, police substations, school construction, and other investments in your neighborhood than I would be if I never went there.

But too little crosstown exchange occurs under the right circumstances. If commercial corridors develop in isolation from residential districts rather than in continuity with them, I can shop, dine, be entertained, and conduct business all over the city without ever entering a neighborhood—meaning a place that passes the kid-on-a-bike test. In the newer parts of town, it is possible to travel many miles geographically while traveling no distance at all culturally or socially. What's the point of driving a dozen miles to your part of town if it has the same chain retailers and franchise restaurants as my part of town?

The problem comes down to this. Telecommunications and air travel have knitted distant countries into a global village, and the automobile and expressway have made distant parts of the city accessible to us, *but there's a hole in the middle.* We have neglected to build or maintain neighborhood structures that encourage us to participate in exchange near our homes.

How did my Evanston neighborhood fill the hole in the middle? The first thing to note is that, while the neighborhood consisted predominantly of detached single-family houses with front and back yards, it also had significant numbers of apartments in low-rise and mid-rise buildings concentrated, for the most part, along major streets. Nearby was a major university with a large resident student population. The medium- and high-density residential development helped provide enough customers to support neighborhood retailing within walking distance of everyone. At the same time the higher incomes and larger range of needs of people in the single-family houses (appliances, gardening supplies) balanced the lower incomes and more limited needs of people in apartments, so that more *kinds* of retailing had sufficient markets. Retailing cannot exist for long without customers. Low density spreads the customers out over a larger area, which means that retailing must also be spread out over a larger (and unwalkable) area unless low density is balanced by high density in the right places.

There were few off-street parking spaces in Evanston's neighborhood retail hubs. People who drove parked on the street. It was possible for small retailers to survive with such limited parking because so many of their customers could come on foot—an advantage of having many apartments near commercial areas. Moreover, the absence of parking lots meant that retailers stood close together on the street. A driver could park once and pick up laundry, buy groceries, and look at furniture all in one trip. One parking space, in this high-density retail setting, did the work of three parking spaces in a low-density arrangement. Indeed, in terms of economic value, the one parking space was worth more. The furniture store, which opened during the time I lived in the neighborhood, gained close-up exposure to the already established clientele of the grocery and the dry cleaner, as well as to the extensive pedestrian traffic. With no intervening parking lot, the store's display window was close enough to the street to allow passing motorists to detect what kind of store it was. Thus the furniture store could get its message to a lot of potential customers at no advertising cost. (The store did take out small ads in *Chicago* magazine, because support from a larger area than the immediate neighborhood was required, but without that neighborhood exposure a larger advertising budget would have been needed in order to keep the store in business for even a few months.)

The absence of off-street parking lots gave small, low-volume, low-margin retailers a significant cost break. None of their rent was paying for asphalt or the real estate it covered. Furthermore, the absence of off-street parking made these sites unattractive to large, high-volume retailers, thus depressing rental rates to a level that small retailers could afford.

The rail transit system was an essential element in the mix. The Dempster Street el station, situated between two small retailing hubs, generated considerable foot traffic and thus exposure to retailers on the pedestrian routes from the el stop to residential streets. And the el stop was a magnet for apartments. The clustering of apartments within walking distance of the station concentrated a pedestrian market for retailers, which could also form tight clusters as a result.

The street system had a role to play as well. While some retailers in our neighborhood hubs relied almost exclusively on a neighborhood clientele, some (such as the Whole Earth Store and the chess club) drew from a far wider area, and could not have survived without a large geographic base. Happily, the retail hubs were located on through streets that allowed access to distant points, but which were not so wide or busy as to inhibit pedestrian crossings or violate comfortable pedestrian scale.

But while the through streets made the retail hubs accessible from distant areas, they also fit into the residential street grid in such a way that they provided easy access to the immediate neighborhood. Predominantly residential side streets intersected the through streets at short intervals, and sidewalks ran continuously from residential to commercial streets. The through streets were a bit wider and busier than the residential streets but were otherwise indistinguishable from the rectilinear grid of the neighborhood. For the most part, commercial buildings were not greatly different in scale or age from nearby single-family houses or apartment buildings. Commercial and apartment buildings were closer to the street than single-family houses, but not much closer—front yards tended to be fairly shallow. Because commercial and apartment buildings stood close to the street rather than being set back behind parking lots, the public space of these neighborhood hubs maintained an intimacy of scale comparable to that of the single-family streets. For all these reasons, the walk from a house or apartment to a retail hub remained within the same neighborhood context, both perceptually and geographically. You didn't feel as though you were passing into alien territory. It was all part of the same varied but seamless fabric.

RINGS AROUND THE NEIGHBORHOOD

A neighborhood is not one big, uniform area, but a series of roughly concentric rings with your front door at their center. The smallest ring, which we'll call A (for Adjacency), encompasses your house or apartment building and the ones next door and across the street—everything that falls easily within your field of vision and all that is most familiar to you as you sit on your front porch or work in the yard. The people who live within this first ring are the folks who keep an eye on each other's houses or apartments, who borrow each other's lawn mowers, who chat across the fence and wave to each other from their driveways, or who snarl at each other over violations of written or unwritten codes of civility.

The second ring is the path you might follow when taking your dog for a walk. We'll call this Ring B, for Bowser, which, by merest coincidence, is the name of my dog. This ring consists of an area of a few blocks. You probably have at least a nodding acquaintance with most of the people in Ring B, while you might not recognize many or most of the people just beyond that ring. If you see someone who lives in Ring B approaching you on the sidewalk, chances are you know immediately whether to feel safe or unsafe—probably the former—because that individual is to some small extent a known quantity.

The third ring, C, may be defined by what used to be called the Constitutional, a leisurely but not short walk for enjoyment or exercise. The path of a constitutional typically covers seven or eight blocks but remains well within the People-Like-Us zone. It may cross a small park or a retail area, pass a school or library, but it is not likely to stray into an industrial or warehouse district or onto a busy road that is not equipped with an inviting sidewalk system. The constitutional is not likely to take you beyond the edge of what you perceive to be your neighborhood, even if you can't precisely define its boundaries on a map, but neither does Ring C necessarily take in *all* of your neighborhood.

On a street map, draw these three rings with your front door at their common center. In reality the rings aren't likely to be perfect circles, but go ahead and draw circles as an easy approximation. Now imagine the map filled with the circles that everybody in your neighborhood would draw, so that you have a pretty abstract picture of lots of circles. Some of the circles overlap each other; many don't. Your Ring A is not identical to your next-door neighbor's Ring A—his is one house further down—but they almost certainly overlap each other. Your Ring B is not quite the same as Ring B for someone in the next block, but these rings, too, probably overlap. Your constitutional, or Ring C, is going to be different from that of the woman who lives several blocks away, but these rings also are likely to overlap at some point—maybe you both end up at the same ice cream parlor or park. The size of each of these rings and whether they overlap or not depend on personal physical and psychological variables. Only your state of mind and physical condition determine how far and where to walk Bowser or where your constitutional will lead you. But these personal variables are affected by geographic variables of the sort discussed in earlier chapters—continuity of sidewalks, width of street crossings, the rhythm of the streetscape, and so on.

You might think of the rings that overlap each other as links in a chain; or, since we're talking about an area that goes for many blocks in all four directions, links in the chain mail fabric that medieval knights used to wear. The fabric of a neighborhood is strongest where the pattern of overlapping rings is densest. The cohesion and continuity of a neighborhood are weakened wherever there is a break in the overlapping of one or two orders of rings; wherever there is a break in all three orders—A, B, and C—the neighborhood effectively stops, at least so far as you are concerned.

If you look at the pattern of overlapping rings as a single continuous area bounded by the breaks in the pattern, you have Ring D, for Daryl, which happens to be the name of the kid on the bike. Considering distance alone, Daryl has a longer range of easy travel than a pedestrian. Thus Daryl's range of travel may cross several Constitutional rings.

But the same geographic features that serve as boundaries for pedestrians also tend to be boundaries for cyclists. Generally speaking, Daryl's progress is stopped, or at least discouraged, by major rivers, expressways, wide commercial roads with few regulated street crossings, subdivision boundaries if there are no street linkages to the adjacent subdivisions, or perhaps a large institution such as a college or hospital. Similarly, when you envision your neighborhood, you probably do not imagine that it crosses such boundaries. Even if the residential district on the other side of the boundary is like your own, chances are the two sides of the boundary do not coalesce, in your mind, into a single neighborhood.

Neighborhoods don't usually cross such boundaries,[3] but people do, of necessity. It may not be easy, convenient, or pleasant, but it is often unavoidable. You shop for groceries and clothes, go to the movies or the bookstore, take classes at the community college, do research at the branch library, work out at the gym, mail packages at the post office, or visit relatives, whether these destinations fall inside or outside the boundaries of your neighborhood. People do things. People are like that. Thus the fifth ring that is relevant to the neighborhood is what I call the *ambit*—the places you go for pleasure or necessity, frequently or occasionally. Your ambit consists of the places where you engage other people in exchange, so if you demand alphabetical consistency you can call this Ring E, for Exchange, Engagement, or Errands.

It is rare indeed for your ambit to coincide perfectly with your geographic neighborhood. Some of the destinations in your ambit fall inside, some outside the geographic boundaries of your neighborhood as you perceive them (Ring D).

Probably you would not wish all your ambit to be contained within your neighborhood; that would be convenient, but limiting and rather dull. It is interesting and useful to get away from one's familiar turf now and then, to see how other people—people not like us—live and cook and do things. Even though you may weep with joy when a good Chinese restaurant opens in your neighborhood, you still want to visit Chinatown on occasion, if your city is lucky enough to have one.

Neither, however, would you wish all of your ambit to lie outside your neighborhood. It would be a drag to have to drive a mile or two every time you wanted to buy a newspaper or a carton of milk. But apart from the matter of convenience, if all or most of the places in your ambit lay outside the neighborhood you live in, then it's hard to see how it could be in any meaningful sense *your* neighborhood. We feel a sense of proprietorship only in the things we use.

Thus we arrive at the first two requirements of a well-formed neighborhood. It is, first, large enough to take in a substantial portion of its residents' ambits, but second, small and continuous enough so that the entire space can be comprehended and owned by the kid on a bike.

What difference does it make? Just as we began, in thinking about cities, by asking what cities are about and what sorts of things cities exist to enable, we need to ask the same questions about neighborhoods. I tried earlier to make a case that cities exist to promote exchange and, thus, value creation, but that claim as applied to whole cities is valid only as a first approximation. In most sizable American cities—virtually any town with more than ten thousand people, and many with smaller populations—an individual doesn't live in the city at large but in a part of it. Just as the gross, worldwide settlement pattern is made lumpy by the appearance of cities, there is a practical lumpiness to the way we live within cities.

Open up a street map of your city and look at the boxes formed by the locator grid. Suppose the grid is labeled A–T horizontally and 1–20 vertically, for a total of four hundred boxes. Suppose, further, that over the course of a year your shopping, business, recreational, social, and cultural activities take you to four hundred destinations, which in sum constitute your ambit. Chances are, these destinations in your ambit are not evenly distributed across the city, one per box. Nor are they distributed randomly. Some highly specialized needs may take you anywhere on the map. If, for example, you drive a 1954 Studebaker and the only mechanic who works on Studebakers is located twenty miles away, you go to that mechanic even though no other place in your ambit falls anywhere near his garage. But most of the places in your ambit probably tend to cluster in a few parts of the city, areas near your home or workplace, or other parts of town where you feel comfortable and that you know reasonably well.

Figure 6.3   Near your home, but not near each other, businesses A and B can't help each other.

The location of points of exchange is not a matter of indifference if exchange is to occur efficiently and if its value-creating benefits in the cultural, social, and commercial realms are to be fully realized. Efficiency of exchange depends first of all on proximity: other things being equal, you're more likely to shop for goods or ideas near your home or workplace than far away. As a corollary, efficiency of exchange also depends on the clustering of exchange sites within your ambit. In figure 6.3, suppose two points in your ambit, A and B, are each a half-mile from your home, but in opposite directions. Both are located near your home, but not near each other. In figure 6.4, the two stores (or offices, or art museums, or one park and one laundry) A and B are located next to each other, forming a cluster a half-mile from your home.

Figure 6.4 begins to illustrate what I call *economies of form*. You are more likely to partake of the exchange opportunities afforded by *both* A and B, rather than *either* A or B, if (1) they are both close to your starting point rather than far from it, and (2) if they are close to each other rather than far apart.

We began this book by talking about economic development and quality of life. If you were to list all the desirable features that constitute these two categories, you would find that most of them are unavoidably linked to physical places—factories, offices, stores, parks, hospitals, schools, concert halls, theaters, sports stadiums, transit stops, airports, and so on. Suppose, to take an extreme and absurd example, you live in Sector A-1 on the top left corner of your city's street map, and all the desirable features you listed are located in sector T-20 in the bottom right corner, twenty-five miles

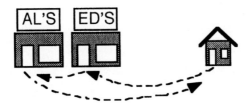

Figure 6.4 Near your home *and* near each other, businesses A and B can support each other and shorten your shopping trip.

from your home. Your city's chamber of commerce could rightly claim that the city contains all the makings of economic development and quality of life, but a lot of good that does *you*.

The city cannot fulfill its promise as an enabler of exchange unless the sites where exchanges can occur stand in some reasonable and usable geographic relationship to people. If people live in all of the boxes on the locator map, from A-1 to T-20, then a wide range of opportunities for exchange must be found in (or very near) all of those boxes as well. But because exchange occurs more efficiently when exchange sites are close together than when they are far apart, they need to coagulate into clumps rather than spreading evenly across the map. Our objective is not just to have a shoe store in "reasonable and usable geographic relationship" to the people in the 1200 block, a hardware store to the 1300 block, and a library to the 1400 block, but to have a cluster of these and other exchange sites standing in a usable relationship to all three (and more) blocks.

Thus we arrive at the third constraint on the well-formed neighborhood. It has a strong center where exchange sites aggregate and support each other. At a superficial level this picture is not very controversial. Zoning regulations and development practice typically produce a map with lumps in it. (In chapter 9 I try to show that common contemporary practice does not produce lumps that work efficiently within themselves and that the benefits of lumpiness are further diffused by the presence of exchange corridors, or ridges, in the map.) But for the moment I want to focus on a more fundamental issue. It isn't sufficient that the lumps (however they are defined) be scattered throughout the city in rough proportion to the population. If you live in sector D-6 on the map, it isn't enough that one or more lumps be located somewhere—anywhere—within that same or adjacent sectors. Raw distance, as the crow flies, is not the issue, or not the only one. The closeness or remoteness of the practical and psychological relationship between a lump and your home is defined by all manner of details—street layout, sidewalk design, building scale and rhythm, landscape, vehicular and pedestrian traffic volume, noise levels, security and safety, lighting, and so on.

Lumps are good. They facilitate communication and exchange. A lump in the fabric of the city is analogous to your Rolodex or address book, which compresses into easily usable form the listings of particular interest to you, in contrast to the phone book's undifferentiated mass of listings, the vast majority of which you will never use. But there are lumps and there are lumps. Most people keep their Rolodexes (Rolodices?) close at hand on their desks, not between the detergent and the bleach in the laundry room. The lumps are more useful in some locations than in others. They are most useful when they are conveniently and pleasantly accessible from your home base.

In a successful neighborhood a lot of the points of exchange that constitute your ambit and those of your neighbors coalesce into a cluster located within the geographic boundaries of your neighborhood. Or, to put it in the negative, you don't have to leave your neighborhood every time you want to do anything that you can't do at home.

It follows necessarily—and this point *should* be taken as dogma—that a successful neighborhood encompasses a variety of functions and land uses beyond the strictly residential. Remember, we're not just looking for repose, comfort, and safety, which can be had in a purely residential compound, but these things *plus* a representative sampling of the exchange possibilities of urban life. And these possibilities must be not merely in the vicinity, not merely nearby in an abstract, as-the-crow-flies sense, but integrated in practical terms with the routine of daily life. We want, as it were, a net that is large enough to capture a good variety of fish, but not so large as to be unwieldy.

First let's consider the types of fish we want to capture. Some are uncontroversial. Even the most antiurban suburbanites, if they have growing families, generally wish to have an elementary school within walking distance. A common amenity in modern subdivisions is a private recreational center with a swimming pool, tennis courts, and assembly hall. More expensive subdivisions—usually only those with perimeter walls and guarded entrances—may include a park, walking trails, even a small lake. These items are uncontroversial because they serve People Like Us, those who share a particular subdivision, a particular income level, a particular range of tastes, and probably a particular type of family. These amenities generate little traffic from beyond the immediate area and entail minimal risk of attracting strangers.

But even People Like Us cannot live on school and tennis alone. We need a loaf of bread on occasion, or a library book, or a video rental, or a pair of pants, or a haircut. We need, in short, places that trade in goods, services, and information.

Moreover, because people are unavoidably social animals, we need places of gathering, assembly, and hanging out, places where we may peacefully encounter, observe, imitate, and influence other people. Through these encounters culture (from fashion to ethics) is both transmitted and transformed. These processes tend to reinforce dominant behavioral norms. Through ordinary public contact we learn not to make too much noise, not to bump into other people on the sidewalk, not to steal or kill, not to break into a line. At the same time, through these processes, diversity is made familiar and may be accepted as part of a larger community of People (Sort of) Like Us. We need places where friends may stroll, but where they share the same social space with people outside their set, a space that is owned equally by many kinds of people. Without such spaces for the normalization of diversity, a society becomes brittle, unadaptable, fragmented, calcified, and weak.

If city planners were to establish a specialized space for the express and sole purpose of hanging out and encountering other people—with a big sculpture in the middle and signs inviting passersby to enter Sociability Square—the space probably would not work very well. Who would go there? Why?

In order for the informal processes of social exchange to work, they must be integrated with the other kinds of exchange that we routinely practice. That is why sidewalks and other kinds of public spaces between stores or other exchange sites are so important. Our individual needs for exchange could be satisfied if we could magically appear in a store, buy what we need, and then magically be transported, in an instant, to the next store or back to our homes. In theatrical terms, the plot of *Madama Butterfly* could be conveyed to an audience if someone on stage merely told us that the lady had killed herself, discreetly offstage. But it is dramatically necessary for Butterfly to display the knife—which we know to be the same one her father had used to kill himself—on the public space of the stage. We must encounter her as she is transformed by the knife and its history. Otherwise, however she may be transformed, we are not—and it is for our transformation that we enter the theater or the city.

So we want to have near our homes a variety of possibilities for exchange. We want a goodly number of them to be organized in such a way that the space between them is an active social space—indeed, a theatrical space—not merely a void. And we want this active social space to be readily accessible to many people's homes on streets that form a continuous and nonthreatening urban fabric, satisfying the kid-on-a-bike test.

These desiderata have certain practical implications. First, in order for stores and other exchange sites to define an active social space, they can't be strung out at wide intervals and separated by large parking lots, or even large verdant landscapes. Exchange sites need to aggregate into compact nodes. But in order for these nodes to satisfy the kid-on-a-bike test, they have to be directly accessible from nearby residential areas on many small, low-traffic streets rather than indirectly accessible only on one or two wide, high-traffic roads.

A node has to be integrated with the physical structure of the neighborhood in such a way that it serves as the neighborhood's perceptual and functional focus. At the same time, the node has to be readily accessible to other neighborhoods and distant parts of town on major through streets in order to provide sufficient markets to sustain a good variety of retailing and services, without which the neighborhood center falls into disuse.

We'll call the retail-commercial node the neighborhood market place (in chapter 8 I discuss the structure of the market place in more detail). A larger area, including the market place, nearby apartments, and perhaps such assets as parks and recreation centers, we will call the neighborhood center. In the rest of this chapter, I treat the entire neighborhood center as a single entity.

A healthy, well-formed neighborhood has a center, a magnet for community life. Indeed, a good neighborhood is defined in large measure by, and radiates from, its center. The kinds of exchange that occur in the center, and the environment for those exchanges, have a lot to do with the loyalty and sense of ownership people feel for their neighborhood. Without a center, a residential area may be a pleasant retreat from the world, the people may be friendly to each other, but some social glue is still missing, the glue of shared experience, of serendipitous meetings, of a common ground that is neither your home nor mine, but ours. Earlier I spoke of the importance of sidewalks as the capillaries of community life. Remember that the sidewalk, especially working in tandem with the front porch, is a transitional zone between public and private realms. It brings pedestrians into the sphere of influence of other people's homes and lives, but in a way that is (usually) nonthreatening to both sides. Sidewalks and front porches are wonderful, even miraculous inventions, and many of our nation's problems would solve themselves if Congress would only pass a law requiring sidewalks and front porches everywhere. But sidewalks make little sense unless they go somewhere. And the place it makes sense for them to go, if they aren't just to go around in circles, is toward the neighborhood center.

What sorts of things should happen in the neighborhood center? No standard menu will serve for all neighborhoods. The general answer is: enough to make people want to go there frequently.

We are aiming at two interrelated goals in a neighborhood center. First, we want it to have enough activity and enough kinds of activity to attract a steady stream of visitors, but not so large a torrent of visitors that neighborhood safety and comfort are jeopardized. Second, we want to attract enough visitors to support the desired range of activities, but not enough to support the high-volume activity that can disrupt a neighborhood. At the risk of sounding circular, we want enough activity to attract enough traffic to support the activity that attracts the traffic, and vice versa, but we don't want too much of either. The neighborhood center has neighborhood-oriented retailing (a dry cleaner, a hardware store, a frame shop, a flower shop, clothing and variety stores), services (a bank, a post office, medical and dental offices), entertainment and recreation (restaurants, a game room, a video store, a YMCA), culture (a theater, a gallery, a bookstore or branch library), and places for mingling, assembly, and people-watching (a park or plaza, a fountain, street benches).

But a particular neighborhood center needn't have all of the specific items in that list, not to mention all the others that could have been mentioned. Probably every neighborhood center would have a dry cleaner and a restaurant; not every one would have a post office or library branch or frame shop. The mix of activities should be such that the neighborhood center is used continuously through the day and evening. It is important to include apartments or town houses in (or very near) the center. The reasons are almost too obvious to need explaining.

First, legitimate activity inhibits illegitimate activity. Burglars and other miscreants do not normally ply their trades when people are around to see them. In a neighborhood center shared by businesses and apartments, store owners and their customers afford protection for the apartments during business hours, and residents afford protection for businesses at night. Similarly, businesses that operate at night lend security to neighboring businesses that close earlier.

Second, parking lots can be used more efficiently (and thus they can be smaller) if they serve businesses that generate auto traffic at different times during the day and evening. The parking spaces that are used by office workers or beauty shop customers during the day can be used by restaurant patrons or video store customers at night. A rich mix of uses allows more commercial and social activity per square yard of asphalt than a narrow range of uses does.

Third, the inclusion of apartments in a neighborhood center puts a lot of customers within walking distance of businesses, helping to keep the businesses alive and reducing the number of miles driven—and the traffic congestion—as a ratio to sales. Apartments or town houses forming a ring around a commercial area can provide a buffer or transition zone between the business district and single-family residential areas. Higher-density housing, if properly designed and oriented to the street, can help pull pedestrians from the low-density residential areas toward the commercial center. The quicker streetscape tempo and more active rhythms that are possible with apartments and town houses can shorten perceived distance for pedestrians. A football field's length of sidewalk bounded by four or six single-family houses seems longer to a pedestrian than the same distance bounded by twelve row houses or sixteen well-articulated apartment bays.

Let's put together what we've learned in this chapter and propose a schematic matrix for the structure of a neighborhood (figure 6.5). The diagram does not show streets or roads but only the general disposition of land uses. Assume the diagram is about one mile on each side.

Following common practice, most of the land area is given to a ring of single-family residential zoning, although this ring could include row houses or apartments. In the real world, the single-family residential zone is likely to be planned and built by several developers, and the houses are likely to be grouped into several distinct subdivisions. That's OK, as long as there are local connector streets (not just major thoroughfares) linking one subdivision to the next and linking every subdivision to the neighborhood center. The heavy arrows indicate that all the subdivisions are oriented to the neighborhood center—linked to it by local streets with generous accommodations for pedestrians and cyclists.

The neighborhood center consists of three distinct types of development, in locales that cannot tolerate true mixed use. The innermost portion of the neighborhood center is the compact, mixed-use core. This core has the highest density, the quickest streetscape rhythms, the smallest blocks, and the most richly developed pedestrian environment. Front doors are close to each other, and parking is dispersed along the street and in small, commonly operated off-street lots. Small retailers, restaurants, professional offices, and other functions that do not require large land areas or drive-through facilities would go here. These are the kinds of businesses that customarily go into retail strips, although some government offices and cultural facilities, such as police substations and branch libraries, would also fit

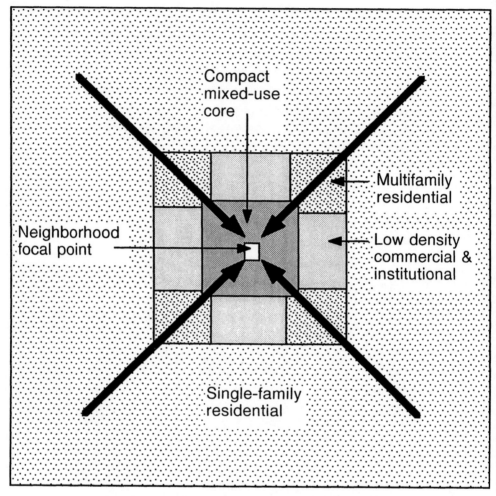

Figure 6.5 Schematic structure of a well-formed neighborhood.

the core. Near the center of the core is a focal point. This might be a small park or plaza, a wide place in the sidewalk for a fountain or sculpture, or maybe just a landmark piece of architecture. The focal point is the neighborhood's version of Times Square, an identifying feature and a magnet for neighborhood activity.

Between the compact core and the single-family residential zone are areas of higher-density residential development—apartments or row houses. These are not just near the core, as the crow flies, but are oriented to it along local, low-traffic streets, some of which will continue into the single-family zone. Small neighborhood parks might best be located where the single-family and apartment zones meet, along the local streets leading to the center.

Finally, the neighborhood center includes places just outside the compact core for large land users—supermarkets, movie complexes, and discount chains, but also high schools, hospitals, and other institutions. These large land users, which draw customers from far beyond the immediate neighborhood, would have parking lots oriented primarily toward major thoroughfares rather than local streets, to avoid disrupting neighborhood serenity. At the same time, however, these large land users should have local street and pedestrian connections with the compact core and with the apartment zones. Alert readers will notice that the nonresidential land uses in this diagram are formed into a cross-shaped plan that is similar to the plan of the shopping mall, which has big department stores at the extremities and little shops in the torso, usually with a focal-point court in the middle. The mall teaches lessons that are worth heeding.

■ urban form
The whole and its parts

If you live in a part of town that was built up after 1960 or so, chances are your neck of the woods doesn't pass the kid-on-a-bike test. There are a lot of large and small, economic and social reasons for the change, but many of the reasons have to do with a changing approach to urban form, the structural skeleton of a city's map, or the process by which the map grows outward.

To understand why suburban growth of the past few decades has tended not to produce functional neighborhoods, we need to see first how older approaches to urban form *did* produce them. One place to start, for people familiar with old centers of Santa Fe, San Antonio, and San Francisco, is the Spanish Law of the Indies.

Published in Madrid in 1681, the Law of the Indies established detailed and intelligent standards for town planning in Spain's American holdings. Some of the standards relating to street layout are illustrated in figure 7.1, based on the original plan for the Villa San Fernando de Bejar, the future city of San Antonio. The Law of the Indies specified a rectilinear grid of straight streets forty feet wide, so that cannon could repel invaders without damaging buildings. These streets linked residential blocks (lightly shaded) to the plaza and the main public buildings that faced it. The plaza's proportions were set at 3:2, and the church was supposed to face the plaza on the

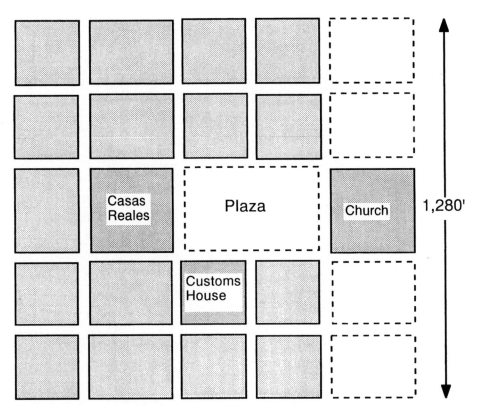

Figure 7.1 Original (unrealized) plan of San Antonio, laid out according to the principles of the Spanish Law of the Indies.

east. (Local peculiarities required the idealized plan in figure 7.1 to be flipped, putting the church on the west end of the plaza, and the rectilinear grid had to be distorted slightly to accommodate the vagaries of the nearby river.) The Casas Reales, seat of local government, faced the church across the plaza, and the customs house was placed catercorner from the Casas Reales. The plaza served as a wagon yard, a market place, and a venue for fiestas and religious processions. Thus the plaza brought church, state, culture, and commerce into intimate relation.

In Colonial New England, too, land was customarily surveyed and divided into rectangles. In 1785 the United States Congress adopted the earlier

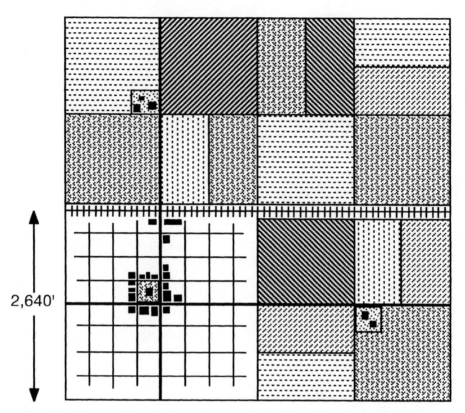

Figure 7.2   Town and farm in the rectilinear grid of the United States' western expansion.

New England practice as the method of surveying and disposing of the nation's western lands. The land was divided into six-mile-square townships, which in turn were divided into thirty-six sections, each one mile square or 640 acres in area. One section in each township was set aside to provide for public schools. This pattern spread westward from the western boundary of Pennsylvania and gained momentum with the building of the railroads in the nineteenth century.

From the window seat of an airplane flying over the Midwest, you can still see how the process worked. Figure 7.2 is a schematic plane's-eye view of one square mile of rural land. The patterned squares and rectangles are farm plots. The grid at the lower left is a hypothetical town in its original nineteenth-century form, perhaps a county seat with its courthouse square bounded by commercial buildings. (In the New England pattern, the central square was occupied by a government building rather than left open as in the Spanish system.) At the town's edge is the rail line, and roads (the slightly heavier lines) pass through the town and connect it with farms and other towns. Houses, schools, and churches would occupy outlying blocks. Businesses requiring large tracts of land—the grain elevator, the feed store or farm implements dealer, later the car lot, the supermarket, the motel, and the Wal-Mart—would fall outside this original quarter-section grid, on the main roads leading out of town. The hypothetical (but typical) street map for the town in figure 7.2 would fit neatly into the neighborhood matrix shown in figure 6.5.

One small town that fits this common pattern is La Grange, internationally famous as the setting for *The Best Little Whorehouse in Texas*, but nowadays just an unusually pleasant town of about four thousand people. La Grange is the seat of Fayette County and the commercial center for a farming area that was settled mainly by Czechs and Germans in the mid-nineteenth century. This was a prosperous town, sprouting magnificent houses, churches, and commercial buildings, many of which have been carefully restored in recent years. The handsome stone courthouse, designed in the Richardsonian Romanesque style by James Riely Gordon (architect of many fine Texas courthouses and of San Antonio's Staacke Building, mentioned in chapter 5), dates from 1892 and dominates the central square. Still an active retailing area, the square is, at this writing, surrounded by a small grocer, a meat market, a bakery, a gift shop, a video dealer, a furniture store, drugstores, clothing shops, a dentist's office, a bank, a couple of restaurants, even a tiny movie theater installed in an old storefront. On Main Street just off the square is the gorgeous old limestone jail, now looking for a new civic use, and the same street continues past big mansions, small cottages, and, at the end, a somewhat dispiriting trailer park—all within a half-mile of the courthouse square. Figure 7.3 zeroes in on the original street grid of La Grange. The town has grown beyond this historic center, of course. Early growth continued and honored the original grid. Later growth, mainly toward the northeast, brought larger blocks and breaks in the continuity of the grid.

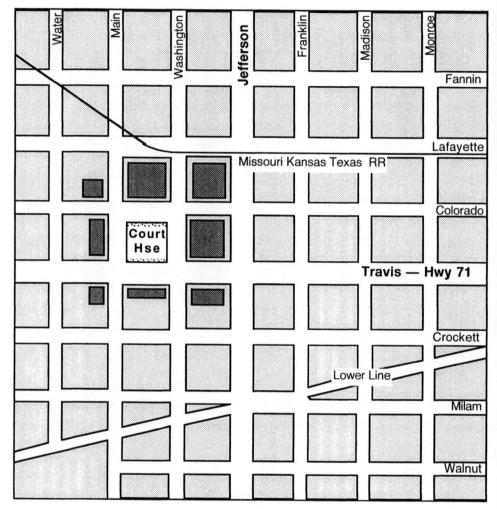

Figure 7.3 The rectilinear grid of La Grange, Texas.

The deep valley of the Colorado River is a barrier on the west and south, a few blocks beyond the edges of the map in figure 7.3. Commercial development—supermarkets, drive-in restaurants, gas stations, convenience stores, retail strips—has extended along the two highways. The magnetic attraction of the center has weakened as a result, and a few disturbing vacancies can be found in the handsome old commercial buildings around the square. Still, most of the townspeople remain within the magnetic field of the center, and most of the street system continues to support that magnetic field.

By assimilating all (or most) of a town's diverse people and activities to the same continuous grid, the small town's street system subtly expressed the notion We're All in This Together. Community solidarity and mutual responsibility were sealed by the town center. The most common destinations (common in the sense of frequency and of universality) were clustered at the center, which was therefore the focus of both commercial and community activity—not just shopping and going to the office, but Fourth of July parades, teenage cruising, old folks' schmoozing, and everybody's newsgathering. The dispersed churches, schools, and VFW halls served as subcenters, but downtown, linked equally and easily to all by the street grid, was the heart and soul—and glue—of the town, the hub of the wheel. The center gave the whole town its identity and tone.

One must guard against over-romanticizing the small town and its focal-point grid. As any observant back-road traveler will notice, many small towns, as they grew, spawned separate street grids for poor people or minorities, often literally on the other side of the tracks. The small-town core has, moreover, been weakened in many cases by the growth of car-oriented shopping centers and discount stores on the highways at the town fringe—the same forces that have so affected urban neighborhoods.

But the image of the small town continues to exert its power over both urban and suburban America. The small town's main street often appears in television commercials when an advertiser (usually an insurance company or a presidential candidate) wants to convey (usually deceitfully) devotion to bedrock values of common sense, hard work, moral rectitude, and community sentiment. These commercials are not usually filmed in the Wal-Mart parking lot or at the new shopping mall on the edge of town—images that would be far more familiar to most viewers (including, alas, many small-town viewers). So powerful is the attraction of the small town as an idea and an image that even an appallingly high murder rate has not dissuaded Americans from returning time after time to the village of Cabot Cove, Maine, the neighborly home of Jessica Fletcher on "Murder, She Wrote."

While few Americans today live in small towns with healthy centers, many Americans still cherish that image and way of life somewhere in the back of their mind. People think that the small town offers a sense of community, mutual responsibility, friendliness, visual pleasantness, ease and convenience of movement, and safety from crime. The small town is not generally regarded as offering much in the way of diversity, either of people or of opportunities, but even on this score the small town has its advantages. While the town of, say, thirty-five hundred or five thousand people can't approach the variety of a big city, the classic form of the small town typically does embrace greater economic, racial, and functional diversity within a perceptually unified, continuously walkable or bikable space than does the typical suburban sector with a comparable population.

The small town's strength is its ability to assimilate whatever diversity it has into a socially cohesive and functionally integrated whole, and this ability derives in part from the type and degree of specialization of the town's spatial organization. The land-use map is specialized in the sense that it has a clear center, the primary focus of commercial, governmental, and social activity, with primarily residential and institutional uses radiating outward from the center; but the street grid on which these land uses arrange themselves is continuous and nonspecialized, setting up no rigid geographic boundary between land uses or, in residential areas, between economic classes. The specialization is in use, not in form.

In the way they function and in their spatial organization, successful urban (and suburban) neighborhoods are very much like successful small towns. The Fell's Point neighborhood of Baltimore, for example, is remarkably like tiny La Grange, despite Fell's Point's cultural diversity and urban density, its streets packed with two- and three-story row houses. Broadway, an esplanade leading down to the old dock area, is Fell's Point's commercial and social spine. The block closest to the water has several high-tab restaurants, a charming little hotel called the Admiral Fell Inn, and nightclubs popular with local collegians, but once you get beyond the immediate dock area Fell's Point is a neighbors' neighborhood. Neighborhood people shop for produce, pastries, seafood, and meats at the municipal market in the middle of Broadway, and you may see regulars passing the day at tables un-

der the trees just outside the market. Jimmy's, a small twenty-four-hour restaurant, is virtually the Fell's Point city hall—not just a place to eat, but a
community center where the staff knows most of the customers, and most of
the customers know each other. Bertha's, across the esplanade, is a popular
neighborhood bar and mussel emporium where a fashionable young woman
is likely to run into the fellow who repairs her shoes; his shop is a couple of
blocks away. The esplanade itself is a convenient place for voter registration
drives, for on-foot socializing and cruising by teenagers, for card-playing by
older people, and, alas, for sleeping by the homeless.

There is some on-street parking for the businesses along Broadway,
but it is the street's predominantly pedestrian character that makes it work.
A driver can park once and visit several shops on foot. People who live
within three or four blocks customarily walk to Broadway. The street grid of
small, rectilinear blocks gives pedestrians multiple, closely spaced routes to
Broadway; the sidewalks, shaded by trees and bordered by row houses that
establish a crisp rhythm, make the trip pleasant and psychologically easy.

A few blocks inland from the old dock, Fell's Point is not an economically privileged neighborhood. Although high-income professionals are beginning to move into some streets, others are determinedly middle class,
most of the old brick row houses still covered by the fake stone siding of the
1950s. Some blocks are immigrant or ethnic communities—Poles here, Ko-
reans there, Greeks a block away. The neighborhood center, in this case a
spine but a fairly short and easily walkable one, is congenial to people of all
ages, cultures, and incomes. The center brings the neighborhood's diversity
into consonance. Indeed, it is the center that transforms an odd-lot assortment of demographic types into a coherent, identifiable, and very pleasant
neighborhood—a community.

To remind you that this book is not just about soft sentiment but also
about hard economics, I will briefly note that the same geographic features
that make Fell's Point and La Grange positive places in the social sense also
make them good places for small businesses. Most of the businesses in both
centers are small and locally owned and operated. As in Evanston, the physical structure of both Fell's Point and La Grange draws customers into a
compact, pedestrian-oriented center that is easy to get to and easy to use.

On-street parking is available for the convenience of those who do not live within walking distance, but there is not so much parking that it breaks the rhythm of the stores. This type of environment does not give an insuperable competitive advantage to national, mass-market chains. The mass marketers can and do locate successfully in such areas—even McDonald's and Burger King can thrive without a single parking space or drive-up window—but local entrepreneurs have an equal shot at success because they have equal access to the market. It is advantageous to a neighborhood to have its locally owned businesses do well. When a small local business does well, both the payroll and the profits remain in the community, and the local entrepreneur has a vested interest in the community's health. The national chain can (and does) easily move out when conditions deteriorate.

The small-town feeling of a good neighborhood has nothing to do with the size of a city. You can find well-formed neighborhoods in places as small as La Grange, where nearly the whole town is the neighborhood, or, as Jane Jacobs has shown in her classic portrait of Greenwich Village, in such huge cities as New York; among the gracious lawns of Evanston, Illinois, or Palo Alto, California; or among the cheek-by-jowl row houses of Baltimore's Fell's Point, where any blade of grass is purely accidental. Good neighborhoods can be economically privileged or modest, ethnically mixed or homogeneous.

What they all have in common is an active, magnetic, mixed-use, pedestrian-oriented center intimately linked by the street-and-sidewalk grid to the surrounding residential areas. They all pass the kid-on-a-bike test.

The well-formed neighborhood is difficult to reconcile, however, with the fragmented development pattern that has prevailed in American suburban rings since about 1960. The reason is that the new city and the historic town differ fundamentally at the conceptual stage of planning. The historic town was laid out from the beginning to be a functionally integrated system, as it had to be. In an era before cars and telephones, it was necessary that the street layout connect homes, jobs, commerce, and culture in a way that was quick, easy, and efficient for pedestrians and horse-drawn wagons, and that all essential goods and services be located close to people's homes. The basic unit of organization, derived from the rectilinear grid of federal land-disposition surveys or from Spanish Colonial practices, was the city block. The block was typically between three hundred and four hundred feet on a side—small enough to allow easy movement and alternative routes between urban functions, but not so small that an unacceptable amount of land area would be given over to streets. The street system was typically an artifact of the optimum block size and section or quarter-section boundaries.

The grid of rectangular blocks was neutral with respect to use, at once dynamic and stable. Commercial uses could expand into formerly residential blocks according to relatively free market forces without disrupting the unity or connectedness of the overall neighborhood structure. Similarly, a growing population could be accommodated simply by adding residential blocks to the edges of the old grid. As these new residential blocks extended farther and farther from the town's original commercial center, market forces tended to form new commercial subcenters in these outlying areas. Because the grid was the same in the new areas as in the old, the same functional integration would be seen. An area of twenty or forty square blocks became a functionally integrated neighborhood with the commercial subcenter as its focus. Furthermore, as long as the city continued to expand by simply adding similar blocks at the edges, the pattern of overlapping rings (Adjacency, Bowser, Constitutional, and Daryl) also expanded in a continuous, unbroken manner.

The pattern of continuous expansion was never absolute, but its breakup accelerated after World War II. Returning soldiers, the baby boom, rising wages, and widely available credit released a huge demand for housing. In the late forties and early fifties, much of the new housing built to meet this demand continued the prewar street grid. But increasingly through the fifties developers built "planned communities" of detached single-family houses beyond the urban periphery—often outside the city limits, where land prices were low and buyers could avoid city taxes.

Increasingly these outlying areas were linked to the central city by limited-access highways. Several thousand miles of toll roads were built in the 1950s, and the 1960s saw the rapid expansion of the limited-access interstate highway system. Together, the rapid building of outlying subdivisions and the spread of limited-access highways fundamentally changed the form of growth. To state the obvious, land that became (sub)urbanized after 1950 was most likely rural before 1950. Because rural land had been subdivided into quarter-section farms, rural roads were typically spaced no closer than a mile apart. Limited-access highways were designed to feed into the existing roads, so suburban exits were at least a mile apart. Meanwhile, tract-housing builders typically bought and developed rural land in quarter-section parcels linked to highways by the old farm roads.

The old mile-apart farm roads and the rural highways would most often become the through roads—not infrequently the only ones—in the suburban ring, whereas in the grid-plan city many streets continued for a considerable distance, and through roads were often spaced a half-mile apart. From the suburban developers' point of view, existing roads provided all the access that was needed. A large tract might be designed with an axial street between the old farm roads, but this street rarely connected with a similar one in an adjacent tract. The widely spaced through roads of the new suburbia carried far heavier burdens of traffic and commercial development than their more closely spaced inner-city counterparts.

Curving "spaghetti bowl" streets and cul-de-sacs became the norm in residential subdivisions in the 1960s. This arrangement slowed down cars and eliminated through traffic, an advantage for families with children, and it reduced the amount of land devoted to streets. But the spaghetti bowls also affected the through roads. Often an entire subdivision of several hundred houses might have only one or two outlets to through roads, which might be the only way to get from one subdivision to the next—or anywhere else. In the old city, Oak Street in the subdivision that Bob built in 1920 would continue as Oak Street in the adjoining subdivision that Hortense built in 1925. In the new suburbia, each subdivision was and is developed in isolation from the rest, with little or no continuity of residential streets. The old city's structural matrix was a continuous but lumpy fabric. Residential and commercial uses were integrated into the same street grid, with retailers gravitating to major nodes roughly a mile apart and (sometimes) minor nodes roughly a half-mile apart (figure 7.4, where the shaded areas represent commercial nodes). The new suburbia's structural matrix consists solely of

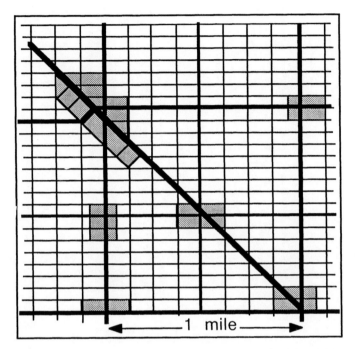

Figure 7.4 The traditional neighborhood was a continuous fabric richly interconnected by a network of closely spaced local streets.

widely spaced major thoroughfares, typically the only through streets. Each subdivision is an island disjunct from the main structural matrix (figure 7.5).

In defense of the insular spaghetti bowls of figure 7.5, it is sometimes said that they have a distinguished lineage in the garden suburbs of the 1920s and their forebears, going back to Frederick Law Olmstead's 1869 plan for Riverside, Illinois. But in contrast to the modern subdivision divorced from commercial and social activity, most of these earlier models included a compact, mixed-use downtown linked by multiple local streets to the entire town. Moreover, while the streets of these earlier suburbs might curve, they still formed an array of blocks—different in shape but not in structure from the rectilinear grid. Riverside, for example, had no cul-de-sacs, and every

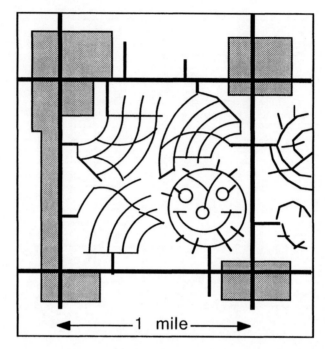

Figure 7.5 In conventional suburban planning, the urban fabric is ripped into fragments that are connected only by widely spaced major thoroughfares.

point in each half of the town (which was bisected by a river and park) was reachable from every other point by multiple direct pathways.

The point of figure 7.4, however, is not to make a case for the rectilinear street grid, although I find that arrangement convenient, liberating, and pleasant. Rather, I am arguing for continuity in the urban fabric—for richness of connections as opposed to the poverty of the insular figure 7.5. Even the rectilinear grid needn't be, and rarely is in practice, as regular and neat and boring as a sheet of graph paper. The regularity is often modulated by diagonal roads that may have predated the city, or by curving streets that follow the path of streams, or by a subdivision laid out neoclassically with streets radiating from a focal park, or by changes in block size from one area to another, or by any number of variants that cause ripples—but not rips—

in the fabric of the city. But the gridiron is not the essential thing. At the risk of being branded a heretic, I would suggest that even spaghetti-bowl subdivisions with cul-de-sacs, anathema to many urban traditionalists but in truth a reasonable adaptation to the noise and danger of auto traffic, are not irredeemably incompatible with a continuous and integrated urban fabric. If cul-de-sacs feed directly into circulator streets (even curvaceous ones) that are integrated into the larger grid, little has been lost, and much has been gained, in terms of serenity and safety for cul-de-sac residents. What is essential is that, however freely a residential subdivision is laid out, it should link up directly with adjoining subdivisions and with mixed-use neighborhood centers. As long as the streets in adjoining subdivisions snap together at the subdivisions' edges, like the lengths of track in an electric train set, their internal perambulations can have considerable freedom without materially reducing the continuity of the city.

In modern suburbia, without links between subdivisions and with only limited connections between subdivisions and through roads, the roughly mile-square grid of major thoroughfares came to have overarching importance in the minds of planners. In effect, all development in the suburban ring was plugged directly into the mile-apart through roads, which came to be conceptualized as the superstructure of the city. The preeminent planning task was to keep auto traffic moving smoothly. It would be an exaggeration to say that city planning became an adjunct of traffic engineering, but not, perhaps, a gross exaggeration.

Because the block was the basic unit of organization in the old city of figure 7.4, the structural matrix penetrated, by definition, to every block, knitting many blocks and their many activities into integrated neighborhoods. In the new suburbia, the widely spaced grid of through roads— which are generally much wider and busier than even the major thoroughfares of the old city—is the structural matrix into which whole subdivisions plug. This structure does not penetrate to the streets where most suburban people live and does not knit homes, stores, offices and institutions into integrated neighborhoods.

It is like redesigning the system of blood vessels in your body to make the major veins and arteries bigger while neglecting the capillaries or eliminating them altogether. This redesigned vascular system might supply enough blood to the vital organs to keep them alive, but eventually you'll lose so much connective tissue that your healthy heart and liver won't do you any good.

Remember that our goal in laying out a city is not just to have a warehouse or filing system for different types of land use (a place for everything and everything in its place), but to encourage exchange. Because the neighborhood is the part of town that is geographically closest, perceptually most familiar, and (in the ideal) psychologically most comfortable to the people who live or work there, the neighborhood is potentially the most efficient nexus of social, cultural, and economic exchange. But in order to realize this potential, the opportunities for exchange must exist within the neighborhood, and these opportunities must be laid out geographically (in relation to each other and to the neighborhood's residential areas) in such a way as to yield economies of form. In order for a city to bring the benefits that cities have traditionally brought, it needs to be laid out as an array of functionally integrated neighborhoods with strong centers. If our goals are to promote exchange and foster a sense of community, and if we agree that active neighborhood centers are necessary to achieve those goals, then it doesn't make sense to regard the residential subdivision as the basic unit of organization, and the grid of major thoroughfares as the structural skeleton, for urban form.

A different organizing principle is required for the many separate cells of an urban vicinity to coalesce and interrelate as an urban neighborhood. We should not and cannot throw out the grid of through roads, which we need in order to go from one neighborhood to the next and to knit many neighborhoods into a city, but we can shift our conceptual focus. Rather than conceptualizing a city's fundamental structure as a grid of major thoroughfares, we can reconceptualize a city's fundamental structure as *an array of neighborhoods, each with its own center*. By doing this we put the neighborhood and its center in the foreground of the city map and push the major thoroughfare grid into the conceptual background. Imagine that a schematic map of a city begins with an array that looks like figure 7.6, where each circle is a neighborhood center, a compact assortment of stores, offices, cultural facilities,

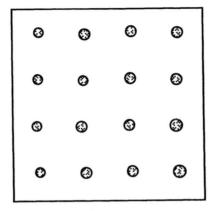

Figure 7.6 The conceptual city begins with an array of neighborhood mixed-use centers.

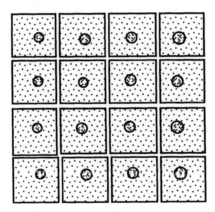

Figure 7.7 Each neighborhood center is the center of a neighborhood.

and gathering places. The connecting roads will come later. The array of circles is the original framework, the basic structure, on which we are going to hang the pieces of a city.

If each circle is a neighborhood center, it follows that each circle is the center of a neighborhood. The tautology needs to be stated because, in common suburban practice, the kind of project that is loosely called a "neighborhood center" is rarely conceived, designed, or located in such a way that it functions as the center of a neighborhood. We need to imagine residential areas, with their schools and parks, radiating from each circle. Schematically, we have figure 7.7, where each shaded square represents the neighborhood that has the circle as its center.

Now, if a neighborhood center is to function as the focus of activity for the neighborhood fabric beyond the circle, the two have to be in intimate relationship with each other, drawn together by a network of streets and sidewalks. The streets in each square must converge on the dark circle and

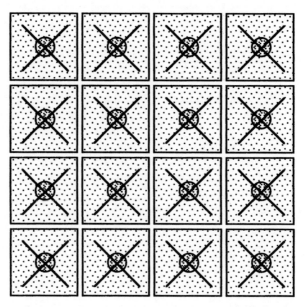

Figure 7.8   In each neighborhood, some local streets converge on its center.

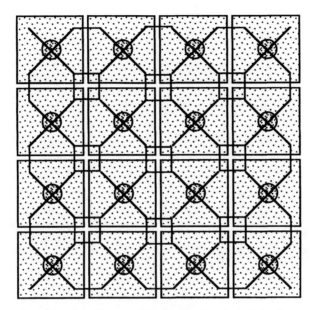

Figure 7.9   Local streets link neighborhoods at their edges,
forming a continuous knitted fabric.

burst through its perimeter. This yields figure 7.8. The radiating lines in figure 7.8 are not, of course, meant literally, but schematically. What is essential is that a neighborhood's local street system allow direct and convenient
access to the center—a condition that can be met with a rectilinear grid of
small blocks, a neoclassical hub-and-spokes affair, or any number of other
design variants.

In figure 7.8, we have an array of neighborhoods, but they don't yet
form a city because the neighborhoods don't connect. Figure 7.9 draws in local street connections—again schematically, not literally—between neighborhoods. In practice, these might be short streets linking back-to-back
residential subdivisions, or they might be secondary arterials paralleling the
major thoroughfares (not yet drawn in) and located halfway between them.

If we now draw in the major thoroughfares connecting neighborhood
centers to each other (figure 7.10), you get something that looks superficially
like the conventional suburban grid of mile-apart roads. But if these roads

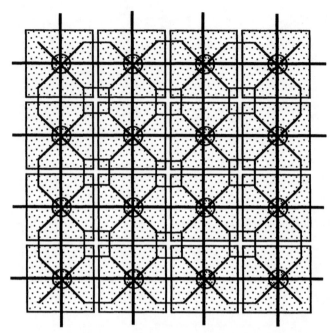

Figure 7.10   Major thoroughfares link neighborhood centers.

come at the end rather than at the beginning of the conceptual process of laying out a city—if our primary objective is good neighborhoods, and roads are designed to pass through them benignly—then the roads we end up with will look different in detail from the suburban roads we have now. We do not aim to end up without major thoroughfares, as we now end up without neighborhoods. Shifting the road grid to the conceptual background means only that as we make planning, zoning, and public works decisions, we design the road to serve the neighborhood, not the opposite.

The pattern in figure 7.10 is complex and, with respect to perceptual neighborhood boundaries, ambivalent. For someone who lives near a corner of one of the shaded squares, is the neighborhood that shaded square with the mixed-use hub at its center? Or is it the square bounded by four major thoroughfares, with mixed-use hubs at its four corners? If the shaded squares are defined as coherent neighborhoods, people who live near the edge of one neighborhood might relate, in their everyday routines and perceptions, more closely to the adjoining neighborhood and its center than to the one they technically live in. The places where four neighborhoods converge would be reasonable places to put elementary schools, neighborhood parks, or small retail centers containing the sorts of stores that can survive on a highly localized customer base. The four-corners areas would thus constitute a secondary (and weaker) array of neighborhood centers. That's just fine. A city, remember, is about manifold options for exchange; the city is the game board on which we play the game of liberty. Freedom of exchange is enhanced by compact and well-defined neighborhood centers, but also by ambiguous and permeable neighborhood boundaries.

Some readers may be disappointed that the major thoroughfare grid has emerged after all as an essential, if perceptually suppressed, component of the urban matrix, and that the primary array of active, strong-magnet neighborhood centers coincides more or less with the intersections of major thoroughfares. That doesn't sound very different from prevailing practice in suburban rings, after all. But in the real world, major activity centers have to be served by major thoroughfares. Some readers may also be disappointed to learn that the matrix of figure 7.10 is compatible with autonomously developed residential subdivisions, including totally private subdivisions surrounded by walls and protected by security gates, so long as a network of public streets provides sufficient redundant linkages within and between neighborhoods. (That proviso probably entails that subdivisions have at least two or three entrances, a requirement that could be justified on grounds of public safety in the event that a quick evacuation is necessary.) Again, in the real world, in the United States, most residential construction is going to continue being organized into cellular subdivisions laid out by private developers.

The question facing urban planners is how to encourage the formation of functionally integrated, strongly centered neighborhoods within these real-world constraints on urban form. The typical residential subdivision of one hundred to three hundred single-family houses does not, by itself, contain enough people to support a vital neighborhood center. But an active center can be sustained by four or five such subdivisions, abetted by higher-density apartment and town house projects near the center, if the physical connections between the subdivisions and their common center are convenient and clearly perceived, and if the center is easily accessible to a citywide market by means of major thoroughfares. Municipal or metropolitan governments can help create these conditions by refining their existing planning tools in ways that do not excessively limit developer prerogatives and thus may be—with effort and time—politically achievable.

Suppose that planners were to figure out where commercial concentrations and residential subdivisions were likely to appear in the natural course of suburban growth—not a difficult task for time horizons on the order of five years. Suppose further that planners were to designate certain of these future commercial hubs as neighborhood centers-to-be. Items in the tool kit for shaping these centers are given below.

• **Overlay zoning districts** can favor higher-density mixed-use development in neighborhood centers.

• **Subdivision standards** can favor continuity of sidewalks and building lines, control the size and location of parking lots, require developers to set aside land for parks and open space, and mandate street connections from one subdivision to the next and between subdivisions and their common neighborhood center.

• **Public works policy** can demand that major thoroughfares be designed in pedestrian-friendly ways within neighborhood centers.

• **Capital improvements plans** can encourage the siting of public libraries, parks, police substations, and other public facilities in places where they are most likely to reinforce neighborhood centers.

• **Transit plans** can be designed so that routes, stationary facilities, and signs support neighborhood centers.

• **Public art programs** can place sculpture, fountains, and other major artworks as neighborhood focal points.

• **Landscape ordinances** can be written not just to promote generalized prettiness and greenery, but to bring coherence to the pedestrian environment of neighborhood centers.

• **Utility policies** can encourage the burial of utility lines in neighborhood centers and (if state law allows) reduce impact fees for neighborhood center projects that meet special design standards.

• **Sign ordinances** can establish special standards for commercial signs in neighborhood centers.

In sum, planners need to measure the whole range of city policies, codes, and practices by how well they work to knit the individual fragments of a city into coherent, functionally integrated, and strongly centered neighborhoods. Over the past thirty years or so, municipalities took responsibility for the grid of major roads, and private developers took responsibility for the individual subdivisions that plugged into those roads, but nobody took responsibility for creating neighborhoods and neighborhood centers. It does not follow that well-formed neighborhoods *cannot* be built on a landscape and a map that are congenial to the requirements of the automobile and modern real estate development practices. It is possible, I believe, to reconcile the neighborhood with modern times, but not if the process is left to chance. City planners have to begin conceiving the map of the growing suburban ring as an array of neighborhoods-to-be, each with its own strong center—an array of La Granges, as it were. If this array of (still imaginary) neighborhoods occupies the foreground or primary level of the conceptual map, then the road system, residential subdivisions, and commercial nodes can be designed—with minimal change from current practice—to support that neighborhood array. The design problem isn't easy, but neither is it insoluble.

▪ the market place
Where exchange happens

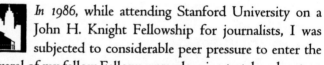In 1986, while attending Stanford University on a John H. Knight Fellowship for journalists, I was subjected to considerable peer pressure to enter the computer age. Several of my fellow Fellows were planning to take advantage of the student discount on computers, and for the first few weeks they talked about nothing else. They invoked the names of mythical deities named RAM and ROM and yammered incessantly about a puppy dog named Floppy, who had learned to drive but was crashing all the time. My Smith-Corona would do. Until . . .

I lived that year in an apartment building two blocks from the main drag of Palo Alto, about two miles from the Stanford Quadrangle, and I usually walked to school. My path took me past the many shops and restaurants of University Avenue—several bakeries, clothing stores, a flower stall, a bank, a bookstore, a pharmacy, a movie theater, a live music club. One day, a particular shop window caught my eye. The display included an enlargement of a page of a full orchestral score. The sign next to it promised that, with a brand of computer software for sale inside, one could "compose a song or a whole symphony" in standard musical notation and hear the results through loudspeakers built into a Macintosh computer. Hmmm. I stopped to examine the display, which included a lengthy text, and then entered the store to ask some questions. I didn't buy anything just then, but the next day I stopped again, and the next day. At last, I succumbed. I would enter the Macintosh generation.

In the intervening years I've spent thousands of dollars for software and peripherals. These exchanges have brought pleasure and intellectual growth to my own life and financial gain to the retailers and manufacturers who sold me the goods. By enhancing my productivity as a writer, the computer has also generated increased income for me. I'm using it now to write this book.

The central event that set off this mutually beneficial cycle of exchanges was the moment that I stopped to look in that shop window on University Avenue. The window display, combined with the opportunity to walk immediately and conveniently into the store to ask questions and familiarize myself with alien territory, broke my sales resistance far more effectively than all of my colleagues' evangelizing.

Now, let's imagine a different set of geographic circumstances. Suppose this computer store were not located on University Avenue, where I would walk past it nearly every day, but in a retail strip on a much wider and busier road where I might *drive* past it every day. The storefronts of a typical retail strip on a major thoroughfare are set back at least seventy-five feet, and often 150 feet or more, from the edge of the roadway, which typically is at least four lanes wide. Suppose I am driving on this roadway, and suppose the computer store in the strip center has a window display advertising music software. What are the chances that I would notice this display? Slim to none. I probably wouldn't even notice the store.

Imagine yourself behind the wheel of your car as you're driving, say, from your home to the supermarket a couple of miles away on a typical commercial corridor. Suppose your route takes you directly past a hundred retail storefronts. How much information about the products offered by those stores do you absorb on this drive? You gain virtually no information from their window displays. They're too far away to be clearly seen. The greatest part of your attention is (one hopes) concentrated on the road. If traffic is moving freely enough to allow your eyes to wander, you have only a couple of seconds at most to see the display, and only in its gross outlines; there are probably so many other visual distractions within your field of vision that a clear message from one store has a hard time coming through.

So the window display isn't likely to grab you. How about the store sign? Seen only briefly as you drive by on the road, a sign, even a very big one, can't tell you much more than the name of the store and the kinds of products it sells: Bubba's Hardware; Night of Ecstasy Salon de Lingerie. At best, a sign might alert you to one or two products, but only by name and price: Deluxe pizza, $4.99! A driver on a major thoroughfare does not have the time or the visual acuity to absorb more information than that.

There are three circumstances under which you might be more likely to enter a store in a retail strip:

• You need or want something that falls into the broad category of products identified by the store's name: You need a new washer for the kitchen faucet, see "Bubba's Hardware" on a sign, and pull into the parking lot. This process works only when you can make a direct, immediate, and unambiguous connection between the product or service advertised and a need or desire that you *already knew you had.*

• Your interest in a particular shop might have been piqued by the recommendation of a friend or by advertising. In that case, you might resolve to visit that store as a *destination.* The sign is not an enticement, but only a locator, helping you find the store you were already looking for.

• You might be visiting another store as a destination in the same strip center, or perhaps an adjacent one. While driving slowly through the parking lot or walking from your car to the destination store, you have an opportunity to absorb information about the other stores you pass. You can see the window displays up close. Maybe you can even see inside the stores. From window displays, architectural design, and a glance at customers entering or leaving, you can make a preliminary (if not necessarily accurate or fair) judgment about the kinds of products the store sells; whether its stock is big or small, mass-market or specialized; its style of doing business; its price range; and the social status of its clientele. Most important, as we have already seen, a window display is an efficient way to introduce you to a new product, *something that you didn't know you wanted,* perhaps because you didn't know it existed. If you like what you see, you may walk inside; you're practically there anyway. You don't have to make a special trip, find a new parking place, or struggle with traffic.

Propinquity plays a vital role in economic activity in the retail sector, which weighs heavily in the economy and livability of cities. But propinquity is little exploited in modern planning. The tendency is instead to isolate stores from potential customers.

In this chapter we will be talking about the market place, the physical and temporal space within which exchanges occur. We will be investigating how that place should best be organized to promote the circulation of money, ideas, knowledge, things, and people. As a kind of shorthand I refer to sites of exchange mainly as retail stores, because retailing is the most dominant and pervasive visible feature of the market place, but whenever I use "store" or "shop," I include more than just buying and selling. A "store" may be a library, museum, concert hall, or university; it may be a playground or picnic table or YMCA; it may be the sidewalk bench where you chat with a friend you hadn't seen in a few months, or the corner where an evangelist passes out religious tracts, or the bus stop where you overhear a fragment of conversation that leads you to a new and useful idea; it may be a public sculpture or fountain or vista where you pause for contemplation or amusement. A "store" could be Al's Appliance Alley, but it could also be Patty's Poetry Pantry, which this week has a sale on anapests (59¢ a foot; no dealers, please).

The market place these days is not as clearly bounded as it once was; it has become global. This means not only that the products you purchase in your local stores may come from all over the world, but also that your local stores themselves may be all over the world, thanks to the telephone, the television, the personal computer, the mail, the facsimile machine, and even the old-fashioned book, a kind of store that gives you access to knowledge, beliefs, styles, and ideologies from the whole world in convenient local form. I used my San Antonio telephone to order a Japanese keyboard synthesizer from a discount retailer in Atlanta and paid for my order instantly with a credit card issued by a New York bank. Hamamatsu, New York, and Atlanta were all integrated into the local market place.

But the event that set that interstate, international transaction in motion was my serendipitous encounter with a musician friend who recommended the synthesizer I then decided to buy. The concert-hall lobby where we met was an essential component of the international trade network, as was the sidewalk where I was persuaded to buy the computer that operates my synthesizer. Without that concert hall and that sidewalk, New York, Atlanta, and Hamamatsu would all go belly up, stock markets would crash, and the whole world would be plunged into the Dark Ages again.

The condition of the hands-on, face-to-face, local market place is thus of some moment. What are the characteristics of a well-formed market place? If you are a consumer—and everybody is—of products, services, knowledge, and information, how must the market place be organized to serve your needs best? By way of answering that question, it might be helpful to think of the market place as an all-you-can-eat buffet. How would you want it to look?

• **Variety/range/competition.** You would want the buffet to include many kinds of foods that you and your dinner companions want to eat. Vegetarians and carnivores, dieters and gluttons, the bold and the meek, must all have an abundance of choices. Similarly, the well-formed local market place offers all or most of the kinds of goods that you and your neighbors might desire, and it offers abundant choices among comparable items and competing sources. You don't just want a bookstore; you want a bookstore that has the books you want, even if your tastes are unusual.

• **Density/continuity/immediacy.** Have you ever been to one of those big, fancy receptions where the roast beef is in one corner, and the teriyaki chicken wings and rumaki are in another corner, and the raw vegetables and fruit are in the middle, and the shrimp are in the hall, and the desserts are out on the verandah, and you pigged out on the stuffed mushrooms near the bar before you realized that moo shoo pork was being offered next to the bandstand? In a good buffet, all the foods are close to each other, laid out in a continuity, and visible at close range. A well-formed market place has the same traits. The stores and other sites of exchange are close together, they form a continuous and coherent ensemble, and they are immediately accessible—that is, accessible without requiring the shopper to leave the market place temporarily and venture out to the main road. Obvious as you might think this principle is, developers in suburban contexts typically do not consider pedestrian access in their site plans, even in densely developed areas where significant pedestrian traffic could, with the merest hint of an invitation, be expected. Indeed, it sometimes seems that developers try to keep customers away. Do currency and credit cards transmit some deadly plague virus?

• **Security/comfort/invitation.** A buffet is not likely to succeed if the staff is surly, the room is filthy and noisy, the chairs fall apart, the air-conditioning is on the blink, the ceiling panels fall on the diners, and the path from your table to the buffet takes you past the Dumpster in the alley. A market place can't succeed if customers aren't made to feel welcome and valued. Sidewalks must be of adequate width, in good condition, and protected from the elements; the architecture and landscaping must create an attractive, well-organized, and distinctive atmosphere; and customers must not feel that they are endangered by traffic or vulnerable to crime.

• **Progression/slow movement.** Some Japanese restaurants have a high-tech version of the buffet. The diners sit at a counter while plates of food pass slowly in front of them on a conveyor belt. The belt does not rush past at forty miles an hour; if it did, nobody could even see the different plates, much less be able to take one. At a normal buffet, people do not don roller skates and dash past the foods. They move slowly enough to examine, consider, compare, and discuss—"What do you suppose *that* is?"—the offerings. At the same time, interesting foods down the line entice the diner not to leave the buffet prematurely. You want to see what's in the next tray, and the one after that. A well-formed market place is laid out according to the same principles. You are drawn along the street or sidewalk by a progression of interesting things, without such wide gaps that momentum cannot carry you past the boring parts. But you move slowly enough to detect, absorb, and weigh the information along your path.

• **Serendipity/surprise/change within a context of constancy.** If a buffet offers only ordinary foods, or the same bill of fare every time you go, your visits are likely to be infrequent. At the same time, however, you don't want it to be completely different every visit. You hope to find some of the same items that you enjoyed the last time. The market place, too, should be dynamic, but not unstable. Window displays change with the seasons, as do the colors of flowers and foliage in the market place's public space. The "peoplescape" will vary with time of day. Some stores will go out of business, and new ones will take their place. Moreover, you don't want every market place to have exactly the same mix of shops and restaurants as every other market place. You want some things to be specific, individual, personal, peculiar to their locale.

The market place is not just the sum of the individual private spaces where exchange occurs. It is all these spaces plus the public space that either draws them into relationship with each other or keeps them apart—just as a person is not just the sum of the individual organs of the body, but also the blood vessels that feed them, the connective tissue that pulls them together, the pattern of organization that constitutes the difference between a collection of biomechanical devices and a living person.

The task of organizing the public space falls first to public entities—city governments, primarily—and secondarily to private developers. The multi-store shopping center, whether a small retail strip or a large enclosed mall or a huge mixed-use megastructure, may be understood as an attempt to create a well-organized public space—civil space, as defined in chapter 4—on private property. In compact downtowns and old inner-city neighborhood centers, small block sizes enforced, and the relatively minor role of automobiles allowed, a continuous building line close to the public right-of-way. Civil space was clearly defined and made coherent by the building line. A single building, no wider than one or two modestly sized storefronts, had only to take its place among others along that uniform line in order to be drawn fully into the social and economic ambit of the civil space. Any given block could accommodate a dozen or more buildings of widely varied architectural style, scale, and purpose, without in any way compromising the integrity of the civil space or lessening its value as a connective medium. But with the rising importance of the car and, thus, the parking lot and the large block, the building line broke up into dispersed fragments, and the public space became correspondingly diffuse, less civil. As streets were widened, sidewalks and parkways were made narrower. In this context, the only way to have even a localized semblance of a coherent civil space is for a private developer to create it, arbitrarily and artificially, on private property. The problem then, of course, is that it is rare for one developer's quasi-public civil space to connect with that in the next lot.

It is customary for inner-city partisans to turn up their noses at suburban shopping strips, malls, and megaprojects, but let's give credit where it's due: in a period when city governments had abdicated responsibility for creating a civil realm in the public space, private developers were, for self-interested reasons, undertaking essential research experiments to determine how the public space should be ordered in the age of the automobile. If public entities are to reenter the arena, as they should, they can learn a thing or two from the failures and successes of the private sector.

THE LESSON OF THE SHOPPING MALL: ECONOMIES OF FORM

In the late 1950s a developer in San Antonio had a good idea that turned out to be a dead end on the evolutionary path leading to the modern enclosed shopping mall. The developer reasoned that San Antonio's intense summer heat and occasionally nasty winters inhibited shopping. A strip shopping center would gain a competitive advantage if it could array a large number of stores along a climate-controlled sidewalk. So he built a conventional, straight-line strip center, with the stores facing the parking lot and a major thoroughfare, but he enclosed and air-conditioned the sidewalk. North Towne Plaza was a sensation when it opened. People enjoyed the novelty. But a few years later when the Rouse Company opened the city's first fully enclosed mall of the modern type, North Star Mall—in what was then a virtually unpopulated area at the outskirts of the city—the air-conditioned, single-loaded (in architectural jargon) sidewalk lost its allure. (In recent years, North Towne has become successful again with expansion, remodeling, and the elimination of the air-conditioned sidewalk.)

The reasons for this eclipse are less obvious than they appear to be. The shopping mall would seem to have violated conventional wisdom about retail location. Imagine yourself a shop owner in 1958. You have a successful business on a downtown street or in a suburban strip center. In either case, your store is exposed to passing traffic on the street. Retail space with more frontage on busier streets commanded higher rental rates than space with less frontage on marginal streets. More frontage on busier streets translated, other things being equal, to more customers.

So your store in 1958 has good frontage on a busy street. Now a real estate guy walks into your store, hands you his card, and says, "Have I got a deal for you!" He's gonna lease you some space with *no* street frontage, out in the middle of nowhere, and you'll pay more than you're paying now. It is not surprising that many retailers said no, to their subsequent regret. North Star Mall has consistently been among the best-performing shopping malls in America and has expanded to many times its original size.

According to the conventional wisdom of its (and our own) time, North Star Mall and its progeny should have been turned inside out. That is, the stores should have faced the street along an air-conditioned sidewalk in order to provide street frontage for the retailers. The next evolutionary step beyond North Towne Plaza should have been, according to this logic, back-to-back rows of stores connected by single-loaded sidewalks, with the storefronts facing two streets and a central axis for loading and support services. But that's not what happened. Why?

The reason has to do with what I call *economies of form*.

Imagine that you are the owner of the Village Bookstore. On a typical Saturday your store is a destination for a hundred customers. Now imagine that I own the Squeaky-Kleen Bath and Shower Stalle. On a typical Saturday my store is also a destination for a hundred customers. If it does not unreasonably challenge credulity, try to imagine that people who read also, on occasion, take baths or showers, and vice versa. By the luck of the draw, if our two stores are located anywhere on the same major thoroughfare in the same part of town, one or two of my customers might, after buying towels and shower curtains at my store, drive to your store to buy the complete works of Jung. That is, both our stores might have been on these customers' destination lists, but the number of destination customers that you and I share is likely to be quite small.

But suppose our stores are located next door to each other. In that case, I have an opportunity to entice your destination customers to enter *my* store, even if they had no prior interest in bath towels, and you have an opportunity to entice my destination customers to enter *your* store, even if they had no prior interest in Jung. Continue this pattern of mutual support several stores in either direction and you have the principle of the strip shopping center.

Now imagine a second pair of side-by-side stores—Val's Video and Pete's Pet Supply—that also support each other. Many people who rent videos also own pets. But many people who rent videos and own pets also read books and take showers. Thus, just as your bookstore and my bath supply store support each other, our two stores *together* could enter a reciprocal relationship with Val and Pete, to the advantage of all four of us. Where should Val and Pete locate their stores, in relation to ours, in order to optimize this reciprocal relationship?

To answer this question, put yourself in the position of one of Pete's customers. Sarah has driven to Pete's Pets to buy a new leash for her schnauzer. Perhaps the path from her car to Pete's front door has taken her past Val's, and she's stopped there to rent a couple of movies for the weekend. When she walks out of Pete's or Val's after completing her purchase, what does she see? Most often, in the typical pattern of retail development along major suburban roads, she sees a parking lot with several rows of cars, and beyond the parking lot a roadway with four or more lanes of traffic moving at about forty miles per hour. Visible on the other side of the roadway might be another parking lot with several rows of cars, and finally another line of storefronts, perhaps four hundred feet away from Pete's front door. Suppose my bath shop and your bookstore are in this strip center facing Val's and Pete's. As Sarah exits Pete's and heads to her car, how much information is she likely to glean about our shops four hundred feet away? Not much. She may be able to read the signs above our stores, and the names alone may arouse some degree of interest in learning more about what we have to offer. But will she be interested enough to cross the road? If she absolutely must have a new set of towels because she has houseguests coming from out of town, she might make the trek to my bath shop despite the physical and psychological obstacles. If her needs or desires are less pressing, she is unlikely to invest the time and effort required to cross the road.

But suppose my bath shop and your bookstore face Val's and Pete's at a distance of just sixty feet, across a two-lane street where traffic is moving at twenty miles an hour, and where regulated street crossings occur at frequent intervals—roughly the situation of University Avenue in Palo Alto. In this case, Sarah can gather considerably more information from the facing shop windows, and the investment required to investigate further is greatly reduced. She may cross the street even if she has only a very low level of commitment to books and towels—just enough interest to see if our shops have anything she might want, even though she doesn't really need it enough to make a special trip. And once inside our stores, she might buy something. Even if she doesn't, she may remember our shops (positively or negatively) when she needs to buy a book or a towel. She may even tell her friends about our places.

Thus one pair of mutually supportive stores (my bath shop and your bookstore) enters into a reciprocal relationship with another pair of such stores (Val's Video and Pete's Pets). Together, we are singing a quartet instead of two duets or four solos. All four stores contribute customers to the totality, and each store, being able to attract some of its neighbors' clientele, is better off than it would be in isolation from the others.

The advantage doesn't derive solely from the four stores' being close to each other—"close" being an imprecise and relative term—but from a set of physical relationships established by the visual acuity, psychological inertia, and physical stamina of the potential customer. If your bath shop and my bookstore hope to attract customers from Val's and Pete's, then our storefronts must be situated in such a way that (1) Val's and Pete's customers are highly likely to see them in enough detail to have their interest piqued and (2) the physical and psychological barriers in the customers' path to our doors are slight enough to compensate for low levels of interest in what we have to offer. In general, the greater the resistance the physical environment puts in the shopper's path, the greater the shopper's need or desire must be in order to overcome that resistance.

Now we're ready to see why the modern shopping mall is more successful than the strip center with an air-conditioned sidewalk. The strip center, with or without an air-conditioned sidewalk, is a single-loaded corridor, with shops that do not face other shops in any effective sense. Even when two strip centers face each other across a major thoroughfare, the intervening roadway and parking lots typically raise resistance to a level where the two strips cannot share customers with each other. The shopping mall, however, is laid out as a *double-loaded corridor*, with shops facing each other across a not-too-wide hallway. The double-loaded shopping mall at least doubles the number of shops the customer can easily see and visit on the way to or from a destination store. The shopping mall has the advantage in economy of form. The physical arrangement of businesses in relation to each other and to pedestrian paths permits the most efficient exchange of information (and money) between businesses and potential customers.

The shopping mall holds valuable lessons for us as we try to reconsider how best to lay out the public pathways of a city. Is it possible to duplicate in the city streets the economies of form that we see in the shopping mall? The answer is an obvious yes, because the question discloses a deep irony of the post-1960 American city: The shopping mall sought to duplicate—but only inside its walls—the economies of form that had been typical of American downtowns and neighborhood centers. The pedestrian-level scale, geography, and retail mix of a large shopping mall are, in general outline, like the pedestrian-level scale, geography, and retail mix of a traditional downtown or neighborhood retail district. The shopping mall does not, of course, come near to duplicating the multiplicity of uses, the visual complexity, or the dynamism of a traditional downtown or neighborhood center, but in general form they are much alike.

BEYOND THE SHOPPING MALL

It does not follow, however, that cities would magically regain their vibrancy if only they would concentrate all of their retail businesses into shopping malls. As they are most often conceived and designed, shopping malls exclude or are incompatible with many kinds of useful commerce—grocery stores or public libraries (which are a kind of nonprofit retailer), for example. Rental rates, and thus volume sales requirements, are typically too high for many kinds of innovative, independent, or start-up retailers. While shopping malls are usually laid out for excellent economies of form on the inside, they typically set up high impedances at their peripheries. A suburban mall entrance is almost never integrated with the pedestrian matrix of the surrounding neighborhood, even when the neighborhood includes thousands of apartment dwellers within an easy walk of the mall. You don't just happen to find yourself in a shopping mall; you really have to want to go there. Most troublingly, if all the retailers were in shopping malls, no retailers would be anywhere else, and, as we have seen, retailers are essential components of healthy neighborhoods.

But the market place is not just about shopping. It is also about socializing. It is about every kind of persuading, from the political to the religious to the amorous. It is about reflection and recreation. And while a geographic orderliness is important to the functioning of the market place, a degree of social disorder is also essential.

Not long ago a young communications student and public-access TV producer named Hondo Aguilar took his video camera and a few friends—all jocular, unthreatening types—to a San Antonio shopping mall. After taping for a short while, they were accosted by a security guard, who, in distinctly humorless tones, insisted that they turn off the camera. I had a similar experience with my still camera—not at an enclosed shopping mall but at a large shopping center composed of factory outlet stores and designed (very well) to emulate the atmosphere, scale, and streetscape of a traditional town center. A security guard asked me to obtain permission from the front office before taking more pictures.

There are more or less legitimate reasons for the no-camera rule in such settings—to prevent burglars from casing the joint, to defend a developer's trade secrets, to protect the privacy of customers. Well, actually, the reasons are flimsy, but property owners have the right to make the rules in their private realms.

And that is the point. Private realms, however open to the public they may be, are no substitute for the public realm. In the public realm of a free country, anyone may take photographs of anything or anyone without fear of legal hindrance. Bans on picture-taking—or distribution of religious tracts and political propaganda, or fundraising for charities not authorized by the mall management, or mere high-spiritedness—in the quasi-public space of shopping malls leave one with a vague feeling of resentment, or bring to mind visions of Red Square in the (not so) old days. Similarly, any legal business may have direct access to the public realm (with geographic limits imposed by zoning regulations) without regard to some preconceived retail mix. Stores, banks, small manufacturers, lawyers, restaurants, churches, schools, political campaign headquarters, street-corner preachers, libraries, parks and playgrounds, theaters and homes—all are linked into a mutually supportive and mutually influential ensemble by a healthy civil space. Information of many kinds flows freely. But when the public realm is supplanted by a succession of small private realms of limited functional and stylistic scope, the market place is fragmented. Exchanges of one sort are segregated from exchanges of another sort. If only some kinds of products, some kinds of ideas, some kinds of decorative or marketing concepts, and some kinds of people are permitted access to the quasi-public space of a shopping mall, then other kinds are excluded, shunted off into other, separate environs. This segregation of exchange brings with it a conservative, consolidating tendency that partially nullifies the dynamic, creative, dialectical function of the market place.

But the dialectical function of the market place is nullified with equal effectiveness in the chaotic public realm of suburbia outside the shopping mall. At least the shopping mall, for all its limitations, benefits from economies of form and scale. Outside the mall, the post-1960 suburban market place fails all of the criteria for a buffet listed near the beginning of this chapter. Let's review that list to see how the normal suburban pattern falls short and, conversely, what traits need to be built into the well-formed market place, whether in a suburban or urban setting:

• **Variety/range/competition.** In order for a market place to offer great breadth or depth in products, ideas, and knowledge, it must be accessible to people who will buy those goods in sufficient quantity to keep the rent paid. Suburban dispersion of both potential customers and commercial districts suppresses effective demand for the unusual and thus reduces the availability of the unusual. Indeed, even demand for the usual is suppressed in diffuse suburban environments.

A pair of contrasting examples may explain what I mean. As a music critic, I buy a lot of compact discs, and my needs and tastes do not necessarily run parallel to the mass market's. San Antonio's biggest record store, a Blockbuster located on a major commercial road that passes between low-density residential subdivisions, is limited in its classical and jazz offerings. Eighty miles away in Austin, a city with about half San Antonio's population, Tower Records opened a store on The Drag, the commercial and entertainment strip across the street from the huge University of Texas at Austin. Here, the jazz and classical offerings are far larger and deeper, more intelligently organized, and more reasonably priced.

Probably the two cities are about equal in the number of people who buy classical and jazz CDs, and about equal in their total college-student populations, but Austin has this signal advantage. A lot of its students and CD-collectors are concentrated in and near the high-density university neighborhood where Tower Records is located, and most of them can easily walk to the store without departing very far from their normal routines— without having to make a special trip by car. (The store doesn't even have its own customer lot. The Blockbuster in San Antonio has ample free parking at the front door.) Concentration provides access to high sales volume, and high sales volume enables the store to stock items with limited appeal. In the more diffuse environment of San Antonio, which has no high-density university neighborhoods, a store like Tower Records would face an uphill battle.

Concentration is especially important in fostering variety in intellectual commerce—not just record stores, but bookstores, video and software emporia, theaters, art galleries and religious spas, and the informal exchanges of ideas that occur on sidewalks, park benches and bar stools.

• **Density/continuity/immediacy.** The characteristics that give the shopping mall and the traditional downtown their economies of form are wholly lacking in most suburban commercial districts. The chief culprit is the parking lot, which—in the most common approach to site planning—interrupts the continuity of the market place, reduces its density, and holds potential customers at a distance from the things they might want to buy. Immediacy of contact between people and points of exchange is further eroded by the mistaken assumption, expressed in site design and location planning, that people driving in automobiles at forty miles an hour will be mysteriously attracted to stores that are separated from the road by a hundred or two hundred feet of parking lot.

A few years ago, the San Antonio Police Department reinstituted foot patrols in certain areas of the city. A TV news report on the change included a brief interview with a patrol officer who cogently explained the advantage that feet have over cars. Driving in a patrol car, the officer said, she found that she was insulated and distant from the life of the city. Her ability to observe, to notice departures from the norm or incipient problems, was impaired by her enclosure in the automobile. The automobile created a physical and a psychological barrier between her and the people she was charged with protecting, the people from whom she must gain information. If the automobile inhibits the observational and interactive abilities of police officers, for whom observation and interaction are central to their jobs, then it must all the more inhibit the observational and interactive abilities of ordinary people as they go about their ordinary routines.

Retailers on major roads attempt to compensate for this distancing effect by erecting the big, tall signs that are so widely disliked on aesthetic grounds. The familiar forests of commercial signs *are* an aesthetic disaster, but, worse than that, they are effective only as symbols that can trigger a memory of something already known. The roadside sign has little practical ability to convey information about the unfamiliar. A pair of yellow—oops, "golden"— parabolic arches says nothing in itself about the restaurant whose presence is indicated, but it is an effective sign because the symbol of the arches has been attached to a meaning through print and television advertising, or through previous experiences at other McDonald's locations. You know what to expect. Suppose, however, that one of your neighbors, Betty, decided to open a hamburger restaurant across the road from McDonald's. What does she put on her sign? Because the venture is new and your neighbor can't afford a big advertising campaign, no mere symbol would be meaningful. Passersby would not have had the opportunity to attach the symbol to information about the restaurant. A picture of a hamburger, or the word "HAMBURGERS," might help, because everyone already knows what a hamburger is, but this stratagem can convey nothing about what is distinctive or innovative or noteworthy about Betty's burgers as opposed to Bob's or Bill's or Beulah's. If Betty has an unusual concept that can be imparted in two or three words—"Betty's Buffalo Burgers"—she has a chance to gain attention, but if she just serves a good burger with no gimmicks, her sign can't easily get that message across.

By contrast, if Betty and McDonald's are located near each other on an urban street with lots of pedestrians, she would have much better chances. A pedestrian walking past her storefront can gain considerable information, quickly, by glancing at the menu posted by the door, eyeing the food being served to tables by the window, or even sniffing the air. Because of this immediacy, new information can counterbalance the already known. The sign in this context is of minor importance. Certainly nothing is to be gained by mounting a huge sign ninety feet in the air, where pedestrians can't see it anyway.

For these reasons, the low density, discontinuity, and distance that characterize the suburban market place suppress competition, innovation, individuality, and variety. The small entrepreneur with a good idea cannot, except in highly unusual circumstances, gain a foothold on the busy commercial corridor. If a city hopes to maintain the dynamism of its economy and productive, creative capacity, then it must have places where such small local entrepreneurs can establish themselves and have a reasonable opportunity to compete with the big chains. It must have functional, lively, neighborhood-oriented market places that are not entirely auto-dominant.

• Security/comfort/invitation. Short of elbow-to-elbow crowds, the best security for people is more people. One feels less safe in a deserted parking lot or walking past vacant buildings or blank walls than one feels in the company of others, even strangers who appear to be going about their ordinary, honest business. To be secure, the public realm needs to have enough honest people around to discourage dishonest people from doing their thing—people walking in the public realm and people observing the public realm from their private realms of stores, offices, and homes. To feel secure in the public realm, we want to see places of refuge at frequent intervals—a store or theater or restaurant or other place of honest activity that we can duck into if we detect a threat in the public realm. Thus the mix of land uses and business types must be such that there is activity in the market place throughout the day, from morning until late at night. Moreover, we want to increase the amount of time that our honest fellow citizens spend in the public realm, so that we may decrease the opportunities for criminals to operate unobserved. We want the public realm to have value as a place for strolling, relaxation, conversation, and play, not to be just a blank space between private realms. The reality and the perception of security are enhanced if the public realm is designed and equipped to invite frequent, extended use, not merely to permit it grudgingly.

Clearly, the usual way of developing suburban property today violates these principles of security. The far reaches of large parking lots, beyond the observation range of the businesses they serve, are fertile fields for crimes against persons and property. Even if the occasional developer creates a welcoming pedestrian environment to connect storefronts within his own project, the stroll is usually interrupted at the property line. (In San Antonio, the property line is often an occasion for a drainage ditch, a fence, or a steep retaining wall at a grade change.) Continuity of pedestrian movement where we want people to be, a step or two away from places where they might want to go, is next to impossible. Moreover, most of the pedestrian environment in suburban commercial areas is distinctly uninviting, a tortuous and disorienting path past parking lots, Dumpsters, and drainage ditches, bereft of shade or solace or places to sit and chat and observe the passing scene. There is no reason for people to be in the public realm longer than absolutely necessary to dash from their cars to the stores where they're headed. Fewer people spending less time in the public realm translates to less security for the people who *are* there.

• **Progression/slow movement.** If I own a store, I want passersby to pass by my window slowly enough to see what I have to sell. Some people will come to the market place just to visit my store, perhaps, but I also want

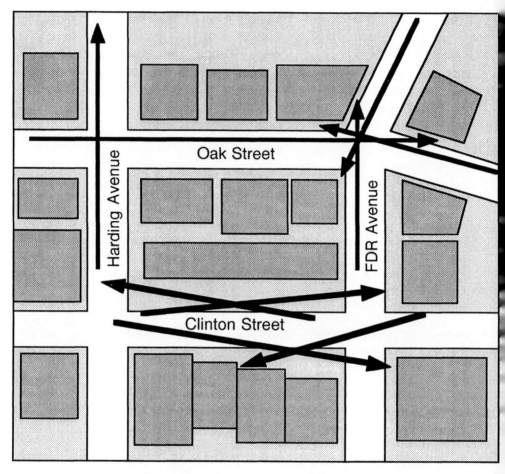

Figure 8.1   The visual terminus is a magnet for pedestrians and motorists.

to be noticed by the larger number of people who came to the market place to visit other stores. That means I want people to move around within the market place—to stroll—and to stroll within a few feet of my window. I want the market place to be designed in such a way that people will want to stroll, and I want the pace of the stroll to be moderately slow.

People won't stroll unless they feel they're getting someplace and they detect, not too far ahead, a someplace to get to. They have to encounter spatial events that are interesting enough and frequent enough to justify the investment in time and energy required to stroll. If people have no reason to expect the next hundred yards to interest them, they have no motivation to continue the stroll.

In chapter 5 we talked about architectural rhythm as a device to enliven the pedestrian's sense of movement along the sidewalk and to sustain the momentum of the stroll. To expand the musical analogy, the market place also needs cadences, melodic contours, episodes of distinctive texture, and an overall structural shape that implies and leads to a climax or resolution—all of which can be understood as higher-order rhythmic events. For example, the market place needs visual termini, destinations that beckon from a distance of two or three blocks. In figure 8.1, the twisted intersection at FDR Avenue has advantages over the strictly right-angled intersection on the left. In the twisted intersection, the lines of sight (indicated by arrows) are terminated by buildings or parks or strategically placed monuments, giving the intersection a visual importance that it would not otherwise have—assuming that the opportunity is exploited by the architects of the properties at the four corners. Even where the streets form strict right angles, a pseudo-terminus can be created with building setbacks, as along Clinton Street in the drawing. An angled or staggered setback, as on the south side of Clinton Street, can lend a sense of direction and procession to the public room of the street.

The visual terminus is a magnet for pedestrians, but they still need a well-spaced sequence of events, localized exceptions to the standard commercial environment, to measure their progress toward the terminus and provide distinctive landmarks that remind them where they are in relation to the whole. One would not want three or four uninterrupted blocks of commercial storefronts of roughly uniform scale and architectural style. At strategic points the well-formed market place introduces exceptions to the norm along the pathway—a vest-pocket park, a conspicuous change in scale or setback, a noncommercial land use such as a museum or library or apartment building, a well-preserved historic structure in the midst of newer buildings, a sidewalk café, a grouping of benches and trees.

One cautionary note: It is essential that the market place, or at least substantial portions of it, have a norm to deviate from. A profusion of discrete, unrelated events is just noise. The well-formed market place establishes a range of expectations for scale, rhythm, style, setback, landscaping, and so on. At strategic points, here and there, it violates those expectations in a pleasant (or at least not repugnant) way.

• **Serendipity/surprise/change within a context of constancy.** This point is related but not identical to the preceding one. Previously we were concerned with the way more or less permanent fixtures of the built environment modulate and direct pedestrian movement along the pathways of the market place. Here we focus on change over fairly short periods of time within the physical space, so that successive visits to the same public place do not result in exactly the same experience. But such change depends at least in part on the built environment. Some design decisions are congenial to change and varieties of experience; others aren't.

A healthy market place has a good balance of local and national, specialty and mass-market, upscale and downscale, normal and weird retailers (or other exchange sites), and thus it must have suitable places to put this variety. In practical terms, a healthy market place mixes large and small spaces and high and low rental rates that can be supported by a mix of high and low sales volumes. Its stores have display windows, so that the pedestrian experience changes periodically with the display. Its sidewalks can accommodate clothing racks, bargain tables, and easels posting a restaurant's daily specials.

While most of the public space would be linear pathways, the design of some special places would encourage, or at least allow, people to use the places in varied ways, at varied paces. In the modern suburban environment, physical opportunities for serendipity and change in the peoplescape are hard to come by except, in a controlled and limited way, in the shopping mall. At best, a retail strip may include landscaping and benches along the arcade that connects the storefronts, but these amenities are intended exclusively for the customers of that specific retail project. Typically, the privately controlled exterior pathways of modern suburbia consist of short, unconnected linear fragments, and there is no usable public space in the interstices between the private spaces. For the most part, privately controlled exterior pathways are overdetermined. The unmistakable message is Do your business and be on your way.

The challenge for the suburban market place is to create a public (or at least common) realm that can support serendipity, surprise, and change along the pedestrian pathways. The first task, of course, is to align and connect the pathway fragments of the many private domains so that they form a usable pathway system. But it is equally important to design into the market place contradictions and complements to the general linearity of the pathways—places that are not tightly programmed for linear movement alone, but that are more open-ended in their use while remaining perceptually a part of the pathway system. That's a complicated way of saying parks and plazas, if these terms are understood to include areas that may be as large as a city block or as small as a wide place in the sidewalk.

In downtown Palo Alto, which I grant is an older and urban-style suburb but one with ample parking in municipal off-street lots, one corner of University Avenue, the main shopping and restaurant strip, is dedicated to a small plaza that serves as a focal point for the market place. There is nothing grand or pretentious about this plaza. One side is bounded by a very nice building that, if you look closely at the small neon signs in the windows, turns out to be a Burger King restaurant with a few outdoor tables on the plaza. A flower vendor's cart is usually stationed next to the sidewalk on the plaza. There are a few places to sit and a little landscaping—nothing very remarkable in itself. But this plaza is tremendously beneficial. First, it creates a major cadence, a punctuation in the middle of the five or six blocks' walk past storefronts of similar scale—a change of pace, a chance to recharge psychic batteries. Second, the plaza provides an informal gathering place, slightly apart from but attached to the main pedestrian pathways, for people young and old. Such places are especially important for the young, who tend to cluster in sizable groups for sociability. The plaza provides a place for sociability that doesn't interfere with commerce or pedestrian movement. Third, the plaza is a convenient site for community celebrations.

The plaza would work less well if it were much larger, and thus less intimate and less engaged with the main pedestrian pathways at its edges, or

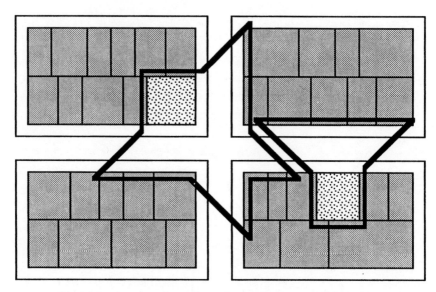

Figure 8.2 A corner plaza affects a larger area than a midblock plaza.

much smaller, and thus less able to accommodate so wide a range of activity. The corner location is an important element in its success. Compare, in figure 8.2, the corner plaza and the midblock plaza. The heavy lines indicate roughly the area of influence of each plaza. The midblock plaza is visible to fewer buildings and a far smaller amount of sidewalk; it can capture the attention of people walking directly past it on its own or the opposite side of one street. Being more enclosed, it is likely to feel less safe, because observable to fewer passersby than the corner plaza. The corner plaza would have an even greater influence over its market place if the streets were slightly skewed to make the plaza a visual terminus, and the plaza's value as the focal point for the market place would be further enhanced if some important cultural or public activity—a library or museum or theater—were part of the mix of uses fronting on the plaza.

That is not to say that all open spaces and departures from the norm in a market place must occupy corner locations or be of civic scale. On the blocks leading to the market place center, the pedestrian's progress can be enlivened by the occasional narrow courtyard leading to a restaurant or

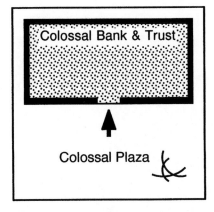 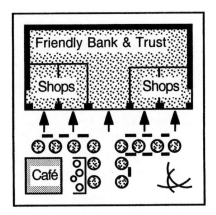

Figure 8.3   The nearly bare plaza on the left is a void in the urban fabric. Differentiation of the space to define areas of passage and repose, as in the plaza on the right, can transform a void into a dynamic, lively civic place.

apartment building, or by a tiny park consisting of one or two tree-shaded benches and a bit of hedge on a wide place in the sidewalk or at the triangle where a diagonal street meets the main grid.

It is important that larger plazas be differentiated internally so they are not just big blank expanses of Italian marble. Consider, for example, the two plazas (hypothetical but drawn from the real world) in figure 8.3. Colossal Plaza is a big, mostly blank space, differentiated only by the big outdoor sculpture (by a Famous Artist) on the corner and the monumental entrance to the banking lobby and office tower (by a Famous Architect) in the middle of the facade. What can people do in that space? They can scurry across it to and from the building entrance, they can pause to admire the sculpture, and kids can use the plaza for skateboarding if they aren't shooed away by security guards, but that's about the extent of it. Happily, Colossal Bank & Trust went belly-up during the banking crisis of the 1980s, and its assets were bought for $37.98 by Friendly Bank & Trust, which had the plaza redesigned to get more cash flow from the real estate. In the new Friendly Plaza, trees organize the space to help define pathways, benches are placed under the trees, and a café with outdoor seating occupies one corner. On the building itself, the formerly blank walls flanking the entrance are opened up to create storefronts, with doors and display windows facing the plaza. By these means a passive and static space has been transformed into an active and dynamic place. Trees and flowering plants were chosen to change colors with the seasons. The storefronts generate additional pedestrian traffic on the plaza. The office workers use the benches for brown-bag lunches in good weather. The café draws customers from both the Friendly Tower and the surrounding area. The outdoor tables keep the plaza in use and under observation during the lunch hour and perhaps the late-afternoon happy hour and dinner. The outdoor dining area also provides a visual diversion for people walking by on the sidewalk or the plaza and, so long as the tables are occupied, reassures pedestrians that the plaza is safe and welcoming.

The trees and benches divide a formerly intimidating, overscaled space into more intimate, human-scaled spaces that may be used in different ways without, however, being tightly programmed or overdetermined. The tree-lined corridor on the axis with the main entrance has the character of a passageway, for coming and going. The long space across the front of the building serves both movement (to the storefronts and the tower entrance) and what might be called purposeful leisure. The tree-shaded benches invite sitting to eat a sandwich or wait for a friend, but the feeling of relaxation is mitigated by the passagelike linearity of the space, the commercial storefronts facing the benches, and the directed comings and goings of people. The corner area by the sculpture, on the other hand, stands apart from pedestrian routes and business entrances, and the benches form a kind of amphitheater with the sculpture as a focal point. This is the area where lovers are most likely to meet and sit for a while after work or during the lunch hour, where tourists and downtown workers from other buildings will stop to relax and observe the passing scene, where (if the security guards don't chase them away) street musicians will sing and artists set up their easels.

FALSE DICHOTOMIES

Talk of street musicians, public art, lovers' trysts, and the design of plazas inevitably leads policy debate into a counterproductive byway, the supposed distinction between essentials and amenities, function and aesthetics. The very term *urban design* is widely misunderstood—by both doubters and proponents—as being about aesthetics, which the doubters dismiss as expendable. This conceptual error is deeply rooted in American culture.

When Americans think of the word *design*, they tend to think of ornamentation—something added to the basic product (house, car, TV set, etc.) to make it prettier or more fashionable. American manufacturing practice tends to think of design as *styling*. Design is shunted into the artsy-craftsy realm of aesthetics, a realm that is frivolous, superficial, and morally suspect.

This attitude has its roots in certain Christian (mainly Protestant) traditions, in which virtue is exemplified by simplicity, modesty, and suspicion of sensual pleasure; and in Platonic idealism, which asserts that the things of this world are more or less inexact manifestations of their *essences*—that, for example, there is such a thing as "essence of chair" to which the human-made chair I am now sitting on inevitably fails to measure up.

What does all this have to do with cities? Modern American discourse on city policy is conditioned by the same polarity between essence and appearance. The services that city governments provide are customarily divided into "essential services" and, by implication, "inessential services"—that is, services that are assumed to be *of the essence* of city government and services that are assumed to be luxuries. Capital improvements are similarly divided between those that are assumed to be functionally necessary *infrastructure*, such as roadways, sewers, and jails, and those that are assumed to be *amenities*, such as parks, theaters, and public art. Furthermore, infrastructure is usually deemed to be the exclusive turf of engineers, who are expected to lay out their projects according to strictly objective, functional, "essential" standards; aesthetic considerations are incidental or extra. The same polarity affects the regulatory framework governing private property. Those types of regulation deemed important for safety and health are found almost universally and are strictly enforced. These "essential" regulations are seen as different in kind from regulations setting standards for landscaping, signs, and historic preservation.

Much of the private sector—which, after all, builds most of the walls that bound the public space—is also governed by the perceived polarity between essence and amenity. Lending institutions dismiss as "architectural embellishment" anything beyond the shell of a commercial building. It is fairly easy to obtain a loan for the plain box, but lenders are reluctant to risk the slight extra cost of architectural embellishment to make the box and its environs more attractive and functional for customers.

In this regard, the modern shopping mall is again a source of instruction. The shopping mall, in its interior at least, is a spectacular exception to the essence-appearance polarity. The common space of a shopping mall is not a bare-bones, strictly "functional" cattle chute. Every successful mall is stuffed with trees and flowers, fountains, benches, sculpture, decorative paving, stylish graphics, fancy light fixtures, colorful banners—all manner of things that are not in any way "essential" to the common space's engineering function of allowing shoppers to walk from one store to the next in a climate-controlled environment. But the people who build and design shopping malls know, from research and practical experience, that these amenities *are* essential to the mall's function as a market place, and thus to the mall's financial performance. The visual diversions in the common space establish the mall's identity as a distinctive and desirable place, one that people will want to come to, and stroll through, even if they have no particular purchases in mind. The amenities support the mall's value as a place of socializing, recreation, and amusement. People of all ages go there to meet friends, exercise, have fun, and, in a very nonspecific way, see what's new in the world, not solely to buy something. But much of the mall's success depends on its ability to convert—on the spot—strollers into buyers. The more people are drawn to the mall for whatever reasons, the more frequently they come, the longer they stay, the more extended their stroll, the more likely they are to spend money and to spend it in more shops.

The shopping mall's environment can be criticized for being excessively contrived and, for all its lushness, antiseptic. It remains nonetheless a brilliant confirmation of the principle that the extrafunctional features of the common space—whether the private realm of the shopping mall or the public realm of streets and sidewalks—have a palpable (if not precisely measurable) effect on the propensity of people to engage in exchange at the many private places that the public space connects. Another way to say the same thing is this: the common-space amenities that make a shopping mall a desirable destination for potential shoppers, irrespective of the offerings of the many individual stores, *create value* for the mall's tenants. By extension, investment in common-space amenities creates value—more, usually, than the cost of the amenities—for the mall's owner, because tenants that sell more goods pay more rent.

Ordinary commercial districts outside the shopping malls do not, of course, have the benefit of mall management to create value for them in the common space. But I would argue that municipal governments are, in effect, mall management. The task of shaping and maintaining the common space in a way that creates value for private businesses falls necessarily and justifiably to city governments—necessarily, because, except in rare and geographically limited exceptions, no single private property owner controls the common space in an entire commercial district; justifiably, because property taxes and sales taxes yield most of the revenues that municipalities depend on to provide services for their citizens. Public investments or regulations that increase taxable value and sales serve the municipality's financial interest. City governments should not be timid about defining and fulfilling their responsibilities as market place management.

The first task is to designate and specify the boundaries of market places, which may be called by many names—neighborhood centers, urban villages, and so on. Money being a limited commodity, few cities can afford to dress the entire public realm in shopping-mall finery. We have to choose our targets strategically. Furthermore, except in areas of Manhattan-like population density, market places are most sustainable, approachable, and efficient in their use of land and resources when they form concentrated clusters rather than stretching out continuously along the road network. In the interest of public convenience and necessity, it makes sense for city governments, in consultation with private developers, civic groups, and neighborhood associations, to decide where those clusters should be and what types of land use should be permitted in or excluded from them. As a corollary, some types of land uses that are permitted within market places might have to be prohibited or limited outside them.

Some may object that, even before the advent of modern zoning codes, urban commercial frontage tended to coalesce into linear corridors along the major thoroughfares, and that zoning for commercial corridors merely ratified what had been happening naturally in cities. This formation could be clearly seen in many cities' 1920s land-use maps, including the map of San Antonio.[1] On the surface, it would seem that commercial *corridor* zoning is more "traditional" than commercial *node* zoning is. But detailed examination reveals that retail activity—grocers, meat markets, bakeries, clothing and hardware stores, beauty parlors, theaters, etc.—did tend to concentrate into short (quarter-mile or so) segments or, at the intersection of major thoroughfares, into cross-shaped nodes.

Because major thoroughfares tended to be spaced only a mile or so apart, these nodes were close to each other; with distribution and supply companies or offices often located along major thoroughfares between the nodes, a land-use map consisting of dots representing commercial sites would make it appear that commercial activity formed more or less homogeneous and continuous corridors. That isn't how the city actually worked, however. Furthermore, differences in scale can produce differences in kind. A linear array of twenty commercial sites in a span of three hundred feet, with ten stores on each side of a two-lane street, yields very different results in actual use from a linear array of twenty commercial sites within a span of twelve hundred feet, with ten stores on each side of a five-lane road. The first, though organized linearly, still counts as a node because all the front doors are close enough to each other, both laterally and orthogonally, to constitute a walkable, mutually supportive ensemble. The strategic error of most zoning ordinances was in failing to recognize the nodal differentiation of land uses that, at a high level of abstraction, seemed homogeneously linear. The error was compounded, paradoxically, by minimum-setback requirements and off-street parking standards that militated even against linearity. The well-formed market place, like the shopping mall, is both nodal and linear—nodal in the sense that consumer activity sites coalesce into a small and walkable geographic area; linear in the sense that, within that concentrated area, activity sites array themselves along shortest-distance paths, or straight lines. The best way to characterize the well-formed market place might be *nodal linearity*.

Once market places have been designated by the zoning code and drawn on the map as overlay zoning districts, cities can apply numerous planning and capital improvements tools to help assure their success:

• Design (or reserve the right of design approval for) the internal pedestrian traffic pattern, street layout, public spaces, and landscaping standards within the market place, including specification of build-to lines and the relation of building entrances to the pedestrian pathways. That is, make sure the designated market places are organized in a way that is both linear and nodal.

• Use the zoning code as a tool to concentrate high-density residential and office populations in or within easy walking distance of the market place.

• Specify street (including pedestrian) connections between the market place and surrounding residential districts.

• Adopt off-street parking standards that favor the sharing of parking lots among property owners, make optimal use of parking spaces, and minimize parking lot frontage along the main pedestrian pathways. For cities whose development standards generally require large numbers of off-street parking spaces, a relaxation of those standards within market places can be an incentive for some kinds of businesses to locate there and avoid spending money on unproductive asphalt.

• As appropriate complements to commercial and residential uses, provide market places with parks, plazas, cultural facilities, libraries, public art, and public services such as police substations, clinics, and mini–city halls. The idea is to give people a lot of different reasons to go to the market place, to extend their strolls within it, to stay longer than is absolutely necessary to buy the item for which they might have come, and thus to increase the likelihood that they will engage in more exchanges and other kinds of exchanges. These public investments need not, in most cases, represent extraordinary spending but simply a more careful targeting of the capital improvements that would be built in any case.

• Locate and design traffic signals, pedestrian crosswalks, vehicular traffic patterns, drainage, and utilities in such a way as to minimize resistance to pedestrian movement within the market place or between the market place and the surrounding area.

• Adopt special sign standards suited to the pedestrian character of designated market places.

• Raise the visibility of market places as transit destinations by locating major transit facilities or transfer stations in market places and by featuring them prominently in printed transit schedules, route maps, and marketing programs.

• Where practicable, create bicycle routes and linear parks to connect market places with each other or with major institutions and employment centers.

All of these mall management design features are a lot easier and less costly to accomplish if they are planned into new development before the earthmovers get to work. Each project that is built in the absence of a unifying plan forecloses some of the options available to the public to create a coherent market place. When all the land in a particular part of town has been developed, all of the options have been eliminated, short of expensive, difficult, and fractious retrofitting that may require condemnation proceedings.

To some degree, however, the necessity for retrofitting is a fact of urban life that local governments have to accept, with or without planning for coherent neighborhoods. Social, economic, and technological conditions change, leaving behind even well-planned (for their time) older neighborhood centers. In its role as mall management, a city needs to be prepared to recognize the implications of change and to respond to it. But retrofitting is much easier and less costly in market places whose fundamental organization and economies of form reflect the unchanging physical constants of the human body than in those that do not. Smart shopping mall owners continuously respond to changing market conditions and consumer preferences by turning big stores into little stores or little stores into big stores or by launching such innovations as food courts and vendor carts. But it is not necessary to change the fundamental structure of the shopping mall because it is based on enduring principles. Similarly, older, down-at-heels neighborhood centers in the inner city require freshening up, renovation, replacement of nearby housing stock to rebuild a concentrated customer base, and some reconfiguration to satisfy modern needs, but if their fundamental pedestrian-oriented structure is retained they have a leg up on revival.

The shopping mall works because it was designed to work. The shopping mall, like the traditional city streets of older urban neighborhoods, is not a free-for-all but a coherent framework into which many private, individual stores must fit for their mutual benefit and the convenience of their customers. The framework of a shopping mall is created, maintained, and, as necessary, altered and expanded by the mall's management. Who will be mall management for market places outside the mall? That responsibility falls naturally to the planning and zoning functions of local government.

THE WELL-FORMED MARKET PLACE

By way of illustrating the general principles examined in this chapter, let's construct, in a rough schematic way, a hypothetical market place. We'll assume a fairly common situation on the suburban periphery. At the intersection of two roads, three quadrants have been developed as subdivisions of single-family detached houses. More such subdivisions (or perhaps an apartment complex or two) occupy the fourth quadrant at some distance from the corner, but a sizable tract—about two hundred acres in figure 8.4—has been reserved for commercial use.

In the normal course of events, if the entire tract is not master-planned by a single developer, the land would be subdivided into many parcels of varying size, each developed independently. Large uses such as supermarkets and discount stores might occupy the interior, with fast-food restaurants, retail strips, and auto-service facilities placed along the roads. Typically the fronts of the big stores would face the backs of the businesses along the roads, with large parking lots and perhaps an internal street between them. The result is usually chaos and congestion because of insufficient and discontinuous internal pathways, the proliferation of driveways along the main roads, and the lack of direct links, either for drivers or pedestrians, between the commercial district and the residential areas that house its nearest potential customers.

Let's propose a departure from the normal course of events—not a revolutionary departure, but a modest and evolutionary one. Rather than just letting things happen randomly, let's design a public framework within which private projects can occur in a mutually beneficial way.

We'll begin by positing a center, a focal point, for the market place

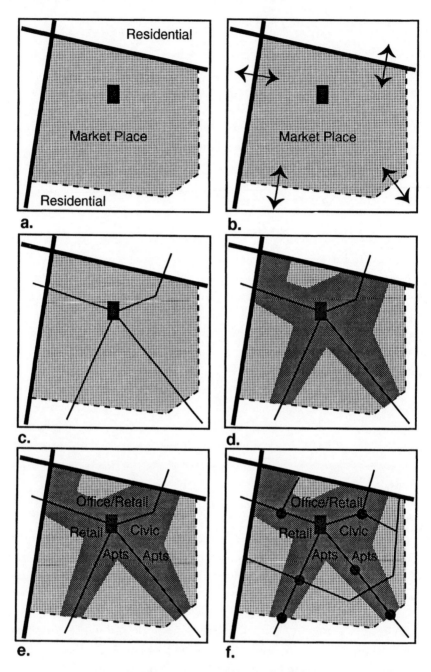

Figure 8.4 Stages in the conceptual planning of a well-formed neighborhood market place: the focal point (a), points of contact with surrounding residential areas (b), links from the periphery to the center (c), areas of high and low density (d), land-use zoning (e), and internal street connections and secondary focal points (f).

(the dark rectangle in figure 8.4a). The center is an open space of public, civic character. Although people may cross the center on their way to some other place, and indeed the center must be located at a junction of pathways in order to be most effective, its primary function is not to be a pathway. The center is a place of gathering and celebration, assignation and rest, greeting and conversation and play. This space need not, and usually should not, be grand or imposing. It should be where the people are, at the routine crossing of their paths. A variety of activities should impinge on the center—stores, offices, restaurants with outdoor seating in suitable climates, apartments, perhaps a theater or a library. The central space should be designed and situated in such a way as to beckon pedestrians from a distance of a few blocks and to invite lingering once they are there. There should be trees and places to sit and open spaces where civic groups may set up voter-registration tables or skateboarders practice their art.

We also need points of local entry (figure 8.4b) between the market place and adjacent residential subdivisions—or, for that matter, apartment complexes, business parks, or large institutions. We want the surrounding developments to have streets leading to the market place, and if the path to the market place must cross a road, we want the resulting intersection to be designed and regulated in such a way as to allow people easily and safely across. Of course the major roads and their sidewalks are also passageways into the market place, and figure 8.4 assumes the presence of a suitable pedestrian environment along the roads bordering the market place.

The next step is to lay out internal streets, sidewalks, and pedestrian ways connecting the points of entry with the center (figure 8.4c). These are the market place's primary pathways. In the diagram, the pathways converge in such a way that buildings or other large features in or around the central public space terminate views down the pathways from the market place's periphery. As we have already seen, in order for a pathway to function as a pathway it has to be defined and bounded, and it has to connect the places that people want to go to. It follows, then, that most of the stores, offices, apartments, and cultural facilities in the market place should have their front doors on (or very close to) the primary pathways. The amoeba-shaped shaded area in figure 8.4d represents the market place's destinations scrunched up toward the primary internal pathways, which thus become double-loaded corridors like those in a shopping mall. The remaining lightly shaded areas, removed from the internal pathways, are where we might put large land-hungry businesses such as supermarkets, discount stores, nurseries, and movie theater complexes; road-oriented facilities such as auto-service businesses or fire stations; and large parking lots, although small parking areas and on-street parking should be scattered throughout the market place.

The amoeba in figure 8.4d reaches one arm to the corner formed by the major thoroughfares. This refinement has less to do with the internal function of the market place than with the way the market place engages the rest of the city and passing traffic. In typical modern practice this corner would be reserved for parking, and businesses—even a stand-alone convenience store or branch bank that might occupy a corner pad site—would be set well back from the streets. I would argue that more businesses need to be placed close to the corner, with their front doors and display windows oriented to the sidewalks along the major thoroughfares. First, the only chance drivers have to spend time looking at what the market place offers is when they are stopped at a red light; we want to put some information about the market place close to where drivers are stopped on the road, at eye level, to give them a reason not to just keep passing through. Second, roughly half the drivers (and some pedestrians as well) approaching a one-quadrant market place from the major thoroughfares will encounter it first at the corner, so the corner affords the first and best opportunity to establish the market place's identity and to create a pedestrian environment that draws people in. A parking lot, even if it is equipped with a great big omnibus sign, doesn't do the trick. Finally, we want the market place to be and read like the public center of a complete neighborhood, not a private precinct isolated from its environs. We don't want the market place to shrink back timidly from people as they approach it. Even though most activities in a sizable market place should be oriented to and connected by internal pathways, the major thoroughfares cannot be ignored.

This being a fairly large market place, it can accommodate considerable breadth and depth of activities—apartment complexes, big and little stores, office buildings, institutional and cultural uses such as a child-care facility, library, or recreation center. We want the city's zoning apparatus to allow a diversity of uses within the market place, even if the local culture won't accept true mixed use, with apartments above and immediately adjacent to stores or offices. Zoning might produce a distribution of land uses like that in figure 8.4e, with retailing and offices close to the major roads, a place for a cultural facility facing the central public space, and apartments deep inside the market place providing a transition between the more commercial, public uses and the single-family subdivisions.

Finally, we need to add some streets to provide redundant means of access, especially for deliveries and services, and create small cadences and transitions—landscaped areas, groups of benches, places for public art or fountains—along the streets leading to the center (figure 8.4f). The schematic market place in figure 8.4f looks very different in some ways from the typical suburban development pattern, but the distance between them is not so wide as might seem at first glance. In figure 8.4f, most buildings are set back from the major roads behind parking lots; with a few exceptions, buildings are located pretty much where they would be in the normal suburban development pattern. The main difference in figure 8.4f is that many front doors face in a different direction. Development is oriented toward internal streets rather than toward big parking lots and, beyond them, the major roads. Figure 8.4f is rather like a shopping mall, but with vehicular traffic allowed on some of the corridors and with mall entrances that effectively meet the surrounding neighborhood. (In principle, the internal streets could be a strictly pedestrian environment, in effect yielding an uncovered shopping mall like Old Orchard in Skokie, Illinois, or the Stanford Shopping Center next to Stanford University. In practice, exposure to vehicular traffic and the presence of at least some parking close to the front door is probably necessary in order to sell parcels or lease storefronts in most market places.)

Even the internal streets do not depart greatly from common practice. Each individual project in the typical suburban commercial area is required, by the building code, to be accessible to emergency vehicles. A fire lane usually stands between a project's front door and the parking lot. But what would happen if all those individual fire lanes serving all those individual projects were aligned and connected across property lines? There would be internal streets. It remains only to arrange some of those streets so that they converge at a usable public space—which might just be the entry plaza for a branch library or mini–city hall—and to do a little more than the minimum to create a welcoming and continuous pedestrian path on the sidewalks that developers would have built along the fronts of their buildings anyway.

The well-formed market place does not, in short, require much additional expense or much disruption from normal practice or much intrusion on the prerogatives of developers—or even much planning. It requires a little thought and consideration, a little design skill, and a good deal of cooperation among public and private entities. But the economic benefits of a coherent, convenient, and welcoming market place far outweigh the modest additional costs. And a well-formed market place could reduce the amount of land used for parking, cutting real estate and asphalt costs or allowing more land to be put to economic use.

It is relatively easy, in principle, to create a market place and its linkages to residential areas—a neighborhood—on raw land at the city's periphery. A tougher case is the revival of the older city's decaying neighborhood centers, which must be adapted to modern business needs while retaining (or recovering) their traditional neighborhood character in scale, architectural style, and pedestrian orientation. But here the basic street grid, the housing stock in the surrounding residential areas, and proximity to the central business district are often favorable to redevelopment of a viable market place, and depressed property values help make redevelopment affordable.

The most difficult challenge is to bring order to the suburban commercial area consisting of many insular projects on streets that do not form an efficient internal circulation system or connect with adjacent residential subdivisions. One such area grew up at the intersection of an expressway and a major thoroughfare on the far North Side of San Antonio. Within a third-mile radius of the intersection can be found a supermarket, a large bookstore, a video and compact disc dealer, a Wal-Mart, a Sam's Club, a Builders Square, a PetsMart, a fourteen-screen movie theater, a bowling alley, a miniature golf course, several fast-food places, numerous shops and restaurants in retail strips, a couple of office buildings—virtually every commercial product and service that might be needed routinely by a large neighborhood.

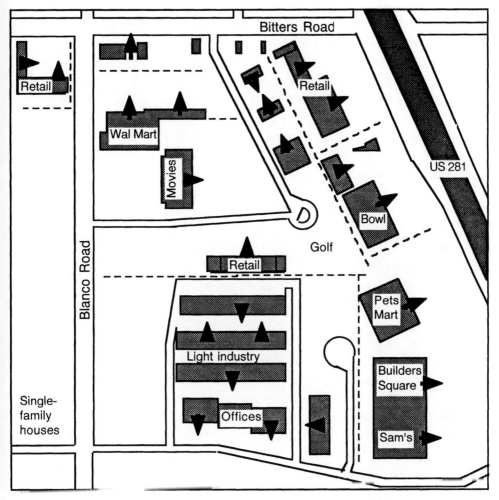

Figure 8.5   In a chaotic market place, the pieces pull apart from each other.

But this commercial area is so fragmented that a movie patron cannot, practically speaking, walk to the bookstore or the Mexican restaurant a quarter-mile away in the same quadrant of the intersection, let alone to the drugstore across the expressway. Walking to nearby apartments or single-family homes is out of the question for all but the doughtiest spirits.

Figure 8.5 maps the streets and buildings of the southwest quadrant of this chaotic market place. Everything that isn't a street or a building or marked "undeveloped" is a parking lot. The broken lines indicate physical or psychological barriers to movement within the market place, and the arrows show which direction the front doors of businesses face. Because the area was built by many developers operating independently over a period of a decade, without benefit of a coherent area plan into which their individual projects would fit, the pieces don't connect with each other. Neither pedestrians nor drivers can go easily from one project to another. More land than necessary is given over to parking lots: even though the movie complex and the big retailers generate their peak parking loads at different times, each has its own parking lot designed for its own peak load; when one is full, the other is empty—resulting in a waste of space and the needless destruction of many mature native trees.

To convert this area into a cohesive unity would require major investments in internal streets and sidewalks, perhaps some demolition of existing structures to make room for those connections, landscaping to define pathways and break up the huge parking lots, and new public amenities such as small parks and plazas, benches, fountains, and public art to give the area focal points and to bridge gaps in the fabric of commercial activity. A useful pedestrian link across the expressway is a lost cause. Direct links to some residential areas would require new streets.

One infuriating feature of the mess in figure 8.5: A large sign next to the expressway access road lists the current features at the movie theater complex. Ah! This must be the entrance! Wrong. Once in this trap, you have to drive down the alley in back of the retail strip that faces the expressway, make a dangerous left turn onto Bitters Road, and another left turn onto a street grandly if unaptly named Embassy Row. This is a splendid example of the Marquis de Sade school of site planning.

■ the asphalt bungle, or:
How can the city cross the road?

 Mr. Bendiner, who for many years was the education director of the synagogue I attended in San Antonio, used to tell a story about a visit to Heaven and Hell. (Technically, Mr. Bendiner's first name was Milton, but old habits die hard.) All the residents of Hell were seated at an elegant dinner table loaded with magnificent foods, but the eating utensils lashed to their hands were all four feet long. The Hellians starved in the midst of plenty because they couldn't maneuver their overscaled forks into their dishes and mouths. The physical circumstances in Heaven were exactly the same—the same dinner table, the same oversized utensils—but here the dinner guests ate to their ectoplasmic hearts' content. The solution? Each diner used her utensils to feed the person seated opposite her at the table. In Heaven, dinner was a collaborative artwork.

What's dinner like in suburbia? In figure 9.1, the intersection of Dante Boulevard and Lucifer Lane represents a common bit of suburban geography. Two roads cross, and developers have built retail strips at each corner. Each retail strip is L-shaped, and the stores face a parking lot on the inside of the L. The idea behind this site plan, which may include a couple of trees and covered sidewalks, is that customers of one shop will be enticed to stroll to

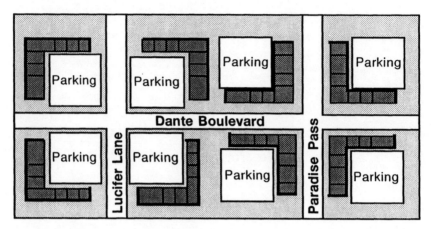

Figure 9.1 The four retail projects at Paradise Pass gain by sharing customers; the projects at Lucifer Lane suffer from insularity.

the other shops in the same strip. The L-shaped plan gives every front door in one wing a glimpse, at an angle, of every display window in the other wing, if both wings are short. This is reasonably intelligent site planning, if you assume that the ten or fifteen stores in a single retail center will generate, among themselves, all the shopping traffic they need to sustain them.

This type of plan is designed to capture a customer for all the stores within a given retail strip, but it also impedes pedestrian traffic *between* retail strips. The circulation of people, money, and ideas is inhibited because the circuit board has been divided into little nonconnecting pieces. This exercise in pure individualism is the urban-geography equivalent of dinner in Hell.

The next corner, where Dante crosses Paradise Pass, represents a plan rarely seen in suburbia. Here are the same retail strips, roads, and parking lots we saw before, but each retail L has been turned upside down, backwards, and inside out. The storefronts line up with the public sidewalks along the roads, and the parking lots are in back. In this plan, a customer walking out of a store in one wing of a retail strip can't see any of the stores in the other wing of the same strip, but he has a direct view of the stores in the strip across the street. Because four rows of parking (a typical configuration for retail strips) take up more space than the right-of-way for a seven-lane road, facing storefronts in these competing strips may actually be closer to each other than stores at the ends of a single L-shaped strip on Lucifer Lane. If the intersection and the sidewalk system are designed to encourage pedestrian movement, a shopper can roam easily and conveniently past all the stores in all four retail strips, dropping money as he goes, before returning to his car. Moreover, because the shopper can visit fifty or sixty stores on one auto trip rather than just twelve or fifteen, the auto trip is more likely to be rewarded. This collaborative type of plan on Paradise Pass can generate more trips, and more sales per trip, than the individualistic plans on Lucifer Lane. The developers are feeding their dinner companions across the table.

But figure 9.1 obscures a troublesome reality, which we must acknowledge and deal with if we hope to apply Mr. Bendiner's parable. If Dante Boulevard and Paradise Pass are two-lane or four-lane streets with a thirty mph speed limit, and if protected crossings occur at close intervals, as in the old city, the four quadrants of the intersection will bind together easily. If, however, the streets are five-lane or seven-lane roads with a forty mph speed limit, and if protected crossings are a half-mile apart, as in common suburban practice, additional measures are needed to help the city cross the road.

In chapter 8 we talked about some of the attributes that a market place needs to have to function as a coherent unity, promoting the movement of people and the exchange of money and ideas. This chapter deals with specific design features and planning techniques that can tie disparate individual projects into a collaborative ensemble. We will seek planning tools to help us avert the chaos that is typical of suburban commercial areas, but we will accept as a discipline the real-world facts of suburban life—wide, heavily trafficked roads, ample off-street parking, huge discount retail stores, fast-food restaurants with drive-up windows. We will assume that the neighborhood commercial hub must cross major thoroughfares. We will accept these facts of life, not because we like them, but because a planning regime that attempts to ignore them is doomed, in most localities, to political failure.

Urban design is unavoidably political, and politics is the art of the possible. The techniques I propose here are the ones that I think are politically and economically possible, in part because I have seen most of them, in one form or another, in the real world. The political give-and-take that necessarily precedes every master plan or policy decision is implicit in this chapter. Drawing from my observations of the political process in San Antonio, I have sought to imagine first what the desires and antipathies of many interests might be and then to imagine what a reasonable resolution of those divergent interests might look like on the ground. I do not imagine that divergent interests will immediately, or ultimately, buy into everything in this chapter. The political process must play out uniquely in every locality. I simply hope that readers of many stripes will gain an understanding that thorough, intensive, innovative design can, in many instances, resolve differences and give seemingly opposite interests more of what they want.

Let me give you an example from the real world. Suppose you want to provide a sidewalk from the front door of a building to the street, or to the adjacent property, but at some point the pedestrian path must cross a fire lane or the driving space of a parking lot. At best, the pedestrian way at this crossing point might be marked visually with painted stripes or special paving, or be protected by speed bumps. Either way, the pedestrian drops down to car level. For a community college in San Antonio, planner Larry Clark resolved the conflict simply and ingeniously by continuing a wide, curb-height walkway through a parking lot's vehicular crossings. At the crossings the walkway's edges slope so that the walkway can act as a wide speed bump. Pedestrians remain at a constant level, protected from fast auto traffic and rain runoff. Drivers gain, too, because the wide space between up and down slopes allows a less jarring passage while still reducing speeds. Clark calls this device a "silent cop."

The problem of making a neighborhood cross a busy suburban road is more complex than this example, and no one simple solution will do the trick. As in the game of chess, winning urban design is a matter of an accumulation of little advantages. We need to deploy many design techniques to do the job. One of those techniques, as we already saw in figure 9.1, is to turn the typical commercial site plan inside out. We need to move the parking lot.

Those are fighting words. Nothing is more sacred to a suburban developer than the parking lot at the front door. But let's try to persuade him that he is worshipping a false god.

Suppose developer Marty McGee wants to build a retail strip. He has his sights set on the corner of Commercial Boulevard and Industrial Parkway, two busy roads with lots of traffic. Suppose that the land he needs for this project is a city block divided into sixteen parcels of identical area with sixteen owners. In the normal course of events, the parcel at the corner of Commercial Boulevard and Industrial Parkway would command the highest price, because it has corner exposure to two busy roads. Other parcels with exposure to one or the other busy road would command slightly lower prices. Parcels on the back and side streets would be the least expensive. This price gradient is represented by darker and lighter shades on the lots in figure 9.2a. McGee buys the property and builds an L-shaped retail strip, McGee's Merchandise Mecca. The outline of the retail building, superimposed on an outline of the original parcels, is shown in figure 9.2b.

Note that the most expensive land closest to the main intersection has the least productive use, free parking, while the least expensive land is where the most productive use goes. But why did McGee have to pay more for the land with major road frontage in the first place? Because the land closer to the road is closer to where more of the people are. Proximity to potential customers is a value that is roughly measured by the price of commercial land. So if McGee is spending so much money for that valuable frontage on two major roads, why is he wasting that frontage on a parking lot and putting his retail strip on the less valuable land farther from the people?

As a variant on this site plan, the corner is sometimes reserved for a pad site, a freestanding business such as a gas station, drive-through bank facility, or fast-food restaurant. Although this arrangement brings productive use to valuable road frontage and may, with good design, have the beneficial effect of filling a void in the streetscape, it also adds a visual barrier to the barrier of distance between the road and the retail strip. With or without a pad site next to the road, most businesses in McGee's retail strip are pushed so far from passing traffic that not even pedestrians, let alone drivers, can see what is being offered for sale. If people don't know what is there to be bought, they

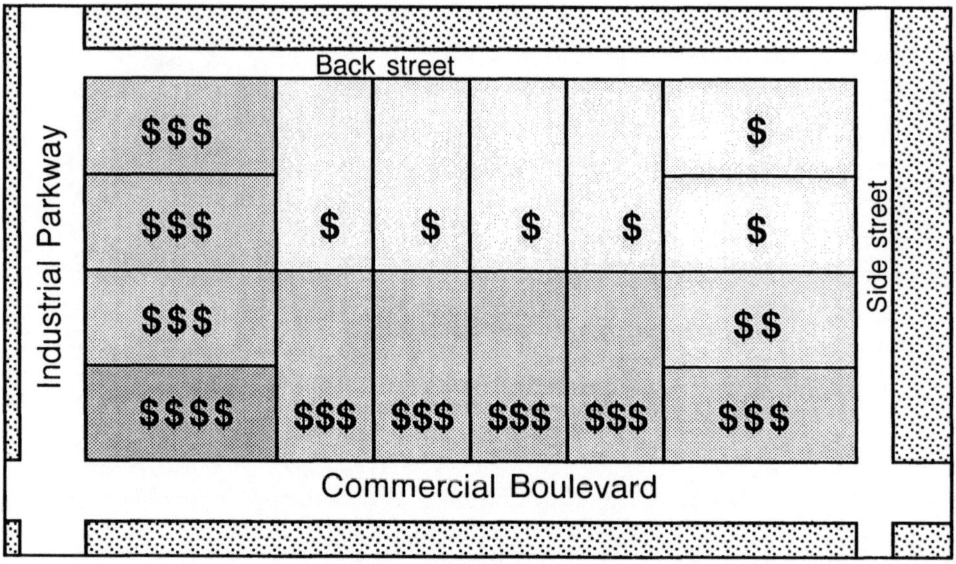

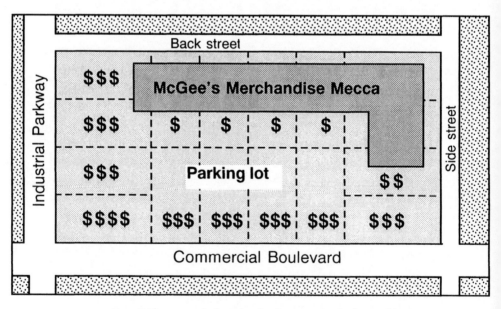

Figure 9.2a Why would a developer devote the costliest and most valuable property ...

Figure 9.2b ... to the least productive use, namely, free parking?

won't buy it. Developers continue to engage in this suicidal behavior because they and we have come to conceptualize roads in the wrong way.

Roads were invented to connect things. A road is a line of communication between point A and point B. But suppose, in figure 9.3, you want to go from M to N. You don't want to travel along the length of the road, you want to cross it. In that case the road is not a line of communication but a barrier. Indeed, the more efficiently a road carries traffic lengthwise, the less efficiently it carries traffic crosswise. Put simply, the busier and wider the road, the harder it is to cross. Whether on foot or in cars, people get killed that way.

Quantitative differences have qualitative implications. The narrow residential street with little or no through traffic isn't much of a barrier. Kids can play softball with impunity in a residential cul-de-sac. The five-lane or seven-lane commercial road (four or six lanes plus a left-turn lane) is another matter. One side of such a road has little functional connection with the other side unless the connection is carefully designed into the road and its environs. Otherwise, the two sides of a busy road may as well be in different counties. A road isn't just a wide street. It's a different genus of animal altogether.

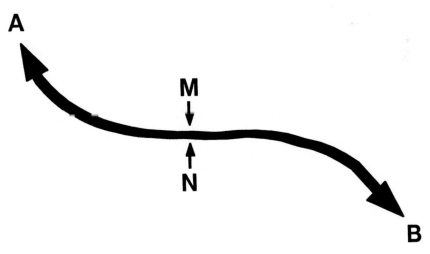

Figure 9.3   A road that connects A and B may be a barrier between M and N.

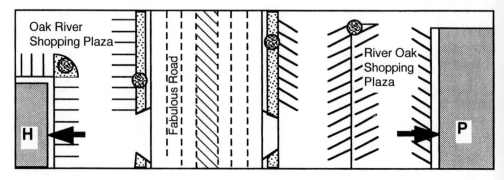

Figure 9.4a In typical suburban site planning, distance and traffic separate Hugo's goods from Philippa's customers—and their money.

By way of explanation, allow me to inject you into a hypothetical but probably familiar shopping excursion.

Winter approaches. To prepare for the cold winds, you have driven to the River Oak Shopping Center, the location of Philippa's Fireplace Follies (marked P in figures 9.4a and b). When you exit Philippa's with your new pair of andirons, what do you see? The proprietor of Hugo's Hobby Hutch (H in the diagram), which is located in the Oak River Shopping Center directly in your line of sight across Fabulous Road, hopes that you will see his display window. Hugo has just received a new shipment of model ship kits, and he knows that if you saw them you'd buy one. And you would—but you won't.

The site plans partially indicated for the two retail strips are typical of suburban San Antonio. The distance between Philippa's and Hugo's is 300 feet, or one football field. (In practice, the distance between such storefronts might be 100 feet or 200 feet wider, but rarely narrower, depending on how many parking spaces lie between the store and the street.) The street pavement accounts for 86 feet, and the total public right-of-way is 110 feet, slightly more than a third of the door-to-door distance. By far the greater portion of the space between the two stores is used for parking.

So, as you walk out of Philippa's with your new pair of andirons, you

Figure 9.4b   To a customer exiting Philippa's, Hugo's storefront occupies only a thin slice of the field of vision.

see, as the song said, the sea—in this case, a sea of parked cars and striped asphalt, and beyond that the deeper, swifter current of the road, and then another parking lot, and finally, off in the far distance, Hugo's Hobby Hutch. You are not likely to be able to make out anything that Hugo is displaying in his window. You probably will see no more than the sign above his shop, and unless the letters are very big and plain you might not even be able to read that. You are not being invited to cross the sea. If you were to make your mind up to cross anyway, you would find no dedicated pedestrian route for getting there—no connection from the sidewalk directly in front of Philippa's to the sidewalk along the curb, and none from the sidewalk on the opposite side of the street to Hugo's front door. And of course you would have to commit the heinous offense of jaywalking (or jayrunning) in order to cross the road at all, on foot. Because traffic engineers want to keep the cars moving, traffic lights may be spaced as much as three-quarters of a mile apart on suburban roads. Even if a regulated intersection were close enough to make a safe crossing possible, you would still be intimidated by the corners' wide turning radius, designed for quick right turns, and by the need to cross seven traffic lanes without an intermediate safe haven in case the light changes before you've made it across.

But the greater barrier is psychological. No safe, convenient, and pleasant path has been marked out to invite pedestrian flow between Philippa's and Hugo's, and the wide space that must be traversed, while an almost orderly environment for vehicles, is almost complete disorder for pedestrians.

Figure 9.4b is a simplified side view of the same slice across the road. The tiny stick figure outside Philippa's front door is you. At this distance, the display windows across the street (assuming the line of sight is not blocked by cars) occupy only a tiny band of your field of vision, most of which is filled by gray asphalt and concrete below and gray skies above. (This is my book, so I can specify the weather.) Furthermore, given the typical one-story scale of retail strips, the facades of the two retail centers bound a ceilingless room (the road and the parking lot) that is too wide and low to hang together as a roomlike place. The furniture and other objects in your living room relate to each other as an ensemble in part because they are yours and familiar, but also because they are close to one another and are bound together by the walls of a fairly intimate room. If the width and length of the room were each doubled, and the objects spaced twice as far apart along the walls, the objects would no longer form an ensemble, and the place would feel alien.

The image of suburban buildings as independent islands in a sea of asphalt, while something of an urbanists' cliché, is nonetheless accurate. The city doesn't cross the road, not with ease or efficiency. The road, as it typically is laid out in suburban contexts, prevents the emergence of functionally and perceptually cohesive neighborhood centers. The road is not only a physical barrier to exchange. It also disperses sites of exchange and diffuses the market place. Furthermore, because the physical structures of the market place are so widely separated by pavement, they cannot aggregate into an identifiable, walkable, and comprehensible whole—a place. Roads make the market place mushy. Yet roads also make the market place possible. Can't live with 'em, can't live without 'em.

By "road," I do not refer only to the ribbon of asphalt on which vehicles drive. When you talk about the street you live on, you don't usually mean just the trafficway itself. You also mean the sidewalks and lawns, the architecture of the houses, the way the houses are sited in relation to each other and to the pavement—everything you can see while driving or walking along the street. Your street is the ensemble of all these things, the entire roofless "room" defined by the houses on either side of the pavement. Similarly, the road is the aggregate of trafficway, sidewalks, parking lots, signs, and buildings; and the pattern of site, scale, and setback relationships. The problem with asphalt is not just that there is too much of it, but that it is in the wrong places, where it impedes economic and social exchange.

MAKING THE CENTER HOLD

Whereas the retail-commercial hub that formed around street intersections of the older city served as a focal point that tied together the four residential quadrants radiating outward from it, the greater dispersal and wider roads that typify suburban market places isolate the four quadrants from each other. Schematically, it's the difference between figures 9.5a and 9.5b, where the big arrows represent the gradient from lower to higher activity levels within the market place (the shaded square), and the little arrows represent the orientation of surrounding residential areas. In traditional neighborhoods, as the little arrows in figure 9.5a suggest, local streets link residential areas with their common commercial hub in a seamless manner, and people tend to think of their nearby commercial hub as an integral part of their neighborhood. In modern suburban practice, in contrast, commercial and residential areas turn their backs to each other and are inaccessible to one another except by way of major thoroughfares.

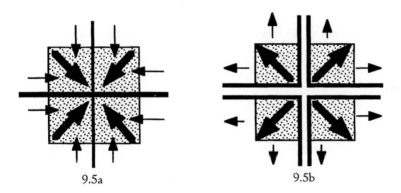

9.5a   9.5b

Figure 9.5a   Because of the compactness and connectedness of the traditional neighborhood, the four quadrants of the major intersection hung together as a unity, a focal point on which the whole neighborhood converged.

Figure 9.5b   In the conventional suburban context of wider roads and insular, dispersed development, the four quadrants of a major intersection pull apart from each other and from nearby residential subdivisions.

While the crossing of major roads is a strong magnet for commercial projects, this centripetal force (toward the center) is countered, usually in much more chaotic ways than are suggested by the four big arrows in figure 9.5b, by the centrifugal force (away from the center) of typical development practice. For the pedestrian—virtually anyone who has business to conduct in the vicinity—the centrifugal force is by far the stronger one. The advantages of concentration are lost to the dispersion effects of parking lots and the fragmentation of pedestrian paths. In functional terms the exchange sites of the four quadrants pull apart from each other and cannot coalesce into a stable unit. The single arrow within each quadrant of figure 9.5b should really be a whole slew of little arrows running in random directions and not connecting with each other.

The design of the conventional suburban road and its environs has consisted of four assumptions. First, all the exchanges that constitute city life occur at considerable distances from the home and from each other. Second, each point of exchange is at the end of a separate automobile trip. Third, nobody ever wishes to shop at both of two adjacent stores if there is a property line between them. Fourth, the road exists solely to allow linear, point-to-point connections across long distances (more than half a mile) by automobile.

The typical pattern of suburban development makes perfect sense if one accepts these assumptions. The priority given to point-to-point travel over long distances yields a wide road with infrequent side-street access points and few stop lights to impede traffic flow. The road is flanked first by parking lots, and then, at varying distances from the road, stores and offices and other points of exchange. The setbacks vary widely, depending solely on the perceived parking needs of individual businesses, because it is a given that no one will wish to walk from one store to the next if they are separated by a property line. Under this model, it is natural for each land parcel to be developed as though it were the only destination in its vicinity, and as though the properties on either side did not exist. It is natural, too, to dedicate the most valuable land—nearest the road and the corner—to parking. Everybody who comes will come by car.

This model turns out to be problematic for several reasons. First, it requires a high degree of motivation on the part of potential customers, for only very highly motivated and informed people aim their cars at a particular parking lot and walk through the doors. If I must have some dish towels and I know that your store has them, I drive there. But if I sort of wouldn't mind having some new dish towels, and I could be persuaded to buy them if I saw good ones in a display window, but my routine doesn't take me within eyeshot of your window, you've lost a sale. And I would imagine that, at any given time, there are a lot more people who sort of wouldn't mind buying dish towels than there are people who absolutely must have dish towels and are willing to make a special trip to buy some.

Second, the conventional model wastes energy and increases air pollution and traffic congestion. I use less gasoline, expel fewer pollutants, and spend less time occupying road space if I can eat lunch and buy a box of floppy disks in one trip by car than if I must add a car trip between the restaurant and the computer store. If I can accomplish both tasks by walking from my home or office—a common occurrence in big cities and even in some urban suburbs—all the better. Roads, under the conventional suburban model, are specialized for moving a lot of people across long distances, but highly inefficient for moving even a few people across short distances. Moreover, the pressures of short-distance auto traffic—the turns into and out of parking lots, the auto trips that would not have occurred if people could have walked—limit the efficiency of long-distance movement.

Third, the conventional model wastes land and money. Because it assumes that all customers will come by car from distant places, and none will come by foot from the businesses or homes next door or in the next block, the conventional model lends a modicum of support to the excessive parking requirements in many city codes. Developers must devote larger portions of their lots to nonproductive uses than if parking demand were reduced and shared among many properties within walking distance of each other. At the same time, the productivity of the productive land is reduced because stores can't effectively share customers.

Fourth, some customers can come *only* by foot or bicycle or wheelchair because they have no other way to travel. The failure to accommodate these people safely and conveniently is both an economic oversight, because their money is as good as anyone else's, and an ethical transgression.

These and other flaws suggest the need for a fundamental shift—in part, a reversal—in our assumptions about roads and development. Traditional downtowns and neighborhood commercial hubs were laid out on the assumption that most people would walk to most points of exchange. Compact commercial hubs are highly efficient for pedestrian traffic over short distances and highly inefficient for point-to-point auto traffic over long distances—the opposite of the case for the road. But in cities where people drive a lot, traditional neighborhood hubs also must provide adequate parking to serve an expanded market area in order to stay alive under modern business conditions. A full reversal to the older model is not practical in most cases. The car and the wide suburban road, for better or worse, are with us for keeps.

The shopping mall is often interpreted as the new version of the traditional downtown. As we have seen, there is a lot to like and to learn from in the shopping mall's double-loaded pedestrian street, particularly its continuity, its definition, and the discipline of the matrix in which individual stores can express their individuality while at the same time aggregating into a coherent whole. But the shopping mall has its deficits and limitations as well. It is basically an exoskeletal creature: All the life is on the inside, while the exterior is a cold, bony shell turned against the rest of the city—even the mall's immediate neighbors. (There are a few exceptions in downtown areas; one of the best examples is Toronto's Eaton Centre, which has small shops and restaurants facing the street and a facade that mirrors the scale and rhythms of its older neighbors.) Furthermore, the shopping mall rarely embraces more than a few types of activity—retailing, a limited range of consumer services such as travel agents and ticket outlets, sometimes movies and night clubs, maybe a hotel, and that's about it. Offices, residences, manufacturing, gas stations, and civic or government facilities—all of which a city must somehow accommodate on its streets—are seldom part of the shopping mall mix. Even many types of retail shops are excluded as inappropriate or offensive. The malls' high rental rates exclude innovative or highly specialized retailers that may not be able to count on high sales volume right off the bat, retailers that could survive or thrive in low-rent, modest, funky neighborhoods. It's rare even to find a good bookstore in a shopping mall. Finally, the shopping mall is a private, controlled environment. Many types of social, artistic, and political expression, permissible in public places, are prohibited in shopping malls. If our objective is to promote the full range of social, cultural, and economic exchanges, the shopping mall is only a partially applicable model. We want the door-to-door connectedness of the shopping mall's interior street, we want its concentration and its placeness, but we do not want its aloofness or its exclusivity. Most especially, we want a greater degree of adaptability and responsiveness than an exoskeleton allows. In sum, we are looking for a hybrid geometry that combines the advantages of the shopping mall and the traditional street grid—a shopping mall that allows cars inside.

Before going on, let me first set off flashing lights, sirens, and gongs to draw attention to this cautionary note. The comments that follow are provocative, not prescriptive. I do not claim that the millennium will arrive if cities just follow my blueprints. I hope merely to present some models—not necessarily *the* model—of a way of thinking about the relationships among roads, sidewalks, parking lots, and points of exchange. How these relationships should play out in practice may vary from place to place, even within the same city or along the same road. What matters is not so much the specific shape of the fantasies presented here, but a mode of thinking about the interlocked consequences of urban design decisions or non-decisions. In real cities, people do many kinds of things in many different ways. In healthy cities with healthy economies—in the widest sense—these many interests and activities, however diverse and random they may be, function as an ensemble. The stage on which this ensemble of interests and activities plays its many roles must also be designed as an ensemble.

The concepts that I present here are not innovative or radical. With one or two exceptions, they merely codify design strategies and happy accidents I've observed in the real world. I explicitly avoid radical departures from the typical suburban development pattern. Much as I admire and cheer the projects of "neotraditional" and "postmodern" planners, some of whose techniques may be recognized as faint echoes in my suggestions, the reality is that most cities will continue building pretty much the way they have in the past few decades, with auto-dominant commercial corridors along wide and busy roads. The gross patterns of suburban form are not going to disappear in the foreseeable future. The question is this: How can we refine these patterns so that they form an ensemble that nourishes rather than inhibits life-sustaining urban processes?

Let's break the problem down into its component parts and see how through traffic, local traffic, pedestrians, nearby residents, developers, retailers (or other points of exchange), and transit operators want their worlds to look, ideally. Then we will see where these ideals conflict and seek workable compromises—but not capitulations.

• Drivers who are just passing through want to be able to just pass through quickly, with minimal interruption or distraction. They want a wide road with as few traffic lights as possible, minimal side-street intersections, and no curb cuts for access to businesses between those intersections. Through traffic doesn't want to be delayed by local traffic.

• Local traffic, meanwhile, doesn't want to be bothered by through traffic. If I'm looking for an unfamiliar store, I want to be able to slow down without fear of being crushed by an eighteen-wheeler. If I need to drive from a store on the east side of the 4300 block to a store on the west side of the 4800 block, I don't want to struggle with fast through traffic to get there.

• Pedestrians want sidewalks of adequate width separated from the danger, noise, and unpleasantness of the major road. Pedestrians want a sidewalk that goes where they want to go, and that goes there efficiently. They want door-to-door and door-to-bus sidewalks. By implication, they also want building setbacks to be uniform, or nearly so, and building facades to be contiguous (give or take a few feet) with the sidewalk. Included among pedestrians are drivers who park in front of Sam's Seaweed Spectacular and, after shopping there, wish to continue on foot to Wilma's Wicker Warehouse in the next block.

• The desires of nearby residents are largely consonant with the desires of through traffic. Residents want limited access from the major road in order to keep out miscreant intruders and limit the noise and danger of vehicular traffic. They want to be buffered from the noise and shielded from the ugliness of businesses. But residents also want easy access, both by car and by foot, to neighborhood service businesses—the ice cream parlor, the hardware store, the card shop, the supermarket—as well as to parks, schools, and cultural facilities. Residents want places to walk or bike to for exercise or pleasure, and they want safe, pleasant ways to do it.

• Developers and their lenders want parking, parking, and more parking. They also want easy vehicular access from the road both for customers and for deliveries. And they want to minimize the up-front costs of development.

• Retailers want paying customers. They want to get their messages across to the maximum number of people with the minimum amount of resistance.

• Transit operators like concentration. They want to pick up and drop off more passengers on the same number of route miles. That requires more destinations and starting points within easy walking distance of the bus route, and more destinations within walking distance of each other, concentrated around transit stops.

Some of these desires conflict. A residential subdivision with limited escape routes for burglars is also one with limited escape routes for residents who may wish to escape only as far as the corner sandwich shop on a Saturday afternoon—or from a toxic chemical spill on a nearby rail line. A road that's highly efficient for linear auto traffic is necessarily inefficient for pedestrian cross traffic. The parking lots that developers and lenders want are in conflict with the concentration that transit operators want. We can't reconcile all these desires in a way that perfectly satisfies everyone. That's life. But it is possible to go further toward reconciliation than our post-1960 building has generally gone.

Before going on to a few ways to bring about that reconciliation, we need to revisit some of the ground we covered in earlier chapters and remind ourselves of the big picture. In post-1960 San Antonio, as in many Sun Belt cities, the big picture of urban form looks, schematically, like figure 9.6. Through roads are spaced roughly a mile apart, and the mile-square spaces inside the road grid are filled with "spaghetti bowl" residential subdivisions. These subdivisions connect with the main roads usually at only one or two

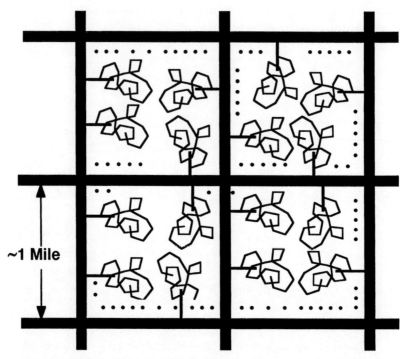

Figure 9.6 Schematic matrix of conventional post-1960 suburban form—insular subdivisions plugged into major thoroughfare grid.

points. They rarely connect with each other or with concentrated retail areas. The little dots denote stores, office buildings, gas stations, restaurants, and all the other points of exchange that are likely to be seen along a suburban road. Apartment complexes also may appear along the major roads, though often apartments appear in clusters along a secondary street behind commercial projects—literally behind, because the stores, restaurants, and offices are likely to turn their loading docks to the apartments.

Figure 9.6 exemplifies the matrix or framework on which suburban development has typically been hung since about 1960. In figure 9.7 I suggest a different matrix. This, I hasten to emphasize, is not meant to be taken literally as a blueprint, but only as a representation of a few general principles. A strictly rectilinear street grid, or many other geometries, could fit this matrix as well as the diagonals, ovals, and chicken scratches I've drawn.

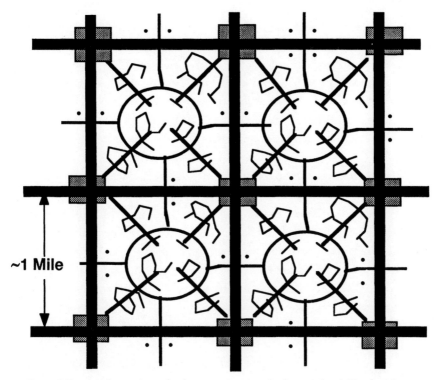

Figure 9.7 An alternative suburban matrix organized around neighborhood centers (shaded rectangles).

In this matrix, the major roads are still a mile apart, the residential subdivisions are still spaghetti bowls (or whatever foodstuff, including waffles, the developers' hearts may prompt), and commercial projects and apartments still gravitate to the major roads. Apart from the occasional demonstration project, these are realities that are not going to change in most places.

The differences between figures 9.6 and 9.7 are fairly modest but important tweakings of conventional practice. First, the ovals indicate that adjacent residential subdivisions, however bizarre and dissimilar their street layouts, connect with each other by way of at least one circulator street. Second, the shaded rectangles, representing mixed-use neighborhood centers, indicate that commercial, retail, and apartment projects—along with small parks and cultural facilities, perhaps—concentrate into compact nodes (probably but not necessarily at major intersections) rather than stretching continuously and diffusely along the road corridors. Third, the diagonal streets (which need not be literal diagonals) indicate direct access between these high-density hubs and the low-density residential areas. Fourth, the dots indicate minor commercial areas—perhaps just a convenience store or a gas station—next to subdivision entrances at intermediate points along the main roads.

This matrix relates to the list of different factions' desires in these ways:

• The concentration of most activity sites into mixed-use hubs allows fewer impediments to free traffic flow in the stretches between hubs. Because these hubs are laid out with internal streets, most parking can be made accessible from those streets rather from the through roads; turning traffic is concentrated at the regulated intersections where circulator streets meet the through roads. Drivers who are just passing through can pass through more easily without being impeded, most of the way, by traffic entering and leaving parking lots.

• The hubs also concentrate pedestrian traffic, so that retailers may share clienteles. The concentration of apartments at these hubs increases the absolute number of potential customers who are able to use the retail district easily by foot, without adding to the parking demand. Concentration of markets helps sustain retailers that residents of low-density subdivisions might wish to have nearby, but which they could not support on their own.

• The walkable character of a compact, mixed-use hub reduces the need for separate auto trips, thus reducing congestion on the through roads, and benefits transit operators, who gain access to concentrated transit markets of apartment dwellers and hub workers. Compact retail-commercial hubs are also more attractive destinations for transit riders, who may be more likely to take the bus if they can accomplish many things at one stop.

• With links between adjacent subdivisions and direct access to the mixed-use hubs, subdivision residents have a place to walk to for pleasure, business, or exercise more safely, conveniently, and pleasurably than if they had to walk or ride a bicycle along the main road between the subdivision entrance and their retail destinations. Whether they walk or drive, residents have more convenient access to a greater range of options—more restaurants and shops—in a concentrated hub than along a diffuse corridor. The links between subdivisions mean that when Bartholomew, who lives in Elysée Estates, wants to study geometry with Wilhelmina, who lives six hundred feet away in Valhalla Valley, he doesn't have to walk or bike a mile out of his way, to the main road, in order to get to her house. Similarly, drivers are given alternate routes to the city at large. Assuming the presence of one retail hub at each corner of a mile-square sector, a driver starting anywhere inside the sector can reach any of the four retail concentrations without suffering, or adding to, congestion on the through roads. In the typical suburban development pattern, in contrast, a driver can reach *no* retail concentration without adding to through-road congestion.

Now, having surveyed an alternative approach to the big picture, let's focus on some of its details. We'll start by trying to bring some sense to the major road intersection, the messiest, most chaotic, most diffuse, and most congested sector of our suburban rings. The problem, as we have already seen, is that while each of the corners of a major intersection is a magnet for commercial and retail projects, these projects do not coalesce into a whole. The citizen cannot conveniently use the entire commercial area the way she could use a traditional downtown or neighborhood shopping hub. Our goal is not just to make it possible to walk across the road, but to design the four quadrants of the intersection in such a way that they coalesce into a functionally and psychologically continuous ensemble, like the four corners of a downtown intersection or the central court of a shopping mall. We want this ensemble to serve as a unified focal point for the residential subdivisions in all four quadrants.

The intersection of two wide, busy roads may seem an unpromising focal point from the pedestrian's perspective, but pavement width and traffic volume alone do not determine the permeability of an urban barrier. Consider, to take one widely familiar example, the convergence of Broadway and Columbus Avenue at Lincoln Center in Manhattan. If these two streets were transplanted to a suburban context, few pedestrians would dare to cross them. In their urban context, however, the intersection accommodates heavy foot traffic in every direction. People by the thousands walk every night between the theaters of Lincoln Center and the restaurants, hotels, apartments, and shops east of Broadway.

Several design features allow this space to work as a focal point of urban life. First, the space is divided into chewable bites. Broadway has a landscaped median with little paved piazzas at the street crossings. A low wall at the prow protects this space from derelict cars, and the piazza usually includes a bench where people sit to eat lunch or take a break from shopping. There are trees in the median and more trees along the sidewalks, so that the huge width of the street is split into several narrower corridors. Except for the broad plaza of Lincoln Center itself, the buildings along Broadway and Columbus Avenue form continuous vertical planes close to the street. The span between facing buildings on Broadway is shorter than the typical span between facing retail strips—each set back behind a parking lot—on suburban roads that may be narrower than Broadway.

In principle, none of these design strategies is incompatible with the lower density and increased open space and greenery that attract people to suburbia. Indeed, the convergence of Broadway and Columbus Avenue is conspicuously greener and more Arcadian than the typical suburban road crossing in outdoorsy, nature-loving San Antonio. (If you want suburbia to feel more suburban, make it look more like Manhattan.)

The conventional suburban model is illustrated in the bottom half of the hypothetical road crossing in figure 9.8a. (You will recognize our old friends Philippa and Hugo from figure 9.4.) In the top half of figure 9.8a, we deploy some of the techniques—none of them radical, many of them commonplace—that can tie the corners together. The side view in figure 9.8b shows how the roofless room of the street acquires more comfortably roomlike proportions and brings facing storefronts into closer relationship with each other, in comparison to the much more wide open space separating Hugo's and Philippa's.

• The buildings, the sites of exchange, are pushed toward the street, with minimal (or no) setbacks from the public right-of-way, which now includes diagonal parking. The public sidewalk provides door-to-door service (the big arrows designate business entrances), and pedestrians on one side of

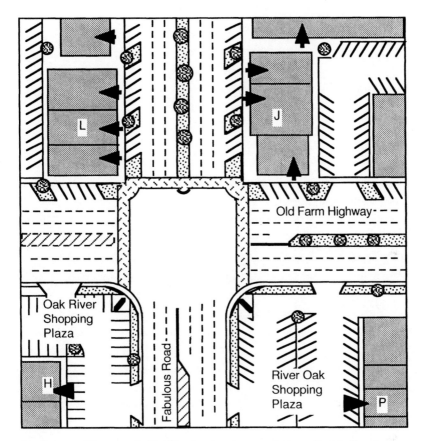

Figure 9.8a The upper half of the drawing shows techniques for binding the two sides of the road together and organizing the public space, in contrast to the dispersal and chaos of conventional suburban planning, shown in the lower half of the drawing.

the street are close to the crosswalks that take them to the other side of the street.

Under this arrangement, even on a seven-lane road businesses can face each other across a distance of less than 150 feet, at most half the typical distance in suburban commercial settings, and the space is further divided into human-scaled segments by lines of trees along the sidewalks and the median.

Figure 9.8b   Street trees and minimal setbacks create a human-scaled ceilingless room in the public right-of-way. The shorter the distance between facing storefronts, the wider the field of vision they occupy.

• Off-street parking lots are moved away from storefronts to sides or rears. Displacing the parking lot from the front of the store can be a risky proposition. Sometimes it works well, sometimes it doesn't. In general, the rear parking lot works fine if it isn't too large (not more than a hundred spaces), if the pedestrian system is in good shape, if there are ample pedestrian passages to the streets, if the location of the lot is prominently marked on the main and side streets by signs with the international parking symbol (which seems to be more reassuring and official-looking than the word *parking*), if the lot itself is communal rather than for the exclusive use of one business or one retail strip, and if the lot borders a street rather than being reachable only through a narrow driveway between buildings. The last two points are important for the perception (and reality) of security. A communal parking lot will have a steadier and larger flow of people than an exclusive lot, and the lot adjacent to the street is more easily monitored by passersby than the hidden one.

Communal parking has another advantage. By allowing parking loads to be shared and averaged out among many businesses, it can reduce the total number of spaces a commercial area needs to have—as opposed to the number of spaces typically required by the formulas in city parking codes. Even with the same number of total spaces, communal parking can make more efficient use of land. One parking lot with fifty spaces and two driveway entrances uses less asphalt than five ten-space parking lots with one driveway entrance apiece.

• The public right-of-way is expanded to include on-street diagonal parking in small groups of spaces punctuated by landscaped areas. Traffic engineers will be horrified by the idea of on-street parking along a major thoroughfare, but on-street parking can be safe even on a seven-lane road if traffic signals are timed to provide sufficient windows of opportunity to back out of a parking space. Safety is greatly enhanced if right turns onto the block with on-street parking are prohibited or limited ("right turn on arrow only").

    • On-street parking and landscaping buffer the sidewalks from the street, and sidewalks are at least eight feet wide—preferably twelve feet—rather than four.

    Figure 9.9 shows how on-street parking, communal parking lots, and landscaping might work in the context of mandatory build-to zones. The outer broken line in the drawing represents the public right-of-way line. The location of the inner dotted line might vary from one block to another, or from one side of a block to another, but probably should be set back no more than twenty or twenty five feet. The space between these lines is the build-to zone. Some specified percentage of street frontage must have building facades and main entrances within this zone. The coverage requirement might be higher on blocks nearest the market place's focal point or along primary pedestrian routes, lower on blocks farther from the focal point or on less important pedestrian routes.

    In figure 9.9, the 90 percent requirement on the west side of the block maintains a nearly continuous line of pedestrian-oriented buildings while allowing ample (possibly landscaped) pedestrian passages to the communal parking lot in the block's interior. The lower coverage requirements on the other sides of the block result in an intermittent line of pedestrian-oriented buildings while allowing substantial gaps for visible, monitorable parking lots, driveways, and such features as the patio café on the east side of the block. A build-to zone, as opposed to an inflexible build to *line*, allows for some variety of setback to accommodate more or less landscaping, and sidewalk cafés or sales racks or special architectural features while at the same time assuring that storefronts remain engaged with the public pedestrian path.

    • Back in figure 9.8: crosswalk in a special paving pattern helps emphasize, for both pedestrians and drivers, the presence of a dedicated pedestrian zone. Brick pavers, especially if laid in a herringbone or fish-scale pattern, reduce the perceptual distance from curb to curb from the pedestrian's perspective. Crosswalks should be equipped with pedestrian signals, and the

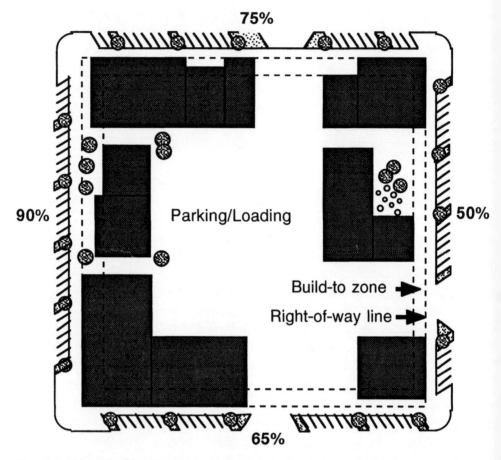

Figure 9.9 How a build-to zone might work in the market place. A specified percentage of street frontage must be occupied by building facades no more than a given distance from the public right-of-way line or public sidewalk.

"Walk" sign should stay on long enough—at least thirty seconds in each cycle—for heavily burdened or infirm pedestrians to cross the street.

• The turning radius at the corners has been slightly reduced from the suburban norm for major intersections so that the crosswalk can meet the curbs at something approaching a right angle. The tighter turning radius also has the beneficial effect of reducing the speed of vehicles making right turns, at corners where turns are allowed.

• Let's reduce the speed limit to 25 mph on the major roads where they cross a market place. Again, the traffic engineers will be horrified. What's the point of a seven-lane road if the speed limit is so low? We need to keep those cars and trucks moving quickly, after all. But in the real world, except in late-night hours, traffic backs up and slows down anyway close to heavily developed intersections. During business hours a reduced speed limit would have little practical effect except on the lead cars in a queue as they accelerate when the light turns green. But that rapid and noisy acceleration can greatly alter the psychological environment for pedestrians. Furthermore, the presence of 25 mph speed limit signs subtly informs drivers that they need to be a little more attentive to pedestrians. A low speed limit for a quarter-mile stretch within the market place would cost little in terms of actual travel times and give back a lot in terms of pedestrian comfort.

• A Manhattan-style landscaped median, with a protected safety island, has been added to help break up the space into more human-scaled sections and ease pedestrian anxiety. To ease the passage of both pedestrians and motorists across the major intersection even more, we will prohibit left turns (eliminating the usual left-turn lane and keeping a full-width median at the crosswalk) and limit or prohibit right turns as well at that point.

What about motorists who need to make left or right turns? Let's recall the overall form of the market place from the previous chapter. To refresh your memory, figure 9.10a shows the conventional pattern of suburban commercial development. Thick lines represent the major roads, thin lines are entrances to residential subdivisions, and little boxes are commercial or apartment projects, each with its exclusive parking lot in front. In figure 9.10b, I introduce hub circulator streets (the big square), tie the adjacent residential subdivisions into these circulator streets, concentrate commercial and apartment projects in the hub, and specify build-to lines within the hub.

In figure 9.10b, the mixed-use hub's internal circulator streets form a big square overlapping the four quadrants of the major intersection. The square could just as easily have been a diamond or a circle or an irregular

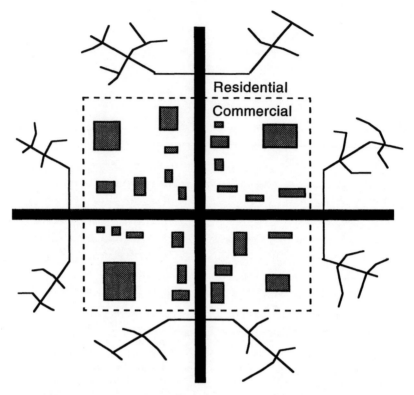

Figure 9.10a   Conventional suburban mixed-use hub, without internal streets or direct links to residential subdivisions.

shape. What matters is that the circulator streets in all four quadrants line up to form a continuous loop. Left and right turns will be allowed where this loop of circulator streets meets the main roads, but not at the major intersection itself. The ensemble of major thoroughfares and circulator loop would work a little like an expressway cloverleaf.

What are the advantages of this arrangement? First, as we have already seen, the absence of a left-turn lane at the major intersection allows the landscaped median to meet the crosswalk at that intersection, giving the pedestrian a pleasant safety island and reducing the perceptual distance across the

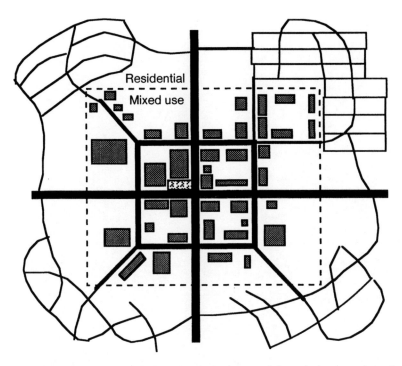

Figure 9.10b Mixed-use hub with circular loop and direct links to residential areas.

road. Second, turning vehicles are forced onto the circulator streets, whose businesses gain exposure to traffic that would not otherwise be there. Third, turning traffic is distributed to four intersections rather than being concentrated at just one; with careful timing of traffic lights, congestion might be reduced. Some of the turning traffic is headed to destinations within the hub anyway, and all of the cars heading to hub destinations are going to have to turn. The circulator streets put those motorists where they want to be without clogging up the main arteries.

Figure 9.11, representing a hypothetical neighborhood center, puts a little more flesh on this fantasy. In the drawing, which is simplified to show only streets, buildings, and parking areas (P), seven-lane through roads

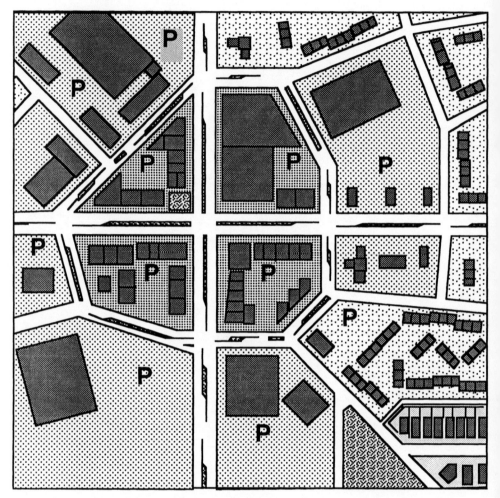

Figure 9.11   A fantasy of a neighborhood center that helps the city cross the road.

(which become six lanes plus a landscaped median inside the right hub) cross at right angles near the center. Five-lane circulator streets form an irregular loop around the four central blocks where most of the small and medium-sized retailers are concentrated.

Very large retail stores—supermarkets, discount chains, movie theater complexes—are located in the outer circle, and the site plans are fairly conventional. Their parking lots are accessible from the major thoroughfares but also from the circulator loop. These parking lots are a little smaller than the norm because of the availability of dispersed parking nearby in the concentrated retail hub. The main difference from standard suburban practice is that the front doors of these large businesses are in closer proximity to the sidewalk system that serves nearby retailers, offices, and apartments. Some outer blocks might also be zoned for gas stations and other auto-service facilities, which require large paved areas and are unavoidably unfriendly to pedestrians, but which are nice to have near the retail center—unless you like having nothing to do but watch soap operas in the tire shop for two hours while your car is being worked on.

Businesses on the central four blocks all face the street and are built up to (or very near) the public right-of-way line. On-street parking (not shown) is provided, and smallish off-street parking lots accessible only from the circulator streets occupy the middles of these blocks. Pedestrian passages, which might include outdoor dining areas, connect the parking lots with the sidewalk and business entrances at several points. I've made the building line pull back at a slight angle from the street on one block to leave room for outdoor dining or public benches and landscaping, and also to give the ceilingless "room" of the north-south street a more interesting and directional shape. On the northwest corner I've put a small public plaza, just big enough for a sculpture or fountain surrounded by landscaping, benches, and a little outdoor café—enough to constitute a focal point for the neighborhood center.

I've shown a larger structure on the northeast corner of the main intersection to suggest that a multistory office building and its attached parking garage can be included in a compact neighborhood center. Indeed, vertical scale within limits can contribute to the pedestrian feel of a street. A six- or seven-lane road bordered by one-story buildings looks, feels, and even sounds emptier and less comfortable to pedestrians than the same road bounded by taller buildings. One technique for unifying the quadrants of a major intersection might be to encourage higher scale by relaxing height limits on blocks immediately surrounding the intersection and imposing lower height limits elsewhere on the road or closer to residential areas. If there is a demand for sizable office buildings in the vicinity, they would do more good in a mixed-use hub, where office workers could walk to stores and restaurants, than in an isolated location accessible only by car. But incentives also should encourage developers to set aside street-level retail space in their office buildings and garages.

Additional retail stores, small professional offices, branch libraries, and other relatively quiet land uses might appear on the blocks that lie between the concentrated hub and residential areas. The next blocks outward from the center might hold apartment complexes. As shown in the southeast portion of figure 9.11, zones of row houses or zero-lot-line houses might mediate between apartments and detached single-family houses. I've tossed in a triangular park as an additional buffer that would also provide outdoor recreation space in close proximity both to the higher-density residential uses and to the retail center. When people have been tossing Frisbees or shooting baskets for an hour, it's nice to be able to walk just a block or two to a store where they can buy a soft drink or a restaurant where they can have a burger.

Time for sirens and flashing lights again: Even if the natural course of things brings about a one-mile grid of major roads with the interstices filled with residential subdivisions, it does not automatically follow that every major crossing point should function as a hub, or that major hubs cannot occupy intermediate locations along the roads, or that every hub must comprise all four quadrants of an intersection rather than just one or two or three, or that any neighborhood center has to look like the hypothetical example in figure 9.11. Local conditions always have to be taken into account. Some hubs need to be larger than others, with more blocks and more circulator streets. Some parts of town may need major hubs no more than a half-mile apart, or no less than two miles. Hubs will have different characters, scales, and mixes of uses, depending on the needs of the local market, the predilections of developers, and the accidents of property ownership and subdivision. Some will be more successful than others. That's fine. We don't want identical neighborhood centers at every mile post.

But neither do we want to encounter no coherent neighborhood centers at all. One task of public planning bodies is to figure out where, in the path of suburban growth, such neighborhood centers would make sense (not a difficult task in cities where residential development is dominated by a few large builders), and then to use all the tools of the planning trade to make those centers function as coherent ensembles. Those centers may look like mine or they may look very different. The essentials are only two: things should connect conveniently with other things, and things should be arranged geographically to support each other best. These essentials can be satisfied in many different ways on the ground, but they are not likely to be satisfied by accident in the absence of a public planning framework. If neighborhood centers are going to work, they have to be designed to work.

BEYOND THE CENTER

Even in my fantasy suburbia, not all commercial and multifamily projects will be concentrated in or near neighborhood hubs. Although I would prefer zoning that favors the development of hubs over continuous corridors, in the real world corridor development is either unavoidable or desirable in some circumstances, whether on arterials or on lesser streets. Can corridor-style development be made to work reasonably well for pedestrians? It can if the sidewalk system is continuous, direct, and inviting from one business's front door to the next, and from the business corridor to nearby residential areas.

Door-to-door continuity entails more or less uniform setbacks—a build-to zone, as discussed earlier. But *where* should the build-to zone be? Several options are possible:

• **Build-to zone along the main road.** The building line could be established at the edge of the public right-of-way, with all off-street parking shunted to the rear or side of the building. The advantages of this arrangement are two. First, the sidewalk is immediately accessible to businesses and to bus stops. Second, the shallow setback puts storefronts close enough to the street to be visible to passing motorists. The disadvantages: Unless traffic lights are spaced more closely than is acceptable to through traffic on the stretches between neighborhood centers, on-street parking would not be

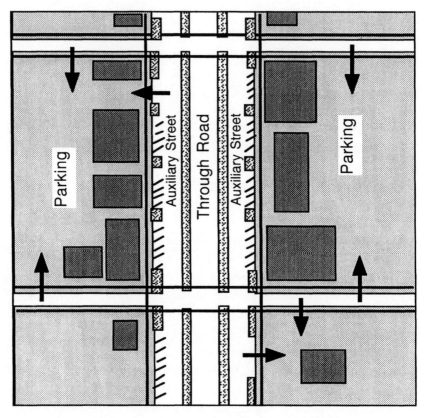

Figure 9.12 Auxiliary streets can allow safe head-in parking at the front door and a pedestrian path buffered from heavy traffic on the main road.

safe. A shallow setback, moreover, may not be practical for some kinds of land uses and may reduce the impact of mixed-use neighborhood hubs with zero setbacks.

• **Build-to zone on auxiliary streets.** Some cities—starting with Paris but including San Antonio on one stretch of road—have widened the public right-of-way to include narrow local auxiliary streets paralleling the major thoroughfare on both sides (figure 9.12). These auxiliary streets, analogous to the continuous frontage roads along some limited-access freeways, usually include on-street parking on one or both sides and (in Paris) are buffered from the main road by a line of street trees. The public sidewalk is usually placed on the business side of the auxiliary street. One advantage for through traffic is that access to individual businesses is possible only from the auxiliary street, not directly from the main road, so that vehicular turns can be concentrated at intersections. Meanwhile, local traffic passes in close proximity to storefronts and at slow speeds. Retailers and other businesses have a chance to communicate with motorists on the auxiliary street without resorting to the enormous signs that are increasingly coming under attack on aesthetic grounds.

This system can work well if setbacks are limited and if off-street parking lots are clearly separated from the auxiliary street. On San Antonio's San Pedro Avenue, only a few short stretches of the auxiliary streets retain their identity as public streets; elsewhere, over the decades they have been allowed to merge imperceptibly with off-street parking lots, and care has not been taken to keep the sidewalks continuous and clearly defined. A standard build-to zone would have helped, but in truth even those blocks that were developed with zero setbacks aren't especially inviting environments—partly because these retail strips were built during a particularly dull period of architectural history, but also because the sidewalk was not designed to be a coherent and inviting system with landscaping, clearly defined crosswalks, standards for connections across property lines, or linkages with adjacent residential subdivisions. Even a perfectly maintained and well-designed auxiliary street, however, has the disadvantage of standardizing a very wide space between facing building fronts—on the order of 220 feet or more for a seven-lane road and two auxiliaries. In general, well-designed auxiliary streets may be most suitable to the kinds of businesses that are appropriate to road corridors—auto sales and service, light industry, wholesalers, large institutions, convenience stores, drive-through restaurants—while being poorly suited to the kinds of businesses that ought to go into compact neighborhood nodes anyway. It's important to recognize these differences in the zoning code.

The same comments apply doubly to continuous frontage roads along limited-access freeways. Because these frontage roads are nearly always one-way, and because distances of a mile or more typically separate crossing

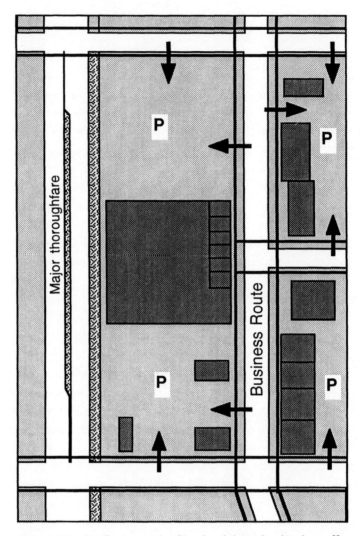

Figure 9.13 Conflicting needs of local and through vehicular traffic and pedestrians can be resolved with a "business route." Businesses are oriented to a local circulator street parallel to a major thoroughfare.

points, frontage roads are abysmally inconvenient and frustrating for retail customers. If you accidentally pass a destination on a one-way frontage road, or if you need to reverse course to stop at another store or return home, you may have no choice but to drive two miles out of your way.

• **The business route.** The analogy here is to the small-town main street paralleling the railroad tracks. In practical terms, frontage on a seven-lane major thoroughfare brings only two real benefits to a business—exposure of the sign to motorists and easy vehicular access. Neither of these goods requires businesses to face the main road. The motorist needs to see only the sign and the access to parking. Thus it costs the business nothing—except perhaps an extra sign—to turn its back to the main road and its front to a local circulator street that would be at most four lanes wide and parallel to the road a block away (figure 9.13). Like auxiliary streets, these local circulators would have on-street parking (not shown in the drawing), but both sides of the streets could be developed. If setbacks on both sides are kept to a minimum and off-street parking is shifted to the rear, the local circulator street would have roughly the same scale as the pedestrian court of a shopping mall. The two sides of the street could form a mutually supportive ensemble. Meanwhile, through traffic can speed along the main road with limited interruptions: Regulated cross streets, which would provide access to the business route and possibly to residential subdivisions, could be spaced widely, on the order of fifteen hundred or two thousand feet, so long as the business route is more generously punctuated by stop signs or signals to allow safe crossings for pedestrians. (The central block in figure 9.13 is only eight hundred feet long to keep the drawing a reasonable size.) Direct vehicular access from the main road to businesses would be limited or forbidden. I've also drawn in a landscaped buffer along the major thoroughfare.

• **The pedestrian corridor.** I haven't seen anything like this (figure 9.14), but it might be worth considering. Suppose a city were to take an easement parallel to the main road's right-of-way and at some distance from it—perhaps about sixty feet, the typical width of a parking lot with two rows of cars, and also the typical depth of a retail strip building. The easement would be wide enough (say, fifteen to twenty feet) to accommodate both a sidewalk and landscaping, which developers would be required to install as integral

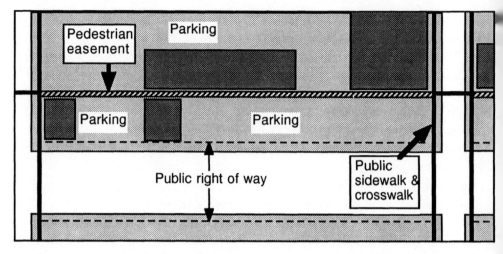

Figure 9.14   One way to reconcile pedestrian connectedness with parking lots—a public pedestrian easement.

parts of their projects. This sidewalk, which would be continuous across property lines and from one block to the next, would be the main pedestrian path, replacing the more usual sidewalk along the road. Developers would have the option of putting buildings or parking on either or both sides of the easement and cutting through it, using the "silent cop" design described earlier, for vehicular access. Development standards could specify how the connections should be made across property lines or streets, and setback limits would be measured from the easement rather than from the road right-of-way. Every front door should open onto this sidewalk.

One advantage to this system, as compared to the auxiliary street, is that the pedestrian corridor could yield a more complex and varied streetscape for both pedestrians and motorists. But in the absence of a local circulator street, vehicular access would be required at intermediate points between cross streets; thus this system might not be appropriate for the busiest and widest arterials.

All of the preceding comments apply mainly to new, undeveloped territory in a city's growth ring, where a matrix can be laid out with forethought and then followed by subsequent development. The more intractable problem is what to do with the chaos that has already been built over the past thirty or more years and cannot in an instant be undone. But in many cases cooperative action between public planning bodies and private property owners could greatly improve the connectivity of commercial districts and create significant value for property owners at an acceptable public and private cost.

The greatest potential for retrofitting may be at very large commercial agglomerations that grow up around the intersections of major roads, or roads and expressways. These agglomerations typically include the full range of stores and services that consumers need, from huge supermarkets and discount retailers to small specialty shops in strip centers, from multiscreen theaters to multistory office buildings, from drive-through burgers to drive-through banks. Developed helter-skelter, piece by piece, without benefit (or restraints) of a master plan, these agglomerations have *many* of the pieces of neighborhood centers—parks, cultural facilities, and funky, individualistic local businesses are usually missing—but the pieces are so scattered, so disconnected that they cannot form a coherent whole. Even in such unpromising locations it may be possible to bring the pieces into some semblance of relationship with each other.

With the cooperation of property owners, separate parking lots can in some instances be aggregated, reconfigured, and made communal, to be owned and operated by a merchants' association rather than by individual property owners. Sometimes fire lanes can be connected across property lines and be transformed, in effect or in fact, into public circulator streets. It may be possible to design a unified landscape and sidewalk plan that could greatly improve pedestrian circulation. (University architecture and urban design classes might find it a useful exercise to study how existing commercial agglomerations in their areas might be retrofitted to function more coherently.)

City government or other planning agencies can make three major contributions: first, by initiating the process of bringing the relevant public and private entities together; second, by offering such capital improvements as better crosswalks and traffic signals, landscaping of the public right-of-way, or parks, libraries, and public art; and third, by offering to reduce total parking requirements in exchange for a unifying master plan.

More than half, and sometimes as much as two-thirds, of the gross land area in these agglomerations is usually devoted to parking lots. The parking code in San Antonio demands one parking space for every 200 square feet of general retail sales or service space. The six spaces required for a 1,200-square-foot shop can cover as much as 1,647 square feet of asphalt if you include the driveway space between two rows of parked cars. Restaurants must have one space per 100 square feet of gross area, and those with drive-up windows must have two spaces per 100 square feet of gross area. Given the prevalence of eating places in major commercial agglomerations, it is entirely safe to say the that current city code in San Antonio, as in many other cities, requires more land to be put under asphalt than into productive use.

The first task is to analyze the real parking need, as opposed to the number of spaces demanded by the formula enshrined in city codes. It is likely that the existing supply in a contiguous group of properties exceeds the demand generated by that same contiguous group of properties. The surplus is land that could be converted to landscaping (not just for aesthetics and environmental quality, but to help organize the total space and shade and define the pedestrian paths), to additional sidewalks or internal streets connecting across property lines, or to additional development.

I am aware of no case where this kind of process has been attempted. Indeed it would be an extraordinarily difficult process, entailing the cooperation of dozens of owners and lessees, most of them large corporations with headquarters in distant cities. But many cities and urban development authorities have amassed experience in forging very complicated real estate deals involving multiple owners, usually for the purpose of creating new mixed-use projects. Cities and property owners have grown accustomed to such stratagems as tax-increment districts, which are commonly used to finance downtown improvements. The sort of process that I have described for suburban commercial agglomerations would be a logical extension of these familiar precedents—difficult, but feasible. The key is for public planning bodies to be able to offer sufficient incentives to capture the property owners' interest.

But that is the key in any planning regimen. Any city's zoning and development standards, its matrix of thoroughfares, sidewalks, and setbacks, its capital improvements policies, its long-range plans for parks and libraries—all of these represent in palpable form some balance of political and economic interests, some direct or indirect quid pro quo.

▪ policy and politics

 In chapter 10 we see how urban design decisions are affected by the political process. Because goals are useless if they are not politically achievable, we discuss the importance of participating in the political process, building alliances, and searching for design solutions that satisfy a wide range of seemingly divergent interests. The appendix summarizes the main urban design points put forward in Part II and lists the policy tools commonly available to cities to translate design objectives into reality. ▪

CHAPTER 10

■ the politics and promise
of poetics

As I write this, I am angry, frustrated, and depressed.

In 1992 some members of the Planning Commission of San Antonio hoped to strengthen the city's sidewalk standards for residential streets. The existing code required developers to build sidewalks, but they could be as little as three feet wide on residential streets, and they could be placed anywhere within the ten-foot public right-of-way between the curb and the property line. In practice the city's largest builder, Rayco, a company specializing in the low-end market, built three-foot sidewalks against the curb. (A sidewalk away from the curb requires extra work and costs a little more.) The planning commissioners hoped to require a four-foot sidewalk set back from the curb. In chapter 5, I explained the virtues of separating the sidewalk from the street.

On 17 June 1993, after several months of meetings and compromises with developers, the Planning Commission presented to the City Council a modest, nearly insignificant change: residential sidewalks would have to be at least four feet wide, with an unobstructed path at least three feet wide, and the sidewalks could continue to be built anywhere within the ten-foot public right-of-way.

Rayco's president, Jack Willome, appeared before the City Council and claimed that the extra foot of sidewalk width would have "no value" and would compromise the "affordability" of his houses. (By my calculations, the proposal would have added between $42 and $69 to the cost of typical Rayco houses, and as little as $30 to houses on cul-de-sac lots.) Willome said he'd never heard from his customers that his sidewalks don't work. Then he admitted to the council that his sidewalks do not, in fact, work by saying, "If you go out and drive the streets and look at the people, you'll see nobody's on the sidewalks. When people are out jogging and stuff, they jog in the street because otherwise they're going around obstacles and cars and dips and so on and so forth."

Inspecting two recent low-end Rayco subdivisions, I found garbage bags at the curb blocking the sidewalk in front of many houses—this on a Saturday evening, with garbage pickup two days away. Many cars were parked on the street, but about half of these were pulled up on the sidewalk. A resident whom I met as she walked with a companion in the street said she wasn't using the sidewalk because she was bothered by the slope at driveway ramps and because the sidewalk was blocked by garbage bags. Children, too, had to walk in the street on the way to school, she said. All the evidence indicated that the sidewalks needed to be at least a foot wider in order to yield a usable pathway. At three feet wide and against the curb, the sidewalk might as well not have existed.

The proposal to require four-foot sidewalks was defeated by a vote of six to three.

One could decry the defeat as an example of politics' outweighing the public interest. But there are two difficulties with that assessment. First, in a democratic form of government, politics is never the problem; it's the solution. One of the great advantages of representative democracy is that those who govern are not insulated from influence by the governed. We elect representatives, not high priests. Nor do we elect mind readers. A representative can represent only the views presented to him or her. If a lot of constituents tell their representative they want X, and hardly anybody demands Y, then the representative will be more likely to vote for X and less likely to vote for Y. The problem in the sidewalk issue wasn't that a powerful developer asked for X. The problem was that the council saw too little countervailing pressure for Y from interest groups representing the handicapped and the elderly, from PTAs concerned about the safety of children walking to and from school, from neighborhood associations. Mayor Nelson Wolff, who voted for wider sidewalks, summed it up this way: "The neighborhood groups were sleeping at the switch."

In a way, the neglect is understandable. The ordinance would have benefited only people who had not yet bought houses in subdivisions not yet built—not much of a political constituency in the here and now. But in failing to act, the community-based interest groups let down the citizens who would live in those future subdivisions.

The second difficulty is that "the public interest" is a fiction, or at best unknowable. It's roughly equivalent to that old utilitarian slogan, "the greatest good for the greatest number," a pleasant sentiment on the surface but impossible to pin down until the end of history, and meanwhile annoyingly adaptable to totalitarian claims. Until such time as everyone in "the public" agrees spontaneously and without coercion what "the public interest" is, we are better off disabusing ourselves of the belief that this abstraction should guide the actions of public officials. In both the theory and the practice of democratic governance, "the public interest" is just what the many variously interested participants in governance, acting through the political process, decide should be done.

Every feature of the built environment in the public realm, and much of the private realm as well, is shaped by the tug of political interests. Decisions about the design of the built environment are not and cannot, in a free society, be made in a vacuum, based on abstract, universally agreed-upon principles. In this book I have put forward an idealized urban matrix, a set of principles for connecting pieces of real estate into a coherent city. I have tried to show how some ways of laying out a city might make more sense, from various points of view, than other ways. But the actual matrix that is enacted into policy in any real city is a reflection of the relative squeakiness of that city's political interests. The built environment, after all, costs money and time and skill. Every urban design policy and practice expresses a particular set of beliefs about how resources should best be allocated and how people are expected to relate to one another—how society is supposed to work. But people differ about what is important. Each of the seemingly mundane details of our cities, the dimensions and layout of streets and side-walks, drainage ditches and bus stops, reflects a particular balance of inter-ests—in rare cases a consensus, perhaps, but more often a messy set of compromises among different people's wishes, or even different wishes of the same people: When you are driving to the supermarket, you may be an-noyed at having to wait for a pedestrian to cross the street; when you are walking to the park, you may have occasion to curse the heavy auto traffic that crosses your route. We can't have everything we want all the time.

People are especially protective of their own resources and preroga-tives. People who fear public controls over their private resources are highly motivated to demand a place at the table when such controls are being con-templated. Developers do not like to be told how and where to build side-walks, how big their parking lots must be, how to landscape their property, how to design their signs and buildings, or where they may and may not build various kinds of projects. Land speculators and real estate brokers do not want zoning controls or development standards that might limit the sell-ing price of property.

Moreover, people are protective of their immediate surroundings. It is easy to mobilize one's neighbors in reaction to a specific, localized, and highly visible threat—a zoning change that will allow a pawnshop near their homes, a dangerous intersection that needs a traffic light, the destruction of beautiful old trees for a Kmart parking lot, or (alas) a proposal for a public housing project in the neighborhood. It is easy to mobilize a neighborhood to demand a sidewalk leading to the neighborhood school.

But it is hard to mobilize people citywide to demand a policy govern-ing the design of sidewalks in general. Such a policy is an abstraction that probably will affect very few people where they live today. People who live in neighborhoods that already have adequate sidewalks have little motivation to demand them for other neighborhoods, especially those that don't yet ex-ist. And in practical terms, existing neighborhoods that don't have adequate sidewalks aren't likely to get them as a result of a new policy for future devel-opment. In either case, a sidewalk policy offers little appeal to self-interest.

Similarly, people may complain about the commercial district in their neighborhood—the kids can't walk safely to the movie theater, the main roads are too congested, the signs are too ugly. But it's hard to motivate those same people to demand policies that could prevent such problems in future commercial districts on the periphery of the city, because what happens out there doesn't affect *them*. Until, of course, they or their children move or work or shop out there themselves. Most people don't think that far ahead. So it is hard to assemble a political constituency for urban design policies—as opposed to specific local projects—that work.

Difficult, but not impossible. Even in San Antonio, a city that has been singularly uncongenial to planning and regulation, a politically effective constituency coalesced around the issue of historic preservation. The preservation movement brought San Antonio a proliferation of historic districts with stringent design controls that are, for the most part, stringently applied even though they often annoy developers and business owners.

The political effectiveness of the historic preservation constituency in San Antonio has been based on two distinct circumstances. First, the movement itself grew out of a powerful emotional commitment to preserving the city's historic legacy, features of the landscape to which many San Antonians had grown attached, seemingly in defiance of reason. The prime example was the San Antonio River's downtown meander. A devastating flood in 1921 killed about fifty people, destroyed thirteen of the twenty-seven bridges across the river, and caused more than $3 million in property damage. Comparable floods had occurred in 1819 and 1865. In 1926 the city's business leaders laid plans to dig a straight bypass channel that would allow floodwaters to pass unimpeded through the business district. They also wanted to turn the original meandering channel into a covered sewer. The San Antonio Conservation Society, formed a few years earlier, wanted to preserve and beautify the original channel. At a legendary mass meeting called by the society, a puppet show adaptation of "The Goose That Laid the Golden Egg" supposedly persuaded the businessmen that the river should be saved. The fact that many of the society's members were the wives and mothers of the men they hoped to persuade probably didn't hurt. Ultimately both sides got what they wanted. A flood bypass channel was built—it remains the ugliest feature of downtown San Antonio—but the original channel was preserved and cut off from the new main channel by floodgates. Architect Robert H.

H. Hugman's fanciful river landscape design, including an amphitheater, stone bridges, water features, and decorative paving, was executed by the city and the federal Works Progress Administration starting in the late thirties. After extensive commercial development of the River Walk began in the 1970s, it became one of the state's most popular and lucrative tourist draws, the centerpiece of San Antonio's billion-dollar-a-year visitor industry.

This economic success leads to the second circumstance that underpinned the preservation movement. Emotional commitment can go only so far. To be politically effective, a movement has to reach beyond its true believers by persuading others, even adversaries, that the movement's goals will serve their interests. Business people and homeowners who may have had no emotional attachment to historic resources were persuaded that design controls and preservation standards, onerous though they might be, would nonetheless add value to their property and put money in their purses.

The same formula—a core group's emotional commitment to a vision, followed by the patient building of alliances based on appeal to the self-interest of others—can create an effective constituency for sound urban design policies.

So you need to get political. To begin, you need a base of operations. For many people the best entrée into the political process is the neighborhood association.

I know what you're thinking. You went to a neighborhood association meeting once. It was boring, it was a waste of time, and you got home too late to catch "Murphy Brown" on television. It is something of a cliché to say "Get involved in your neighborhood association," but clichés often get to be clichés because they are true. Neighborhood associations draft neighborhood plans that can influence local government decision making. In many cities neighborhood groups are given an opportunity to support or oppose zoning changes and capital improvement projects. Associations with large active memberships can produce crowds of supporters at city council meetings. Local politicians often appear at association meetings and get to know the more active members, who may gain consideration for appointment to important government boards and commissions. Associations are pools of knowledge, experience, expertise, and connections, all of which need to be marshaled in order to achieve common ends. In the absence of a current hot-button issue, association meetings may seem dull and fruitless affairs, not worthy of your time. In the big picture and the long run, however, associations can, if they are sufficiently active, be vital to the maintenance and improvement of neighborhoods. More important still, a citywide coalition of neighborhood associations can—with the right leadership and a sufficient number of active component associations—claim an influential place at the table where urban design and planning policies are made.

Other kinds of civic and special-interest groups also afford entrée to the political process and are natural allies in the struggle for more user-friendly cities—PTAs, organizations of the elderly and the handicapped, groups with pet causes such as historic preservation or trees, professional associations of architects and planners, university student associations, and civic groups that support parks, libraries, and recreational activities. In Portland, Oregon, the Willamette Pedestrian Coalition, something that deserves to be imitated in every sizable city in the country, has been highly effective in raising that city's consciousness about urban design problems and goading local government to correct them.

Potential allies aren't always obvious. The search should not be limited to the usual suspects. Effective alliances can be forged by searching for coincidences of interest among groups that may have been traditional adversaries or at best unconcerned about one another's issues.

In San Antonio, for example, the City Council in 1993 passed an ordinance enabling modest standards for signs and landscaping along specified "urban corridors." The ordinance was achievable even in its very weak final form only because a large locally based insurance company, USAA, pressed for it in order to prevent visual blight from encroaching on the routes to its Fiesta Texas theme park. That was a case where the interests of a politically influential developer coincided with the interests of neighborhood associations and other groups concerned with aesthetics. Other developers and such trade associations as the San Antonio Board of Realtors and the San Antonio Restaurant Association fought to emasculate the ordinance, largely succeeding, but even so the ordinance is a foot in the door, a necessary first step toward stronger and more broadly applicable controls. USAA and the neighborhood interests are not natural allies; on other issues they have been adversaries. But progress was possible because, on this issue, they were able to work together.

Other kinds of alliances are waiting to be forged. As in many cities, San Antonio's community-based organizations are divided into several camps along ethnic, economic, and geographic lines. One of the more powerful groups, Communities Organized for Public Service (COPS), is a Catholic parish–based group that presses for jobs, new housing, and infrastructure improvements in the inner city's poorest Hispanic neighborhoods. One concern of long standing for COPS has been the need for drainage projects to correct chronic flooding in its neighborhoods. Acting skillfully in the political arena, the organization has dominated local allocations from the federal Community Development Block Grant program, which in San Antonio has been used largely for street and drainage projects in COPS neighborhoods. But the flooding problem continues to spread and get worse because the COPS neighborhoods are downhill from the bulk of the new suburban development. Runoff from new middle-class subdivisions and commercial parking lots is funneled into COPS neighborhoods.

Yet COPS has never seen—or at least never acted on—the connection. COPS has held itself aloof from community-based planning initiatives, refusing even to participate in the drafting of a city master plan. In practice, City Council members from COPS-heavy districts have sided with the suburban developers and opposed planning or controls that might have addressed flooding problems at their source. One ostensible reason for this bizarre alliance is that council members from poor districts are interested in job creation, and thus oppose policies that might inhibit job growth. Their position might make sense if the job growth stimulated by laissez-faire policies occurred in the poor neighborhoods. Instead, it sucks economic activity out of those neighborhoods. The real reasons for the alliance of these City Council members with suburban developers are complex, but one factor may be a cultural clash between inner-city Hispanic leaders and the forces that favor strong urban design policies—generally a highly educated, professional, well-off crowd that's interested in downtown revitalization, historic preservation, trees, aesthetics, and neighborhood character. The latter group is concentrated partly in inner-city neighborhoods that are gentrified or at least upwardly mobile, and partly in suburban subdivisions whose residents feel threatened by the sprawl and ugliness of uncontrolled growth around them.

But there are unrecognized commonalities between the goals that COPS hopes to achieve and those advocated by groups with very different interests and demographics. Landscape requirements for new development are not just aesthetic but functional as well, helping to retain rainwater and reduce stress on the inner city's drainage system. Zoning and subdivision policies that promote walkable neighborhood centers could provide more opportunities for local entrepreneurs to compete effectively with national chains. Historic preservation controls help to stop or reverse the flight of wealth from old neighborhoods and create jobs and business opportunities in close proximity to low-income areas. Growth-management policies can help reduce the strain on public resources and improve the efficiency of public transportation to connect the poor with jobs.

The lines of interdependency run in both directions. Economic, social, and physical decay in poor inner-city neighborhoods threatens heavy investments in downtown and gentrifying historic neighborhoods, increases the stress on fire, police, and medical services, and diminishes the pool of educated and skilled workers needed by industry. Nobody is fully insulated from problem neighborhoods. It is shortsighted and counterproductive to draw a conceptual line around your part of town and say, "I'm concerned about whatever affects my neck of the woods and will let other people worry about what affects *their* neck of the woods." Fire spreads quickly from one neck of the woods to another.

Alliances across social, economic, and interest boundaries are more than just politically useful; they're necessary. But alliances don't just happen. You have to work at building them. It may take long, determined, and patient courtships to break down barriers of distrust or indifference. It may require the informal cultivation of sympathetic individuals in other groups. It will certainly require careful analysis of joint interests, a willingness to compromise, and the maturity to continue working together for common purposes even when conflict is unavoidable on specific issues.

Politics doesn't refer only to the jostling for advantage in campaigns for elective office. Politics is the process by which differing points of view contend with each other and reach equilibrium from time to time, regardless of the forum in which the game is played.

Policies governing the shape of your city are made in many places by people with many different jurisdictions, functions, and interests—not just by your city council and mayor, but also by the engineers in the public works and traffic departments, the planning and zoning commissions, the folks who run the parks and libraries, the fire and police departments, the sallow fellow who checks building plans in his basement office; by bureaucrats, specialists, engineers, legislators, and lobbyists in the state and national capitals, and in district offices of state and federal departments; by actuaries and financial analysts and loan officers at banks, pension funds, and insurance companies; by the boards, real estate vice presidents, corporate design teams, business strategists, marketing experts, and number crunchers of retail chains and land developers; by the National Association for This and the American Society for That and the Commission on Standards and Practices for the Other Thing. Policy travels under many aliases—"procedure," "code," "variances," "waivers," "technical analysis," "the computer," "the form," "staff size," "the flowchart," "the schedule," "the budget."

Policy often hides behind "hard, objective economic realities," which upon closer examination turn out to be squishy and subjective. The line between policy and economics is exceedingly blurry. Why is the sidewalk blocked by utility poles? The superficial answer the utility company might give is that it's cheaper to do it that way than to put the lines underground or to buy enough right-of-way for an unobstructed pedestrian path—"economic realities." But the outcome of the economic calculation depends on the kinds of information that policy makers decide to plug into the equations—what sorts of costs to consider and how to measure, weigh, and order various kinds of benefits. "Economic realities" may dictate a very different conclusion if policy makers decide to measure the economic costs of traffic accidents that might occur because the utility poles block drivers' vision; or if they decide to consider how the utility poles inhibit foot traffic, commerce, and tax collections; or if they weigh the effect of aesthetics on property values and neighborhood stability.

Most of the people who make policy—or, rather, their little pieces of policy—are not evil or incompetent. They may, however, be narrowly focused. The director of public works needs to fill as many potholes and build as many drainage ditches as he can within the budget allotted him, and he's likely to regard any other concern as a nuisance. The director of traffic is concerned, by training and job description, with making sure the streets are wide enough to handle all the vehicles that will use them; a demand that she also consider the needs of pedestrians is likely to be met with incomprehension.

Bureaucracies, no less than legislative bodies, are politically dynamic. In any large bureaucracy there are diverse views about how things ought to be done. The view expressed by the director as the institution's official position on any issue, including such a seemingly objective datum as how much something will cost, reflects a momentary and changeable equilibrium in the internal dynamics of the organization. Those dynamics can be influenced from the outside.

The electric utility's official policy may be to string utility lines on poles planted in the middle of sidewalks because that's the cheapest way to do the job, but chances are that some strategically placed individuals in the organization are arguing for other options. The public works department's official policy may be to engineer street and drainage projects that, in the interest of short-term economies, ignore the needs of pedestrians and aesthetics, but chances are that someone in the organization takes a broader view of its responsibilities.

An important part of the political process for neighborhood associations and other community groups is to find and support these sympathetic fifth-columnists within the bureaucracies that decide how your city and your neighborhood will work. Your hidden allies may need to stay in the closet in order to protect their jobs, but they can be invaluable sources of advance information about projects or policy changes that may run counter to neighborhood interests. More important in the long run, persistent pressure on public-sector bureaucracies, either directly or through the elective bodies that ultimately control them, strengthens the hand of your allies and may—through leadership changes or evolution of opinion—eventually tilt the organization's formal policies.

People in bureaucracies have a trump card to play when they don't wish to change policy: they can claim to be the experts. Indeed, they usually do know more about the technical and legal aspects of their jobs than outsiders do. But you needn't be intimidated. You, too, are an expert. You know better than anyone else how you wish to go about your daily affairs, how you want your city and your neighborhood to work, what you like or don't like about the world you live in, and what level of risk or inconvenience you are willing to accept in some features of your world in order to achieve benefits or added convenience in other features. And you have power. You vote, you spend money, and you can make noise.

But other people also vote, spend money, and make noise. In every city powerful interest groups are arrayed against planning initiatives. Conservative business groups may condemn planning and urban design initiatives as socialistic interference with free enterprise. Our cities are the way they are, it is often claimed, because of "the market" or "economic realities," and of course "the market" is always right. I don't mean to dismiss such claims out of hand. To some degree developers do respond to the wishes of their customers. The residential cul-de-sac is a case in point. Developers lay out their subdivisions today with cul-de-sacs partly because they discovered that cul-de-sac lots sell faster than lots on open-ended streets. The other reason, of course, is that cul-de-sacs enable a developer to squeeze more building sites onto the same acreage and spend less money on streets. These are, legitimately, economic realities.

But the real-world domain in which "the market" and "economic realities" express themselves is never fully free. The playing field isn't level; it's bumpy. A lot of times what looks like a preference of "the market" or a requirement of "economic realities" turns out to be a product of artificial constraints, not of freedom. One of those constraints is implied in the very term *the market*, which obscures the great diversity of preferences by dumping all consumers into one statistical basket. The observation—valid or not—that many people looking for single-family houses prefer to live on cul-de-sacs in single-entry subdivisions is expressed in the shorthand statement that "the market" for single-family houses prefers cul-de-sacs in single-entry subdivisions. Never mind those other people who might prefer another arrangement.

People can buy only what is offered for sale. Usually the choice is among several compromises between what one wants and what is available. If you choose to buy a house in a particular location because it offers, say, three of the things that are most important to you—for example, good schools, security, and the right price—it does not necessarily follow that all the other characteristics of that location are to your liking. If all the available locations that meet your three most important criteria happen to be in areas where you cannot walk to the park, the library, and the ice cream parlor, it does not follow that you *prefer* to live in a location where you cannot walk to the park, the library, and the ice cream parlor. We are not justified in elevating an accidental annoyance to a positive virtue.

In the real world we have a lot of accidental annoyances to contend with, and most of them are consequences of a complex mixture of economic constraints and policy (political) decisions in both public and private sectors. The suburban pattern of commercial development, for example, wasn't created solely by the free market, but also by a host of public decisions about how cities should be zoned, how auto traffic and parking needs should be managed, how growth should be promoted, where roads, universities, and major economic generators should be built, how utility extensions should be paid for, and how the risks of entrepreneurship should be shared. It simply is not historically accurate to say that the suburban development pattern reflects market forces. It *is* accurate to say that the suburban development pattern reflects the market's response to particular public decisions—one might even say the market's *rational* response to poorly considered public decisions.

If, for example, the public has decided that commercial zoning should occupy narrow corridors running the length of major thoroughfares, that decision leads logically to other consequences. Compared to commercial nodes, commercial corridors place fewer destinations within walking distance of each other and thus generate more auto trips, which require more parking spaces and more parking lot entrances, which exacerbate congestion on the major thoroughfares, which thus have to be made wider, enabling traffic to move quickly again so yet more miles of roadway can be developed as a commercial corridor, generating yet more auto trips and more congestion. And so it goes. Zoning that concentrates neighborhood-compatible businesses into commercial nodes leads to a very different logical chain for both public policy and private development practice. That is not to say that a sudden shift to node zoning would by itself suddenly produce pedestrian-friendly, neighborhood-linked market places. In the absence of other changes, a McDonald's in a node is likely to have the same site plan as a McDonald's on a corridor. But if a city has established the commercial node as a norm, then other decisions and learning tend to follow. A node needs to be penetrated at more frequent intervals by local public streets that allow circulation within the node, because many of the businesses in a node will not directly face a major thoroughfare. For the same reason, businesses in nodes have a greater need to capture their neighbors' customers, so node overlay zoning with development standards that promote internal walkability and aesthetics becomes more easily achievable politically. Because a node occupies a confined area, by contrast to indefinitely extensible corridors, available land is limited in nodes, and parking can be more easily shared, promoting more compact styles of development. Nodes are natural foci of attention for public capital projects such as libraries, parks, schools, and low-income housing.

One way or the other, nodes or corridors, private sector development is shaped by public decisions. On this and other planning issues, a policy change does not entail trading freedom for bondage, but rather one set of limitations for another. The new set need not be, on the whole, more burdensome than the set it replaces. Politically it is essential to drive home this point, or else change will not be achievable in most cities.

YOUR CITY IS YOUR RESPONSIBILITY

It is possible, with sustained, coordinated, and informed action, for citizen groups to sway city hall. But that possibility is both a promise and a problem. Persistence is most often seen only in reaction to narrow, specific circumstances that are perceived as immediate threats. The neighborhood association rises up in anger against multifamily zoning in a single-family area, or demands a street closure to reduce auto traffic. Only rarely do interest groups—whether neighborhood associations, building industry groups, or the various specialists in city hall—place their narrow, immediate concerns in a larger context.

In the absence of that context, achievement of one immediate objective can have unintended and undesired consequences. A residential subdivision, for example, may have been attractive in part because of its convenient location near a retailing district, which is accessible both from the major through road that borders the subdivision and from a local street. The people who live on the local street near the retail district become upset because of all the people from the other end of the subdivision who drive past their houses to get to the retail district, so they agitate successfully to make the local street a dead end. The retail district is now less accessible to the neighborhood than it had been. Forced onto the through road, potential customers might as well keep driving to the next retail area, or to the big regional mall two miles away; maybe there's a difficult and dangerous left turn discouraging them from using their own retail center. The neighborhood retailers find themselves with less business. Some of them close, others become marginal. Five years later, the neighbors complain that their once-vital retail district has become a little seedy, less of an asset than it had been before. And they complain about traffic congestion on the through road, which now has to handle traffic that had previously been using internal streets. They and the traffic engineers want to make the road wider. There go the parkways, and with them the trees. The neighborhood is a little harsher, a little less inviting.

It is important to ask for the right things, to understand how the parts fit into the whole, and how the whole affects the parts. Before you do anything else, you must begin with active, thoughtful, and inquisitive looking around. You have to get into the habit of noticing things that are so commonplace, so much a part of the givens of your environment, that you might never have thought about them before. Much of this book has been concerned with bringing these commonplaces to your attention and putting them into a larger context. It is helpful to acquaint yourself and your neighbors with various types of development in other locales, to be aware of options and models beyond those available locally; slides and videos from travel to other cities can be invaluable educational tools. Critical and engaged looking around can help you to ask the right questions about your city and your neighborhood. I can't ask all the right questions about your city and your neighborhood, because I don't live there. That's your job, in cooperation with your neighbors. Don't forget to include the kids in this task. They live there, too.

■ the stakes

 In the final chapter of *Sustainable Communities: A New Design Synthesis for Cities, Suburbs and Towns*, Peter Calthorpe gives a brief survey of new-town planning concepts and practices in the twentieth century. A few lines before the end, Calthorpe laments: "Meanwhile, most growth continues in sunbelt suburbs, in patterns which bear little resemblance to the proposals outlined in this chapter."[1]

Indeed. The planners' job would be a lot easier if it weren't for all those ignorant and pigheaded people who *like* cul-de-sacs, automobiles, low-density sprawl, and radical segregation of functions.

In San Antonio, as I write this, more than eight hundred acres of raw ranch land, incongruously surrounded by upper-income residential subdivisions on the city's far North Side, awaits development. Many years ago the Voelcker Tract, as this extraordinarily beautiful thicket of live oak, juniper, and prickly pear is called, was bisected by a major road running northwest. Recently, when the state highway department announced plans to build an east-west arterial across the property to link intensively developed areas on either side, eleven neighborhood associations banded together and successfully demanded that the City Council zone a major portion of the tract, 361 acres, for detached single-family residential use—R-1, in the city's zoning code.

Several members of the planning commission saw this acreage as an opportunity to develop a model project based on Andres Duany's "neo-traditional" planning concepts—a mix of housing types scaling up to multifamily use in the vicinity of a "village square" of retail and office space. The opportunity beckoned in the practical sense because this large block of land was held by one owner, located in one of the city's priciest areas, and soon to be easily accessible to the freeway system. The planning commission saw it as an ideal site for a didactic exercise because it was raw land. The commission could demonstrate to developers on the outward-spreading fringe of the city a new, resource-efficient, and—presumably—marketable method of site planning. The design standards that emerged from the Voelcker Tract study would become an alternative development code, parallel to the existing sprawl-producing standards.

Well, as soon as the surrounding neighborhoods got wind of this vision for the Voelcker Tract, they were up in arms. One of the opponents of the "neo-traditional" proposal described it as a "neoneanderthal subterfuge" for junking up their neighborhood with commerce. They would not stand for one flower shop, one restaurant, one apartment duplex.

Now, one can put forward any number of rational arguments for allowing a certain amount of retail, commercial, and multifamily residential development to take place on the land in question. Properly designed and situated as part of a total development scheme, a small commercial hub within the Voelcker Tract could provide added shopping convenience not only for its immediate neighborhood but for the preexisting subdivisions surrounding the site. It could be a center for social and community life for the entire area. It could give neighborhood children a place to ride their bicycles. By obviating the need for car trips to retail districts farther afield, it could help hold down traffic congestion. Multifamily housing near the hub could include subsidized or affordable market-rate units close to the city's biggest job centers, and the additional density could help justify more frequent bus service to the area (not that the residents of the nearby subdivisions ride the bus, but their maids do).

That's all well and good, but the neighbors bought into the surrounding subdivisions precisely because they offered a total separation from the congestion and ugliness of suburban commercial corridors and from the economic diversity (seen as a threat to security, property values, and schools) of the larger city. Some of the subdivisions are entirely private, with guarded entry gates and high walls or fences all around. But obsessively secured or not, all are inward-turning enclaves, semiarcadian and strictly controlled retreats from the sometimes frightening uncertainties of city life.

It is tempting to ridicule these prosperous people cowering in their self-imposed prisons, and a little later I will note the social and political dislocations that result from so complete a physical separation of upper-middle-class professionals, the primary market for these walled enclaves, from the rest of the city. At the same time, however, planners and policy makers need to understand the conditions—some real, some perceived—that turned the professional class, or a part of it, against the city. People don't like having their houses burglarized or their children assaulted, so they choose to live in secured subdivisions, or in those where the street pattern discourages quick escapes. They don't want vehicular traffic disturbing their serenity or endangering their children, so they choose to live on cul-de-sacs. They have seen their parents' neighborhoods in the inner city degraded by commercial encroachment paradoxically combined with the decay and disuse of the old retail hubs, and they have seen the congestion and visual blight of suburban retail corridors, with their towering forests of garish signs and their wastelands of asphalt. It is not surprising that they choose to isolate their homes as fully as possible from commercial development.

In a lecture in San Antonio, Duany observed that suburbanites "like their house and their lot. They like their private realm. What they don't like is the public realm. As soon as they step out of their front yards, they enter a situation which is essentially harsh, stressful and ugly. . . . In the suburbs, the public realm is a tough place to be."

In self-defense, such suburbanites extend their private realm beyond the walls of the house, beyond the front and back yards, to include the entire residential subdivision with its internal streets and, often, private park areas and recreation centers as well. Ultimately, individual subdivisions may bond together as a vast cluster of private cells and, acting together, seek to draw nearby undeveloped land into their private realm by opposing commercial or apartment development. Yet the result is only an ad hoc cluster, not a living neighborhood. The individual subdivisions are as private and impermeable in relation to each other as they are in relation to the larger city's commerce and human diversity. The outer perimeter of the cluster, the third defensive line guarding the sanctum sanctorum of the home, does not in any way dissolve the defensive lines within it.

The defensive wall of the medieval and classical city created a space within which the bonds and exchanges of community life could take place freely and safely. The defensive wall—often a real wall—of the suburban subdivision or cluster of subdivisions has no such creative force. It encompasses a multitude of private realms rather than defining a shared public realm. The recreation center or park that might be built into some subdivisions and be made available only to residents of that subdivision partially mitigates the insular quality of suburban life while simultaneously underscoring it. Even public activities are drawn into the private realm and cut off from the diversity of the city—diversity of people, opportunities, learning, pleasure.

The planner or policy maker who wishes to channel development into a more communitarian and connected pattern is likely to meet heavy resistance. The preponderance of residential subdivisions built since 1960, at least in the Sun Belt, has followed the private, cellular, protected pattern, and that pattern has become identified with suburban arrival, the American Dream. It is difficult to persuade people that any other development pattern could be livable, especially given the "harsh, stressful and ugly" public realm that is almost universal in suburbia.

Yet most reasonably large cities that have been around awhile have models of communitarian planning close at hand, eminently successful old neighborhoods that break most of the rules of new subdivisions. Some of the most prestigious and expensive neighborhoods in San Antonio, for example, have retail and commercial districts cheek by jowl with residential streets. The area's ultimate prestige neighborhood is Olmos Park, an incorporated suburban city that was built up in the twenties and thirties and is now an island in the middle of San Antonio, just a few miles north of downtown. McCullough Avenue, a north-south arterial, runs along the western edge of

Olmos Park and is lined with a mixed bag of high- and low-end stores, offices, and even light industrial buildings. For much of the street's route along the edge of Olmos Park, retail and commercial uses occupy the west side, modest fourplex residences the east side. The suburb's only east-west arterial, Olmos Drive, encompasses in sequence neighborhood-service retail, expensive condominiums, low- to middle-income fourplex apartments, sizable single-family houses, and million-dollar mansions on large wooded lots—all within the space of seven-tenths of a mile. Nobody in Olmos Park lives beyond walking or easy biking distance of a convenience store; few live more than a mile from the nearest grocery store. Alameda Circle, the tiny isle of the most blessed, lies just two blocks from a mechanical contractor and a paint-and-body shop, and four blocks from one of San Antonio's poorest residential areas (literally on the other side of the tracks, and outside the Olmos Park city limits). Somehow all of this functional and demographic variety manages to coexist in close proximity without depressing property values. Much the same is true of a neighboring island suburb, Alamo Heights, which has a successful retail corridor running through it, and two near-downtown historic districts—Monte Vista, which lies just south of Olmos Park, and King William, just south of downtown San Antonio.

How can these older areas tolerate (and even thrive in) the presence of social, economic, and functional diversity, without walls separating them from the rest of the city, while newer areas require—or so their residents and developers believe—physical and geographic protection?

Particular circumstances may help to explain the difference. Both of the incorporated cities, Olmos Park and Alamo Heights, are quite small in population—about 3,500 and 7,000, respectively and their governments are thus highly responsive to residents' concerns. A homeowner in either town can be reasonably confident that commercial and multifamily zoning will not expand onto viable single-family residential streets, so existing commercial and multifamily uses do not constitute a threat. Most of the businesses along McCullough Avenue are small neighborhood-service retailers. Whatever doubts anyone may have about living within a few blocks of a retail district are offset by the convenience of being able to run down to the corner for a quart of milk and an authentic Queen Anne writing table. Some retailers—such as the little Olmos Pharmacy with its soda fountain and lunch counter, just outside the Olmos Park city limits—have become much-loved neighborhood institutions and gathering places, contributing greatly to the tone and livability of Olmos Park. In the case of Alamo Heights, where modest single-family blocks adjacent to the main commercial road have been converted to apartments, increased density helped to turn a marginal retailing area into one of the most vibrant in the city, with the kinds of upscale restaurants and shops that are welcomed by residents of the single-family areas, but that could not exist without the increased housing density to support them. At the same time that Alamo Heights's retail strip was growing busier, its single-family streets were growing more desirable, as evidenced by the remodelings and expansions of formerly modest cottages.

In each suburb, roughly half of the city is laid out as a rectilinear grid, and the other half has garden-suburb curving street patterns. Generally the grandest houses are situated on the curving streets. In Alamo Heights, the spaghetti bowl is particularly confusing to strangers—thus to potential miscreant strangers—and this may be one reason why wealthy people have no difficulty living only a single short block from an intensively developed retail strip.

Monte Vista and King William are laid out as rectilinear grids entirely open to their less exalted adjacent neighborhoods, but both are protected from commercial encroachment onto residential blocks, or from insensitive development in commercial zones, by their status as historic districts. The local Historic and Design Review Commission must approve all new construction and exterior alterations—even paint jobs must go before the board—and ordinances give historic structures some protection from demolition, whether by bulldozer or by neglect. Signs, site planning, and landscaping are also controlled, so the visual jumble of suburban retail areas cannot be duplicated in the historic districts. As in the cases of Olmos Park and Alamo Heights, residents can enjoy their neighborhood retail and commercial districts without fearing their spread. (Expansion of a large church and a university at the northern end of the Monte Vista district proved unstoppable, but the neighborhood was at least able to obtain aesthetic compensation for the loss of houses. The church's new parking lot is beautifully landscaped and shielded from the street by a low wall; the university's new athletic field is a magnificent park.) King William residents even wish that more retailers would move into some of the district's disused or underused commercial buildings. The *shortage* of neighborhood-service retailers, such as an adequate grocery store, is what compromises quality of life in King William, not the proximity to retail and commercial property.

In part, the older neighborhoods keep or regain their cachet because they *are* older, and their housing stock has the kind of unreproducible character that valorizes itself, almost irrespective of the surroundings. They don't build houses like that any more. Old neighborhoods often have an advantage in being located near central business districts and cultural facilities, or commuter rail stops. But the most important reason old neighborhoods can tolerate diversity is that their design, regulations, and development practices *normalize* diversity. Visit a neighborhood that was built in, say, the 1920s and remains largely intact. Study the transitions between single-family, apartment, institutional, retail, and commercial land uses. Imagine yourself walking or driving from one of the single-family houses to the retail-commercial hub. Typically, you will see a nearly seamless transition from single-family houses to apartment houses. The apartment houses probably are not radically different from the nearby single-family houses in scale, architectural style, setback, and landscaping. The next transition, usually to institutional, office, or retail uses, again will not bring a sharp change in character. Nonresidential uses typically occur in buildings of residential scale; the scale may even drop between an apartment building and, say, a doctor's office or fire station. Moreover, because big parking lots do not lie between the buildings and the sidewalks, and because buildings of whatever type stand in close proximity to one another, the sidewalk is a genuine public space that binds diversity into unity, visually, psychologically, and functionally. A schematic map of solids, voids, and pathways would reveal only minor difference between single-family residential blocks and the mixed-use neighborhood center. The resident of a single-family home can perceive the mixed-use hub a block or two away as an integral and attractive part of her neighborhood.

In contrast, typical commercial suburbia is radically unlike single-family residential streets in scale, architectural character, landscaping, setbacks, and the relationships of solids, voids, and pathways. Modern retail buildings tend to be very much larger than their older counterparts—a modern supermarket or hardware superstore might occupy 70,000 square feet rather than 5,000—and determinedly plain in design, having no visual affinity with nearby residential architecture. With big stores come big parking lots, which mean larger voids on the map, greater distances between destinations, more traffic congestion, and less continuity of urban fabric. Ugliness is advanced above by enormous signs on tall pylons (which are themselves ugly at ground level), and below by wide drainage ditches, needed to capture rain runoff from those big parking lots and wide roads. It is no wonder that suburbanites wish to isolate their residential streets from *that* reality. Commercial development is seen as synonymous with all that is ugly, tacky, and frustrating, a necessary evil to be kept away from the space they are willing to acknowledge as their own.

It should not be surprising, then, if suburbanites oppose new commercial zoning anywhere near their homes and resist planning schemes that attempt to integrate diverse land uses and form coherent neighborhoods. Who wants to see those golden arches looming above the backyard barbecue pit? Before they will accept an integrated approach to urban form, suburbanites must be persuaded, by a demonstrable local track record, that the regulatory regime will protect their interests—that nonresidential projects near their homes will be designed and built in a way that adds value to their property and their lives.

But business interests are likely to oppose the kinds of controls—governing signs, landscaping, parking, scale, and site planning, for example—that are necessary to make commercial zoning more palatable to residents. The business people have a good case. Design controls to make commercial projects neighborhood compatible could be economically disadvantageous in the absence of a neighborhood context to be compatible with. If all your customers must drive to your store from beyond its immediate vicinity, then the typical suburban development pattern makes sense.

It is extremely difficult to find politically achievable ways to intervene in this vicious cycle. Probably no city can undertake a sudden and comprehensive reversal of policy. An accumulation of incremental changes, most of them in narrow policy areas, is needed. The chronology of achievable change will differ from city to city depending on historical accidents and mobilizing issues. In San Antonio, for example, widespread anger was aroused when three discount chains bulldozed, in quick succession, beautiful stands of old live oaks to make way for needlessly huge parking lots. These events created a political climate in which it was possible to pass a landscape ordinance that mandated new plantings and provided incentives to preserve existing trees in new commercial projects. That ordinance has no effect on larger questions of urban form, but it can be the first link in a logical and political chain—a virtuous cycle—leading to wider change.

THE STAKES

The map of a city is not just an arrangement of concrete and asphalt, power lines and drainage ditches; it is more than an outline of where we live and work and play. Embedded in the map of a city is a model—an ideal, a set of assumptions—of what it means to be a citizen and a human being. The shape of a city is inextricably bound to our ideas of personhood and society. When we decide where to live, we also decide how to live and how we relate to others. Our decisions about streets and sidewalks and utilities and zoning have far-reaching consequences, not just for the practicalities of life but for its very meaning.

A person who lives in a walled-and-gated, demographically homogeneous subdivision is a different kind of person from one who lives among a diversity of people on a public street. A person who must drive a mile or two for the most routine errands is a different kind of person from one who can walk a block or two to the neighborhood center. A person whose home life is radically disengaged from the public realm is a different kind of person from one whose home is part of the continuum, the fullness, the totality of the city.

Whether because of neglect, indifference, ideology, or fear, we in America have devalued our public realm, our shared life, our sense of community, as we have elevated privacy, security, and separatism as our highest goals. No longer a nation of citizens, we have become a nation of taxpayers, unified more by grumbling under our burdens than by joyful acceptance of each other's gifts.

It is impossible to state the case more eloquently than Lewis Mumford did a generation ago in *The City in History*:

> In a recent study in Boston, a survey showed that only one male resident out of three spends any time on community or civic activity in his dormitory suburb, and that he likewise fails to participate actively in his professional or business association. In effect, the suburbanite renounces the obligations of citizenship at both ends; and the farther he goes from the center the more dissociated he becomes. Neither neighborhood nor city give cohesion to the suburb of the "motor age." The suburban shopping centers, the suburban factories and business office and research institutions, provide a minimum of facilities for association while imposing through their random distribution a maximum exertion of effort—whether counted in time, mileage or cost.
>
> Those fast moving particles are the fallout of the metropolitan explosion. They are no longer held together either by the urban magnet or the urban container: they are rather emblems of the "disappearing city." But this movement from the center carries no hope or promise of life at a higher level. Just as our expanding technological universe pushes our daily existence ever farther from its human center, so the expanding urban universe carries its separate fragments ever farther from the city, leaving the individual more dissociated, lonely and helpless than he probably ever was before. Compulsory mobility provides fewer, not more opportunities for association than compulsory stability provided in the walled town.[2]

In the decades since Mumford wrote those words, large metropolitan areas have begun to reorganize around large commercial subcenters oriented in many cases to expressway interchanges, a process chronicled in Joel

Garreau's *Edge City*. These subcenters have partially replaced what Mumford called the "urban magnet," though not the "urban container," and restored a bit of focus to suburban life. But Edge City remains an automotive environment. One can't easily walk from one's office building or hotel to a restaurant or shopping mall a quarter-mile away, or just across the road. Nor does Edge City link coherently with residential districts. Lacking effective pedestrian pathways, the increased density of Edge City relative to ordinary suburban sprawl has brought untenable levels of congestion. A special case of Edge City, the self-contained corporate "community" planned by a single developer (an example is Houston's Greenway Plaza), answers the internal congestion problem, but at a price. The results inevitably are sterile, placeless, and vaguely totalitarian, like the old robber barons' company towns dressed up with smiley faces. The architecture of such places tends to be dully uniform. Their retail, restaurant, and leisure components are conceived narrowly as extensions of the corporate domain, their main function being to keep corporate tenants' employees on a short leash. They typically do not attract users from outside the "community." Like the shopping mall, the self-contained business park is a privately controlled and patrolled realm, without a truly public space in which the citizen can be a citizen and escape corporate scrutiny. A city or a neighborhood really does have to be a collaborative artwork, because collaboration implies the freedom and creativity of the individual collaborators.

Edge City has not negated the most damning aspects of Mumford's critique:

> Suburbia offers poor facilities for meeting, conversation, collective debate and common action—it favors silent conformity, not rebellion or counterattack. So Suburbia has become the favored home of a new kind of absolutism: invisible but all-powerful.

> The metropolis, in its final stage of development, becomes a contrivance for . . . giving those who are in reality its victims the illusion of power, wealth and felicity, of standing at the very pinnacle of human achievement. But in actual fact their

lives are constantly in peril, their wealth is tasteless and ephemeral, their leisure is sensationally monotonous, and their pathetic felicity is tainted by constant, well-justified anticipations of violence and sudden death. Increasingly they find themselves "strangers and afraid," in a world they never made: a world ever less responsive to direct human command, ever more empty of human meaning.[3]

What sort of world is this for children, and what sorts of adults will they grow up to be? If one day you are feeling excessively cheerful, take a driving tour of some of your area's newer suburban subdivisions—rich or working class, it doesn't matter—and imagine what life there would be like for a kid. With occasional exceptions, we are warehousing children and their families in homogeneous compounds with little access to human diversity and sensual or intellectual stimulation. Homes are isolated from places of commerce, learning, socializing, and recreation. The anthem of the American teenager, "Drive me to the mall," is not just a declaration of an intent to shop; it is a plea for access to the world of experience—or what passes for a wider world in the absence of the more diverse, surprising, risky, and free space of the collaborative city.

Suburbia is advertised as enhancing the security and autonomy of family life. In the mythology of suburbia, the home and the family unit now take precedence over—and turn decisively inward, away from—the community and public life. But the family is not strengthened by isolation from a community. Far from it. Family bonds are strengthened when family members do things together—trivial things like taking a walk to the ice cream parlor or the branch library after dinner, or biking to the park. Bonds between people, in or out of the family, are strengthened when they encounter things in the world and share with each other their reactions to those things. Even in the most fragmented of suburbia, people still have experiences outside the home, but the geography and economic structure of suburbia make these experiences less and less routine, more and more divided from home life. To go anywhere requires a significant investment in time and psychological energy.

One must drive long distances, plan one's route, fight traffic. There is more resistance in the circuit. It is so much easier just to stay at home and watch television, play video games, or listen to the stereo—electronic substitutes for human experience.

Even in happy, well-adjusted families, people need on occasion to escape from each other. Scope for independent activity is especially important and especially out of the question for suburban children under driving age. Where, in practical terms, can they go? What can they do? Too often the answers, even for children in wealthy subdivisions with private parks and country clubs, are vandalism, burglary, drug use, and other antisocial or self-destructive diversions.

Urban form also affects the vitality of cultural institutions. Like any other business, a cultural institution must have customers to survive, or even to have a reason to survive. If potential customers can't easily get to a cultural institution, or are afraid—justifiably or not—of the institution's neighborhood, they won't go. If the institution is readily accessible to lots of potential customers, it is more likely to thrive. Chicago's Near North Side has supported a plethora of professional theaters producing new and interesting work. Why? In large measure, because their neighborhood is densely populated with residents who are interested in what the theaters have to offer. Many of the patrons on any given night are likely to have walked to the theater from their apartments or from a nearby rail transit station. Those who drive from greater distances know that, once past the trauma of finding a place to park, they have plenty of options for pre- or post-theater dining, drinking, socializing, and entertainment within walking distance of the theater and their cars, because the neighborhood is organized in a way that can support those things as well as theaters.

In contrast, many cities have found it increasingly difficult to sustain such major institutions as symphony orchestras because the people who could afford to buy tickets are moving farther and farther away from the concert halls. With the rise of Edge City, even the workplaces of upper- and middle-income professionals, the traditional bedrock of support for major cultural institutions, are increasingly dispersed from the center, where the institutions tend to be located. Downtown workers can easily, conveniently, and with little forethought walk to dinner after work and then walk to the theater or concert hall before returning home. Edge City workers must make the long drive downtown.

A special case of the culturally vital neighborhood is the university neighborhood. Densely developed and walkable university neighborhoods are uniquely able to support excellent bookstores and music stores whose stock is not limited by the desires of the mass market. Such neighborhoods can also support theaters, art-film houses, and other cultural businesses. But new college and university campuses in suburbia—and sometimes even in the inner city—rarely spawn these kinds of neighborhoods, because zoning codes and modern development practices don't give them a place to happen. Often the land that might have become a university neighborhood is used instead for parking lots.

So our cities are becoming increasingly uncongenial to the arts and cultural reflection. But theater, opera, music, dance, literature, film, and painting are among the ways we talk to each other most effectively and thoughtfully about things that matter. They are invaluable sources of intellectual and conceptual variation, fuel for the evolution of our understanding and our social and political arrangements. Electronic media partially fill the void, but these do not respond well to local conditions. The act of congregating in a public place and sharing an experience with friends and strangers alike helps to solidify connections between art and life, between artist and audience, and among the members of the audience, who are not merely observers but actively engaged participants in the cultural experience. Congregating is not just an archaic way to gain cognitive access to art; it is of the essence of the cultural experience, which does not carry the same weight or meaning when it is apprehended in solitude, away from a social context.

But the same can be said of other manifestations of culture beyond the glamorous special case of the arts—even so mundane a task as buying a tube of toothpaste. People are necessarily social animals. We are interdependent. Culture, in its largest sense, is the map of our interdependencies as much as it is the sum of our individual achievements and creations. The objects and processes of culture derive much of their value from the social interdependencies that are inscribed within them. The map of a city is also a map of interdependencies. The richer the map, the finer the weave, the more freedom of movement allowed by its matrix of connectivity, the greater is the city's ability to produce culture. Much of this book has been concerned with culture in its economic sense—with the city's ability to promote the circulation of people, money, knowledge, and ideas. But I can't leave the subject without stressing that pathways are not just for circulation. They are also, like the theater and the concert hall, places of congregation and shared experience. The city at its best is a kind of theater. By virtue of the experiences we share in the public, civic space of our pathways and gathering places, we, our fellow citizens, and the artifacts we create for one another are de-objectified, transformed into something more than an assortment of objects for cognition and use. We are involved with one another. Yet we do not give up our individual selves. As individuals we are larger, more potent, more effectual, because in the well-made city our sphere of action and participation is enlarged. The boundary of the self expands to include the entire gift community. That, above all, is the promise of the city.

appendix
Creating an urban matrix

    The urban matrix is not a new concept. Every city that has zoning, setback requirements, and standards for streets and sidewalks—which means just about any American city—is built according to a matrix or, more to the modern point, a conglomeration of matrices. The jumble, congestion, and disconnectedness of typical suburban development reflect a fragmented matrix that has evolved over many years as an accumulation of unrelated components. Each component was developed to meet a narrow objective; none has a sufficiently fine structure to answer the need for connectivity at the human scale. Part II of this book was concerned with developing a comprehensive matrix that, like the arteries and capillaries of the human circulatory system, allows nutrients—in this case ideas, knowledge, and money—to flow easily throughout the city and penetrate its fibers.

    Because the components of that matrix were scattered across six chapters, I would like to pull them all together in more compact, telegraphic form in this appendix. I want to stress, as I have before, that I am not proposing a Handy-Dandy, One-Size-Fits-All, Universal Ready-to-Wear Urban Matrix. The diagrams in this appendix are schematic, not cartographic. They are not to be interpreted as actual maps, but as simplified representations of underlying structural principles. Some of the diagrams appear superficially neoclassical, but they should not be interpreted that way. We are concerned with how the parts of a city are related and connected, not with pretty symmetries and regular geometry. When translated into the real world, the conceptual scheme is meant to be influenced by geography, terrain, historical accident, local culture and preferences, and political negotiation.

That last influence, political negotiation among diverse community interests, is especially important. The planning strategy that I advocate is to seek development patterns that accommodate a wide variety of interests and uses. The planning framework illustrated by the diagrams in this appendix should be understood as the end point of a long and complex process of negotiation and accommodation. I think the schematic matrix that I propose represents a reasonable end point to that process and a framework that cities might usefully consider when they formulate master plans and urban design policies. The end point envisioned in this book is not all that far from the starting point in standard suburban practice. But in the real world what I think is less important than what you and your fellow citizens think when you come to the policy-making table. What matters is that political interests in a particular community think comprehensively and with foresight about how to arrange their city's geography to best satisfy their diverse needs. The matrix or matrices they come up with might not look like the ones in this book. Certainly many details of geometry and scale need to be filled in according to local needs and conditions.

During the course of the book we started at the front door of my house (or yours) and worked outward to the big picture. In this appendix the procedure is reversed to show better how the parts need to fit the whole, as a nested ensemble. At the end of each section I list some of the policy tools that can be used to achieve the objectives of that section.

Urban form. The city is conceived as an array of richly interlinked complete neighborhoods, each with a clearly defined mixed-use center. The array as a whole also has an identifiable center, usually called "downtown" or "the central business district," which serves as the most important focus of the city's business and cultural life; large cities may also have regional subcenters. The neighborhood centers are linked to each other, and with downtown and the regional subcenters, by a network of major thoroughfares and transit lines. Minor streets, for short-distance movement, connect neighborhoods across their common boundaries. The major subcenters are connected to each other and with downtown by the network of expressways and transit trunk lines.

The conceptual framework is shown schematically in figure A.1. The lightly shaded boxes are complete neighborhoods, which may vary greatly in shape and size. The spaces between the boxes are neighborhood boundaries, which might include natural boundaries such as rivers and ravines, artificial boundaries such as railroads or expressways, or large institutions and industrial districts. Special cases of neighborhoods are the city center, or downtown, designated by the heaviest shading, and large commercial subcenters, or "Edge Cities," shown in an intermediate shade. The heavy lines linking the city center and major subcenters are expressways, which also function as neighborhood boundaries because neighborhoods don't easily cross expressways. The lighter lines forming a square grid are major surface streets linking neighborhood centers (the shaded circles, which need not be circular). The lightest lines represent local streets linking one neighborhood to the next and bonding residential areas to their neighborhood centers.

This scheme differs from the modern suburban norm mainly in concentrating neighborhood-compatible businesses and apartments into integrated, walkable nodes inside neighborhoods rather than spreading them out along continuous corridors that form effective boundaries between neighborhoods. Of course, even the node is not wholly alien to modern suburban practice, but suburban nodes are rarely organized internally as coherent unities, nor are they compact enough to allow a fully functional pedestrian system, nor do they connect well with their surrounding neighborhoods. All three faults derive from a subtle conceptual difference between the scheme of urban form that I am proposing and the one that is more often seen. In figure A.1, the array of neighborhoods and their centers is conceived as primary, the road network secondary, even if (as is common) the roads were built before the neighborhoods. In the more usual practice, the network of major thoroughfares and expressways is conceived as primary, and the territory between them is conceived as residual space to be left to its own devices.

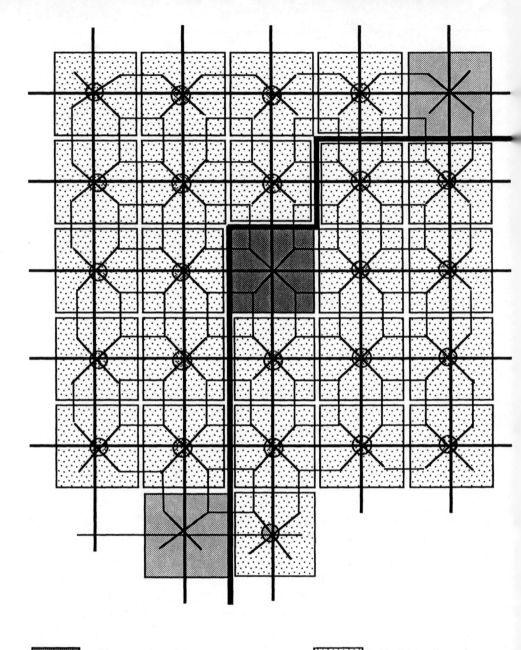

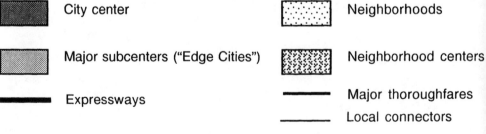

	City center		Neighborhoods
	Major subcenters ("Edge Cities")		Neighborhood centers
▬▬	Expressways	——	Major thoroughfares
		——	Local connectors

Figure A.1 Urban form

This conceptual difference leads to very important differences in details, which will be addressed as we focus more narrowly on the neighborhood, the neighborhood center, and the market place.

Some policy tools that can translate this concept of urban form into reality are the city master plan, the zoning code, the transportation plan, and the major thoroughfare plan.

The neighborhood and its structure. A complete neighborhood consists of single-family and multifamily residences serving a range of incomes and family types, plus schools, parks, shopping, professional offices, services, and recreational and cultural facilities sufficient to provide many routine needs within the neighborhood.

The dimensions of a complete neighborhood depend on population density, natural and artificial boundaries, and other variables. An area of about one square mile probably is optimum in practice, given the overall density that is normal for modern suburban development, and the outer limit is probably about two square miles—the largest size that places all residents within a vigorous walk or easy bike ride of the center.

Apartments, neighborhood compatible businesses, parks, and gathering places—including a public focal point—are concentrated into a compact, walkable ensemble at or near the neighborhood's geographic center, which is directly accessible to the surrounding lower-density (mostly single-family) development by means of local streets (the diagonal double-ended arrows in figure A.2). Standards governing scale, setbacks, landscaping, and architectural design provide for a smooth transition between single-family residential areas and the center they radiate from.

Local streets (the vertical and horizontal double-ended arrows) also link residential areas in adjacent neighborhoods, to enhance the residents' freedom of movement and reduce traffic pressure on the major thoroughfares. Parks and elementary schools serving two or more neighborhoods might best be located at neighborhood boundaries or "four-corners" areas, helping to bind distinct neighborhoods into a unified city.

Major thoroughfares (the heavy lines in figure A.2) connecting one neighborhood center to the next may cross the center or pass by its edges, but in any event major thoroughfares and their adjacent development must

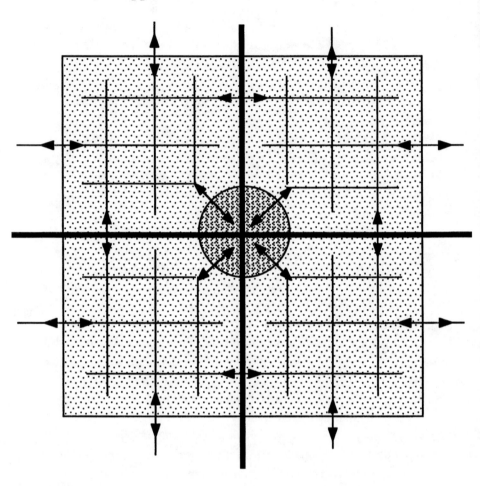

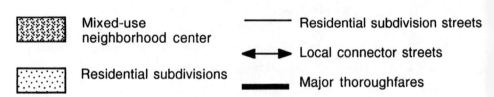

	Mixed-use neighborhood center	—— Residential subdivision streets
	Residential subdivisions	Local connector streets
		Major thoroughfares

Figure A.2 Neighborhood structure.

be designed in a way that encourages pedestrian, bicycle, and automobile crossings in the vicinity of the center and at one or two points between neighborhood centers. Some segments of major thoroughfares, especially those near expressway ramps, may be designated for corridor land uses—businesses and institutions that generate a lot of automobile traffic, require large land tracts for parking or grounds, or are otherwise incompatible with the medium or small scale of neighborhood centers. Some of these land uses might also be confined to special districts between neighborhoods, away from the major thoroughfares that link neighborhood centers. Whatever the width of the major thoroughfares, and especially if they are more than five lanes wide, extraordinary design measures are needed to carry the neighborhood center and thus the neighborhood as a whole across the road perceptually and functionally.

Policy tools relevant to neighborhood structure are the zoning code, including overlay zoning that triggers special development standards for neighborhood centers; the major thoroughfare plan; capital improvements plans governing the location of libraries, parks, service centers, and so forth; and subdivision regulations having to do with the location, dimensions, and continuity of streets and sidewalks.

The neighborhood center. If true mixed use is not politically feasible, the neighborhood center is organized generally as concentric zones with a civic space as the focal point. The concentric structure of the neighborhood center is shown schematically in figure A.3. The dark gray circle represents the highest density of retail and commercial development—the smallest stores, quickest architectural rhythms, smallest blocks, and most richly developed pedestrian paths concentrated around the focal point. The star-shaped zone farther removed from the focal point, but still within walking distance of it, is reserved for parking lots serving the high-density center and for businesses and institutions requiring larger land tracts. By extending arms along the major thoroughfares, such a configuration allows a high volume of auto traffic to reach the lower-density zone without encroaching on the neighborhood character of local streets linking the center with residential areas. A zone of apartments, town houses, parks, and schools (the lightest shading) may mediate between the retail-commercial core and single-family residential areas.

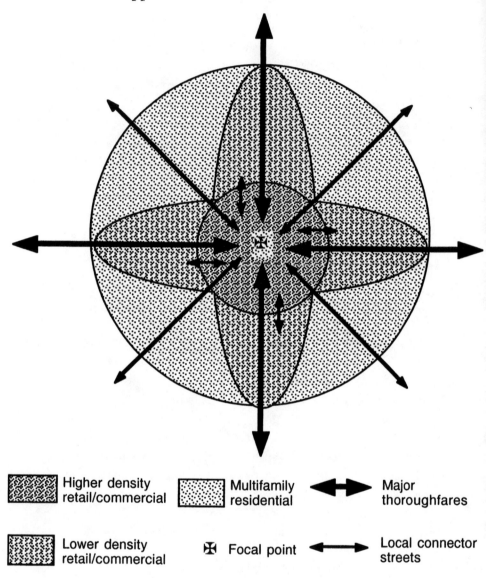

	Higher density retail/commercial		Multifamily residential	⬌	Major thoroughfares
	Lower density retail/commercial	✠	Focal point	⬌	Local connector streets

Figure A.3   The neighborhood center.

The core zone of highest density is directly linked by local streets to residential districts. These local street linkages should include designated bicycle lanes or bicycle paths separated from the roadway, and the integrity of the pedestrian paths should be preserved along these local streets even as development density shades off farther from the center.

Public policy tools for achieving a well-formed neighborhood center include zoning and subdivision regulations; a public process for defining the location and boundaries of new neighborhood centers as the city grows outward; a requirement for public review and approval of neighborhood center master plans; and subdivision regulations that establish a minimum spacing of local circulator streets and maximum block sizes within the neighborhood center.

The market place. The nonresidential core of the neighborhood center is called the market place. Retailers, professional offices, and other consumer-oriented destinations (the branch library, the YMCA, the cultural center, the health clinic) are arranged within the market place in such a way as to optimize economies of form. As in the shopping mall and the traditional business district, front doors are close to each other, both along one side of a street and across the street. Front doors are intimately engaged with the main public pedestrian system, not separated from it by parking lots. Parking lots of more than a dozen or so spaces are treated as common areas for the entire market place to reduce the total amount of parking needed, and large parking lots are located away from the local streets linking the market place with its surrounding residential districts.

Figure A.4 illustrates schematically some important features of the market place. The highest density is concentrated near the focal point (the darkest circle), and density may shade off toward the periphery in order to accommodate parking. Major thoroughfares, linking this neighborhood center with others, pass through or immediately next to the market place, but special care is taken to assure that major thoroughfares in the vicinity of the market place are functionally and perceptually crossable by pedestrians, cyclists, and drivers. Landscaped medians can reduce the perceived scale of the roadway, help tie the two sides of the road together visually, and provide

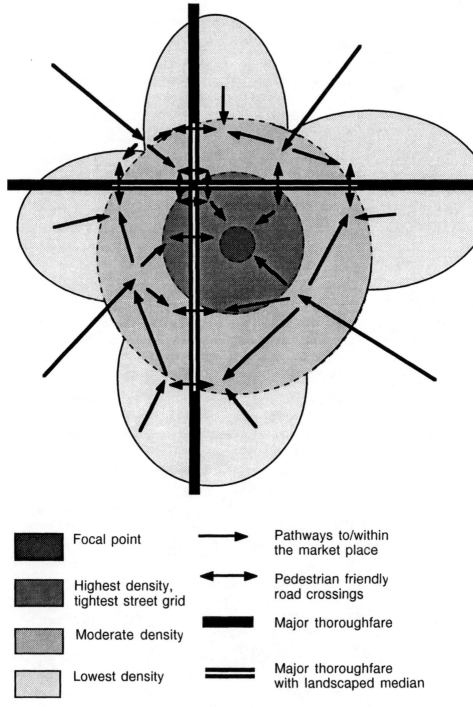

Focal point

Pathways to/within
the market place

Highest density,
tightest street grid

Pedestrian friendly
road crossings

Moderate density

Major thoroughfare

Lowest density

Major thoroughfare
with landscaped median

Figure A.4 The market place.

a safety island for pedestrians. Traffic lights and stop signs provide safe crossing points (the double-pointed arrows) at frequent intervals (300 to 600 feet) along major thoroughfares in the vicinity of the market place's higher-density core. Internal streets (which may include pedestrian esplanades) provide ample freedom of movement on redundant pathways within the market place center, and this pathway system is directly linked with the street systems of adjacent residential subdivisions. To reduce traffic congestion on the major thoroughfares and improve pedestrian connections at their intersection, left turns (and possibly right turns as well) are prohibited at the main crossroads and directed instead to circulator streets that form a loop around the high-density center. Where feasible, parking should be allowed on the market place streets, including major thoroughfares.

Policy tools for achieving well-formed market places include tax-increment districts or mandatory merchants' associations (patterned on mandatory homeowners' associations) to pay for and maintain common areas, including parking lots; overlay zoning to allow mixed use and mandate special standards for architectural design, landscaping, signs, parking, and density within market places; capital-improvements policies that favor designated market places as locations for branch libraries, parks, public art, and other public facilities; and planning guidelines that favor rhythmic pathways, visual termini, usable public spaces, and the preservation of attractive natural features such as waterways and groves.

Pathways. The entire neighborhood is interconnected by a continuous network of sidewalks. The sidewalks are designed as part of an ensemble that includes designated zones for public necessities such as traffic signs, mailboxes, light poles, fire hydrants, benches, and landscaping. To the extent practicable, awnings, arcades, or trees shelter the pathways from rain and sun. The sidewalk is either set back some distance from the curb, or it is wide enough to place the property side of the pathway at least eight feet from the curb to provide a safety buffer from traffic and limit the intrusion of driveway slopes. In business districts, a flexible build-to line is established along the public sidewalk and its associated zone of amenities. The build-to line is flexible enough to allow architectural variety and private landscaping or entrance courtyards, while still assuring that front doors and display windows remain effectively engaged with the pedestrian path. The sidewalk and the building line are locked together, but need not be located adjacent to the street. In cities that have architectural design standards, these should pay particular attention to the rhythm of bays, windows, setbacks, and shadows along the pedestrian path.

Figure A.5 illustrates some features of a matrix of connectivity for the pathway system of a well-formed market place. (Residential areas would be subject to a simpler matrix, governing only sidewalk width, parkway width, and the designation of parkway zones for public necessities.) Dimensions will vary somewhat with local preferences, climate, anticipated development density, traffic patterns, and types of land use. Public policy makers, in collaboration with developers, business groups, and neighborhood associations, need to decide what each of the dimensions described below should be for specific blocks of specific market places.

Dimension A is the maximum allowable distance between buildings that face each other across a street or road. For purposes of easy pedestrian circulation, this distance should be as short as possible—ideally no more than eighty feet. It is possible, however, to allow greater distances in limited applications, and with very careful design, without unduly fragmenting the market place.

Dimension A is the sum of four other dimensions. Dimension B is the roadway width, including median strips and bicycle lanes, if any. If the roadway is to have more than four vehicular traffic lanes, it is highly advisable to introduce a landscaped median where the roadway passes through or beside the market place. Dimensions C and C' (which may vary from one side of a block to another) indicate the zone of sidewalk or parkway designated for public necessities, including on-street parking, and must be wide enough to accommodate all anticipated public objects in an orderly way. This zone may be broken into linear and lateral subzones—one for traffic signs and utility poles, one for trees and benches, one for telephone booths and news racks, one for head-in or parallel parking, for example. Dimensions D and D' indicate the width of unobstructed and continuous public pathway, which in neighborhood centers should be no less than eight feet and preferably twelve feet wide on the most heavily developed blocks. Dimensions E

A Maximum distance building line to building line

B Roadway width, including median

C Zone for public necessities, including landscape and on-street parking

D Width of continuous unobstructed pedestrian path

E Build-to zone

F Percentage of frontage within build-to zone

G Percentage of frontage allowed outside build-to zone

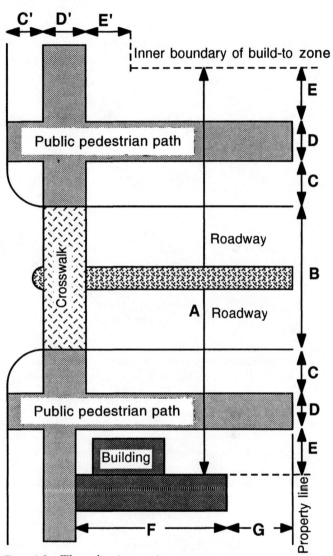

Figure A.5 The pedestrian matrix.

and E' indicate the build-to zone, a band that, in most applications, shouldn't be more than twenty feet deep from the property edge of the pathway to the maximum setback line. Dimension F is the minimum portion of a property's public pathway frontage that must be occupied by building wall within the build-to zone. Dimension G is the maximum portion of a property's public pathway frontage that may be unoccupied by a building wall within the build-to zone.

All of these dimensions need not be, and probably should not be, the same on every block of every street or road within a single market place, but they should not vary from one property to the next on the same block. The matrix may vary from one side of a block to another, or from block to block along any given street, especially for streets that extend from the mixed-use center to the residential periphery, but continuity should be maintained by holding some dimensions constant from one block to the next. In general, the pathways closer to the center should be more densely developed: F would be larger, G and E smaller; D would be wider, to accommodate heavier foot traffic; and C would be wide enough to accommodate a rich menu of landscaping and street furniture. Secondary pathways and those farther removed from the center might be less intensively developed: F would be smaller and G larger, to allow for parking lots, more landscaped open space, and a smooth transition to residential blocks; D might be narrower; C might be either narrower or, in sections with on-street parking, wider.

Public policy tools for achieving functional pathways include ordinances governing the dimensions and location of sidewalks, parkways, parking lots, and build-to lines; landscaping regulations that favor the placement of shade trees along public pedestrian paths; public review procedures that require continuity of public pedestrian paths across property lines; architectural standards or guidelines designed to bring a varied and lively rhythm of architectural features to the pedestrian paths; and public works and traffic-engineering policies that attend to pedestrian and bicycle needs in the design and placement of traffic signals, crosswalks, landscaped medians, drainage, and other infrastructure.

notes

chapter 1

1. Aristotle, *Poetics*, trans. Kenneth A. Telford (South Bend: Gateway Editions, 1961), 1 n.

chapter 2

1. Peter Stallybrass and Allon White, *The Politics and Poetics of Transgression* (Ithaca, N.Y.: Cornell University Press, 1986), 136.

2. Lewis Hyde, *The Gift: Imagination and the Erotic Life of Property* (New York: Vintage Books, 1983).

3. Houston is the most notorious exception, although even that city flirts with the idea periodically. Houston voters narrowly defeated a zoning proposal in 1993.

chapter 3

1. Aristotle, *Nichomachean Ethics*, trans. Martin Ostwald, The Library of Liberal Arts (Indianapolis: Bobbs-Merrill, 1962), 124 (5.1132b). In the W. D. Rouse translation, "city" replaces "state," and "exchange" replaces "mutual contribution" (Chicago: Encyclopaedia Britannica, 1952).

2. Ibid., 125–26 (5.1133a), 127 (5.1133b), all emphasis mine.

3. Lewis Hyde, *The Gift: Imagination and the Erotic Life of Property* (New York: Vintage Books, 1983), 84.

4. Ibid., 78.

5. René Girard, *Violence and the Sacred*, trans. Patrick Gregory (Baltimore: Johns Hopkins University Press, 1979), 146.

6. Ibid., 148.

7. Jane Jacobs, *Cities and the Wealth of Nations: Principles of Economic Life* (New York: Random House, 1984), 224–25.

chapter 5

1. Grosvenor Cooper and Leonard B. Meyer, *The Rhythmic Structure of Music* (Chicago: University of Chicago Press, Phoenix Edition, 1963) 2, 9.

chapter 6

1. David Finkel, "What's in a Neighborhood," *Washington Post Magazine.* 5 Jan. 1992, 22.

2. Robert B. Reich, *The Work of Nations: Preparing Ourselves for 21st-Century Capitalism* (New York: Alfred A. Knopf, 1991), 277–78.

3. In chapter 9 I suggest some strategies by which the urban fabric can be connected, with minimal disruption, across wide suburban roads.

chapter 8

1. See, for example, the 1934 Harvard City Planning Studies, cited in Edgar M. Hoover, *The Location of Economic Activity* (New York: McGraw-Hill, 1963). Hoover reproduces the Harvard maps of five cities, including San Antonio, to demonstrate the "typical disposition of commercial areas" into downtown shopping centers and "ribbons of commercial development along principal thoroughfares."

chapter 11

1. Sim Van der Ryn and Peter Calthorpe, *Sustainable Cities: A New Design Synthesis for Cities, Suburbs and Towns* (San Francisco: Sierra Club Books, 1986), 234.

2. Lewis Mumford, *The City in History* (New York: Harcourt Brace Jovanovich, Harvest Edition, 1961), 502–3.

3. Ibid., 513, 546.